Weird

Carolinas

Your Travel Guide to the Carolinas' Local Legends and Best Kept Secrets

BY ROGER MANLEY

Mark Sceurman and Mark Moran,
Executive Editors

WEiRD CAROLiNAS

STERLING
New York

An Imprint of Sterling Publishing
387 Park Avenue South
New York, NY 10016

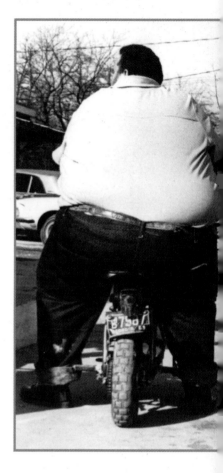

© 2007 by Mark Sceurman and Mark Moran
Photography and illustration credits are found on page 255 and constitute an extension of this
copyright page.

ISBN 978-1-4027-3939-2 (hardcover)
ISBN 978-1-4027-8827-7 (paperback)

Library of Congress Cataloging-in-Publication Data Available

Distributed in Canada by Sterling Publishing
c/o Canadian Manda Group, 165 Dufferin Street
Toronto, Ontario, Canada M6K 3H6
Distributed in the United Kingdom by GMC Distribution Services
Castle Place, 166 High Street, Lewes, East Sussex, England BN7 1XU
Distributed in Australia by Capricorn Link (Australia) Pty. Ltd.
P.O. Box 704, Windsor, NSW 2756, Australia

For information about custom editions, special sales, and premium and corporate purchases, please
contact Sterling Special Sales at 800-805-5489 or specialsales@sterlingpublishing.com.

Printed in China

2 4 6 8 10 9 7 5 3 1

www.sterlingpublishing.com

CONTENTS

DEDICATION

Dedicated to all the fine Carolinians who live in Anomaly, Boogertown, Catch-Me-Eye, Dark Corner, Erect, Flop-Eye, Grabtown, Hard Pinch, Iron Duff, Jollystreet, Ketchuptown, Last Chance, Matrimony, Nevadum, O.K., Purgatory, Quarantine, Rotalata, Sugar Tit, Twitty Prong, U-No, Vegetable, Whynot, X-way, Yorick, and Zirconia—and in all the lesser-known places in between. And to Teddy, my patient companion for this whole long, strange trip.

Our *weird journey* began a long, long time ago in a far-off land called New Jersey. Once a year or so, we'd compile a homespun newsletter called *Weird N.J.*, then pass it on to our friends. The pamphlet was a collection of odd news clippings, bizarre facts, little-known historical anecdotes, and anomalous encounters from our home state. The newsletter also included the kinds of localized legends that were often whispered around a particular town but seldom heard outside the boundaries of the community where they originated.

We had started *Weird N.J.* on the simple theory that every town in the state had at least one good tale to tell. The publication soon became a full-fledged magazine, and we made the decision to actually do our own investigating to see if we could track down where all of these seemingly unbelievable stories were coming from. Was there, we wondered, any factual basis for the fantastic local legends people were telling us about? Armed with not much more than a camera and a notepad, we set off on a mystical journey of discovery. Much to our surprise and amazement, a lot of what we had initially presumed to be nothing more than urban legends turned out to be real—or at least to contain a grain of truth, which had sparked the lore to begin with.

After a dozen years of documenting the bizarre, we were asked to write a book about our adventures, and so *Weird N.J.: Your Travel Guide to New Jersey's Local Legends and Best Kept Secrets* was published in 2003. Soon people from all over the country began writing to us, telling us strange tales from their home state. As it turned out, what we had perceived to be something of very local interest was actually just a small part of a larger and more universal phenomenon.

When our publisher asked us what we wanted to do next, the answer was simple: "We'd like to do a book called *Weird U.S.*, in which we could document the local legends and strangest stories from all over the country," we replied. So for the next twelve months, we set out in search of weirdness wherever it might be found in the fifty states. And indeed, we found plenty of it!

After *Weird U.S.* was published, we came to the conclusion that this country had more great tales than could be contained in just one book. Everywhere we looked, we found unwritten folklore, creepy cemeteries, cursed locations, and outlandish roadside oddities. With this in mind, we told our publisher that we wanted to document it *all* and to do it in a series of books, each focusing on the peculiarities of a particular state.

We knew early on that the Carolinas were one region where we wanted to delve deeper into the weirdness. During our research for *Weird U.S.*, we found the two states, North and South, to be a real hotbed of unusual legends and odd historical happenings. Our only problem was figuring out who we could find to collaborate with us on *Weird Carolinas*. Obviously, it would have to be someone who knew both states intimately and had a voracious curiosity for off-the-beaten-path stories.

As luck would have it, the perfect person would come to us—in a roundabout sort of way. We had a book at Weird Headquarters called *Self-Made Worlds: Visionary Folk Art Environments* by Roger Manley and Mark Sloan. It's a glorious collection of personal living environments designed by folks who definitely travel to the beat of their own drummers. One day one of the authors, Mark Sloan, a curator at the School of Arts at Charleston College, sent us an e-mail suggesting that we cover one such unique property in one of our books. We recognized his name right away and began corresponding with him on the subject of weird environments and other things out of the ordinary. Mark told us that if we were ever thinking of compiling a Weird book on the Carolinas he knew just the guy to do it—his friend and collaborator Roger Manley.

We soon learned that Roger was a true kindred spirit who harbored a deep-rooted fascination for the weird. Having lived in both North and South Carolina, Roger has spent years collecting unusual tales known only to the locals. Best of all, Roger has the rare gift of being able to recognize a site or story that is intrinsically unusual and to convey its inherent uniqueness to his readers. This is a quality that we refer to as the Weird Eye.

The Weird Eye requires one to see the world in a different way, with a renewed sense of wonder. And once you have it, there is no going back—you'll never see things the same way again. All of a sudden you begin to reexamine your own environs as if for the first time. And you begin to ask yourself questions like, "What the heck is *that* thing all about, anyway?" and "Doesn't anybody else think that's kind of *weird?*"

So come with us now and let Roger take you on a tour of the Tar Heel and Palmetto states, with all of their strange sites, forgotten history, and lasting legends. Together they comprise a state of mind we like to call the *Weird Carolinas.*

— *Mark Moran and Mark Sceurman*

Whenever anybody says, "There's nothing weird around here," I take a deep breath and wonder where on earth they've been. I mean, this is the *Carolinas*, practically a world vortex for weirdness. This is where the Lost Colony got lost, where the wild Wanderoo once wandered, and where giant sand geysers once spouted. UFOs seem drawn here like bees to nectar, along with oddball inventors, flimflammers, moon-shiners, street preachers, eccentric artists, imperial wizards, and interstate smugglers. We're the home of giant topiary cats, haunted sheriff's offices, the Moog Synthesizer, Krispy Kreme Doughnuts, and the Gatling gun.

Jules Verne obviously considered the Carolinas plenty weird, since he made this the setting for his science fiction tale *The Master of the World*. And no wonder. After all, giant sharks once swam where peanuts and cotton now grow.

We've still got rivers of sand, lost gold mine tunnels, and the most sunken ships, the most species of fungi, and the most salamanders—including waterdogs, newts, mudpuppies, sirens, and hellbenders—found anywhere on earth. We're not only the only state with an Official Carnivorous Plant (NC's venus flytrap), but the only one with an Official State Insect that practices sexual cannibalism (SC's Carolina mantid). What could be weirder than that?

No one can say we haven't provided our share of unusual characters. We're where Napoleon's finest general may have gone into hiding after allegedly facing the firing squad. We've had full-blown pirates, voodoo-practicing sheriffs, card-carrying witches, die-hard Rebels, and downright nuts.

Over the years, many books have helped me see the weirdness. Books like John Harden's *Tar Heel Ghosts* and Nancy and Bruce Roberts' classic *Ghosts of the Carolinas* kept my hair on end from sixth grade on. Later, I kept copies of Jerry Bledsoe's *North Carolina Curiosities* and William Powell's *North Carolina Gazetteer* in the glove compartment to make driving around more interesting than just cruising mindlessly down the interstate.

I'm indebted now to writers like Lew Powell, Roger Kammerer, Harlan Greene, and Tally Johnson for giving me permission to follow their leads, and to Billy Arthur, Terrance Zepke, Daniel Barefoot, Janet and Colin Bord, Nancy Rhyne, and Richard Walser for the clues they provided in their books too. Edward Meyer is great for unlocking the concentrated peculiarity at *Ripley's Believe It Or Not!*'s amazing archives. I thank Mark Sloan for hooking me up with Mark Moran and Mark Sceurman, and I thank the two of them for entrusting me with writing this oddball guide. I can't thank enough all the local historians, librarians, teachers, researchers, paranormal investigators, reporters, and sheriff's officers in all 146 counties in both North and South Carolina, who took time to write me back and send me leads. I wish I could have found space for everything they sent.

As far as I've been able to determine, the materials found herein are factual—or at least the individuals who passed them along to me believed them to be true, and I found no reason to question them. I regret any omissions or misstatements, and especially anything that may not have been properly credited.

So let's warm up the car and grab the maps. Maybe we'll stop by Piggly Wiggly to pick up something for lunch, but let's get going—we've got some weird stuff to go see!

– Roger Manley

Local Legends

Mention legends to anyone from the Carolinas and you'll hear stories of killer hurricanes, phantom white deer, and discoveries of buried treasure. Legends are the explanations we come up with when we really don't know how something came to be or why it behaves the way it does. And sometimes they may have just that little kernel of truth to them. For example, when people in Darlington, SC, talk about the Civil War, they don't talk about troop movements or battles. They like to single out the story of Union soldier J. L. Klickner. He was ordered by General Sherman to burn the home of Confederate Colonel Samuel H. Wilds. Klickner was unable to bring himself to do it. Why? It turns out that before the war he had been an architect, and the Wilds home had been one of his fondest commissions. He just couldn't bring himself to destroy his own labor of love. This nonevent has become a local legend in ways that reveal far more about the complexities of that conflict than any straight historical record.

For more fascinating twice-told tales from the Carolinas, read on.

Bloody Boulder at Gimghoul Castle

Freshmen at the University of North Carolina at Chapel Hill can scarcely make it past their first few weeks without being bombarded with legends about the campus.

The one most likely to stick is the tale of Peter Dromgoole. Dromgoole's wealthy Virginia family sent him to Chapel Hill in 1831, the story goes, to enroll at the university. However, he failed his admissions exam, and rather than return home, he stayed on and hired a tutor in order to acquire the skills he needed to get admitted. However, he spent his time drinking, playing cards, and chasing girls, all of whom were "townies," since the university was male-only.

One of the girls he began flirting with was a local lass named Fannie. Unfortunately, she had a long-term beau in the village who objected to Dromgoole's taking an interest in his girl, and objected even more when the interest seemed to be reciprocated by her. Without Fannie's knowledge, the now former boyfriend challenged Dromgoole to a duel.

The two challengers met east of the campus at a place called Piney Prospect. They squared off back to back, each holding a loaded pistol, and began taking the counted paces in opposite directions. Then came the command to turn and fire. Dromgoole missed. The other young man's bullet struck him in the chest, and Dromgoole stumbled and fell, his body draped over a large boulder.

As often happens, it occurred only too late to the small gathering of students and townies watching the proceedings that something truly serious had taken place. Up to this point, the spectacle of it all had been entertaining. However, now there was a genuine corpse in their midst, and they panicked. Several of them rolled aside the boulder on which Dromgoole had fallen and dug a shallow grave under it. They rolled the boulder back over the grave and, after swearing each other to absolute secrecy, left the scene as quickly as they could.

Fannie, meanwhile, had found out about the duel and began frantically trying to find out what had happened. She was told conflicting stories, and the poor girl was never able to sort them out. All she knew was that her beloved Peter was gone, without a word of farewell. The realization that she might never know for sure what

had become of him slowly drove her mad. As she sank deeper and deeper into insanity, she would wander back to Piney Prospect and sit on the boulder that, unknown to her, hid his corpse. She didn't last long, dying within months, of a broken heart.

The duel had taken place early on a cold spring morning in 1833. Fifty-six years later, in the fall semester of 1889, UNC students Robert Bingham, Shepard Bryan, William Davies, Wray Martin, and Andrew Patterson founded a secret society based partly on the mystique surrounding the legend of Peter and Fannie, naming it the Order of Dromgoole. They soon changed it to Gimgoole and finally to Gimghoul, because, according to Davies, it sounded more like "midnight and graves and weirdness." Martin came up with the rituals and the constitution, which combined the secret pact of the legend of Dromgoole with the chivalric ideals expressed in the legends of King Arthur and the Knights of the Round Table. Only male upperclassmen and faculty could be invited to join, and the order's membership was kept strictly secret—and remains so today.

In time, the group prospered through some real estate moves, which included buying up the area of Piney Prospect that surrounds the "Tomb of Peter Dromgoole" (as the large boulder had already come to be known). By selling parts of the property for residential lots, they were able to finance the building of a meeting place, officially called Hippol Castle but known throughout Chapel Hill as Gimghoul Castle. The castle was built in the mid-1920s of rough field boulders, and many believe it is haunted by the ghost of Peter Dromgoole. In front of it is the boulder that hides his body. It is still spattered with splotches of the blood, they say, of the would-be student who died for honor and the love of a Chapel Hill girl.

FeeJee Mermaid

Folklorists interviewing ex-slaves in Charleston in the early 20th century recorded their old stories about heavy rains that would not stop, until the mermaid caught in the bottle was set free. The mermaid they spoke of was from Fiji—and had once appeared in Charleston, but as part of a great hoax.

In August 1842, "English naturalist Dr. J. Griffin" arrived in New York with a "mermaid" supposedly caught off the coast of the island of Fiji. P. T. Barnum ran ads that depicted it as a beautiful naked woman. In January of 1843, Alanson Taylor, in the employ of his nephew P. T. Barnum, offered the public the chance to see for a mere fifty cents, the "FeeJee Mermaid," an object that Barnum himself described as an "ugly, dried up, . . . diminutive specimen, about three feet long."

People in Charleston were anxious to see it. Lutheran minister John Bachman went to see the specimen. He wrote a letter to the newspaper *Mercury* proclaiming the mermaid "a cruel hoax." It was so badly put together, he wrote, that one could still see the seams where the body of a monkey was clumsily joined to the tail of a fish.

Barnum's uncle replied in the *Courier*, calling such an attack malicious slander. He allowed the *Courier*'s editor, Richard Yeadon, to examine it. Yeadon wrote that the mermaid was real, thus selling both more papers and more tickets.

Eventually, the mermaid—or whatever it was—went on to Savannah and the controversy faded.
—*Harlan Greene*

Vollis Simpson's Whirligig Park

It isn't often that someone has a legend grow up about him while he's still alive to refute it. But that's what's happened to Vollis Simpson. The story goes something like this. A number of years ago, Simpson's daughter was out partying with her friends when someone produced some hits of LSD. After taking the acid, the carload of teenagers went on a wild driving spree out through the countryside near Wilson, NC. At a particularly dangerous intersection, the driver lost control of the car and smashed it headlong into a tree, killing several of the passengers, including the young Miss Simpson. Crazy with grief, her father began nailing reflectors to all the trees in the woods surrounding the intersection, and then began building a series of huge machines to replicate the experience of being high on LSD. "Acid Park," as the site finally became known, was eventually made up of nearly thirty of these gigantic wind-driven mechanisms.

Lest anyone doubt the truth of the story, the storyteller (usually a college kid from nearby Rocky Mount or Greenville) could gather up a carload of buddies from the dorm and drive them out to the intersection where the machines actually stood. Here he could not only show them how all the trees really are adorned with reflectors that glow in the headlights, but could point out the actual wrecked car where the daughter died, still wrapped around the tree where her anguished father discovered it.

Fortunately for the Simpson family, none of it is true. Vollis Simpson's daughter is alive and well and raising her own family nearby. Simpson himself was never crazy with grief, but did have a long-term interest in wind power. He built his first wind machine during World War II, when he was stationed in the Marianas Islands, and used it to operate a washing machine at a

base with no electricity.

After getting out of the army, he opened a welding shop and continued to tinker with whirligigs, mostly for his own entertainment. One day he brought an old car to the shop to strip it of its engine and ball bearings. When he was finished with it, he dragged it off into the woods. Eventually a tree grew up through the hood, thus giving rise to the "daughter's death car" of the legend.

At the age of sixty-seven, Simpson built his first giant whirligig, purely for his own visual amusement. He'd closed his welding business but still felt too vigorous to retire completely. And besides, there was a huge array of used parts, and junked machinery lying around the old shop, which he hated to let go to waste. "I just couldn't see throwing it all away," he said. "So I decided to do something big with it. I was just trying to make something out of all that mess!"

The intersection where the crash is supposed to have happened is pretty amazing. Though they're becoming a bit rusted, a number of four-story-tall windmills atop immense structures still groan as they slowly turn into the wind to power life-size animals and mechanical people that ride bikes and strum guitars, saw wood, and wave at passersby. Reflectors and chromed parts still sparkle, and pieces picked for their sound tones still chime together as the hundreds of parts spin. Teams of mules pull full-size wagons, dogs wave flags, and birds flap their wings — all of it springing from the happy spirit of Simpson's creative joy, not his sorrow.

A Bad Trip at Acid Park

Four of my friends here in North Carolina took a road trip to a local legend out in Wilson—Acid Park. After about five miles and a few hundred abandoned, scary-looking shacks, we were sure we had missed it. Then I saw what looked to be a massive Christmas tree covered in blue lights. It's hard to describe what we saw, other than just huge towers with windmills, trains, bicycles and every other thing you can imagine on top. And everything was covered in millions of reflectors.

We turned off the lights and it was grotesque—silhouettes in front of a full harvest-moon sky. Even with heat lightning in the background, I can't say I was that scared. It was just amazingly cool. At only one point for me was it scary, when the wind started to blow and the frogs stopped croaking. Suddenly the area was filled with the creaking and whispering of these huge towers. Sure enough, you drive down a dirt road to the left of the towers and there is an old car wrapped around a tree . . . draw your own conclusions.

—RockintheCasbah

Pentagram of Acid Park

Ok, first off, I've heard both stories about Acid Park. I've heard the myth and the story that some say is the truth. Really, I can't tell which one to believe. The thing I don't understand is why they say it's a myth, yet there is a Pentagram in front of the site with the girl mentioned in the story, Valerie, in the middle of it. There are really just too many questions that could be asked about this whole mysterious place. And I don't have all the answers to them. —Scott, LostPlayground.com

Cameras Mysteriously Rewind

I live in Winterville, NC, which is about 30–40 minutes from Acid Park. The other night a couple of people and I went out to look at it. Yes, it was pretty intense. One of my friends took her camera to take pics of it, and when we did, the camera broke and rewound automatically. We had only taken three of 27 pics . . . pretty weird, huh? Why do you suppose it did that? Just coincidence, maybe? I don't think so . . .

—Legacy, LostPlayground.com

White Deer

Albino deer, perhaps because of their eerie beauty, figure prominently in Carolina folklore. Dozens of local legends tell of how hunters, wounding a white deer, track the drops of blood to a lonely cabin where a woman is found dying of a gunshot wound. In some of the tales, the woman is described as young and beautiful. Sometimes she's something of a social outcast

or an elderly person long regarded as a witch.

One of the more specific of such stories has to do with Virginia Dare, the first English child born in the New World (see **Ancient Mysteries**). There are many variations on the legend, but most of them share the same basic plot points. The "lost" Roanoke colonists end up living with or being rescued by a local Indian tribe. As the years wear on, two men of the tribe fall in love with the pale but blossoming Virginia. The older one is a medicine man, who realizes she is more smitten with the younger fellow, so he uses his magic to turn her into a white deer in order to keep her away from his rival. There is a remedy to unlock the spell, however, should the need ever arise: If wounded with a magic arrow, the white doe will change back into the girl.

Everything goes along fine for a while. The old magician encounters his beloved deer in the woods from time to time, satisfied that though she can never be his girl, she won't belong to any other guy either.

Then a young man from a neighboring tribe decides to hunt the deer. The medicine man realizes he has to use his magic arrow to unlock the spell before the other man kills her; but, sad to say, his arrow and that of the young hunter strike the deer at the same time. This has the effect of turning the doe back into a girl, but only just in time to die. No happy ending to this old story.

Despite the legend's depressing climax, many people think Virginia Dare still wanders the Carolina woods in white-deer form. Recent reports of a white deer spotted along the Eno River near Durham, NC, include the disconcerting detail that it can sometimes be heard speaking in a woman's voice. A more down-to-earth manifestation of the pale creature can be found in The Little Storytelling House of Garner, NC. There the town has lovingly stuffed and preserved a small albino doe, accidentally killed by an automobile.

Untouchable Tree of Comingtee

On the grounds of the old Comingtee Plantation, on the Cooper River near Cordesville, SC, was a peculiar tree called, for reasons that now seem to be forgotten, the Old Robintation Tree. Employees of the plantation, both enslaved and free, long regarded it as haunted. The trunk of the tree emerged from under a huge flat boulder — in and of itself a rare item in the swampy Low Country — which some of the older folks on the property said was the grave slab of an Indian chief. A ghost lived in the tree, they claimed, and as long as the tree stood untouched, no serious harm could ever come to those who lived in the house or on the property.

For two hundred years the plantation remained in private ownership, then was sold to a paper company in the 1930s. Not long ago, thousands of acres, including the vine-covered ruins of the old house that Elias Ball built here in 1738, were sold to the Conservation Fund of South Carolina. The state hopes eventually to reopen lands that have long been closed to the public. The tiny plot of land surrounding the old tree will have been untouched longest of all, if they can ever locate it.

Two centuries ago, bits of the ancient stone slab, pounded together with leaves found fallen from the tree, were in such demand by root doctors among those of African origin and by the medicine men of the remnants of the local Native American tribes that the Ball family, which owned the plantation (and believed in the lore as well), was eventually forced to fence it in and declare it off-limits to all but themselves. Thereafter, for as long as they owned it, neither they nor any of their people dared touch it. We wonder what could happen if any unsuspecting hikers or forest conservationists were accidentally to touch it now.

Grey Man of Pawleys Island

Before every major hurricane in the past century, people on Pawleys Island have reported encounters with the infamous Grey Man. He warns people of the impending danger and urges them to leave the island. If they heed his warnings, their homes survive unscathed. If they ignore him and stay on the island to weather the storm, great damage is inflicted upon them.

According to legend, the Grey Man is a former resident of the area who suffered a gruesome and untimely death. He had been overseas for months and upon his return was in a hurry to reunite with his fiancée. On his way to meet his beloved, he took a shortcut through some marshland and rode his horse into a patch of deadly quicksand, where he met his end.

The Grey Man has continued to patrol Pawleys Island, warning the unsuspecting whenever danger approaches.

A few days later, this man's fiancée was sadly walking along the beach when a figure appeared before her. She thought it was her fiancé and ran toward him. Instead of a happy reunion, however, she was met with stern warnings. The figure shouted to her, telling her that she was in grave danger and had to leave the island at once. She and her family did so, and they were spared from a raging hurricane.

Since that first warning so many decades ago, the Grey Man has continued to patrol Pawleys Island, warning the unsuspecting whenever danger approaches.

Another Version of the Grey Man Legend

Howling winds, torrents of rain, lightning streaking across the sky, and night as black as the deepest hole—this is what the Grey Man warns is coming when he meets you on the dunes of Pawleys Island. He does not need to speak; his mere presence is warning enough.

Who is the Grey Man and why does he warn selected individuals of impending storms? Some say that he is the ghost of Perceval Pawley, the founding father of Pawleys Island. Others say he is rice-plantation heir Plowden Charles Jeanerette Weston, whose home is now the Evans Pelican Inn. Both men loved the island and their homes, making them good candidates for a ghost on storm watch.

Others believe that the Grey Man is the lover of a beautiful Charleston belle. The man, however, was unacceptable to the woman's family and was sent away to France. But he vowed he would return for his beloved and make her his wife. When it was reported that the man had died in a duel, the grief-stricken woman went into mourning for him. She eventually married another man, and the couple made Pawleys Island their home from May through October each year.

One night, the banished lover turned up again, after the brigantine he was sailing in sank in a storm off Pawleys Island. As luck would have it, he was rescued by one of the woman's manservants. He was brought to the woman's door, and she fainted when she saw that the bedraggled man standing in front of her was her former lover. The man realized that his love had married another and he fled, later dying alone on the mainland of a deadly fever.

The woman resumed her life, but she was frequently troubled by the presence of a grey figure that watched her from the dunes. At one point, he appeared and told her to leave the island immediately, which she did. A devastating hurricane followed shortly after she left. The grey figure had saved her life.

Whoever the Grey Man is or was, he continues to warn residents of hurricanes. Prior to Hurricane Hugo in 1989, an elderly couple encountered him as they walked in the dunes. They did not speak with him but were familiar with the legend and fled. Their home was the only one in the area not demolished by the hurricane. Their kitchen door had opened in the storm, but the towels on the railings of their porch were still hanging undisturbed. —*Karlie*

Witches' Keyhole

The outdoor sign in front of Trinity United Methodist Church at 901 Seehorn Street in Lenoir, NC, has a curious feature. There is a keyhole shape made of dark brick embedded in the lighter-colored brick of the sign, which doubles as a planter. Nothing calls attention to its earlier use or explains what it is doing in front of a modern suburban church.

The keyhole, according to local stories, once provided an escape route for witches.

The details of the story are sketchy, but here's what we've pieced together. George Powell's first house was a log cabin, and when it burned, he blamed the fire on an accumulation of witches and evil spirits that had entered through the keyholes in the doors and then had been unable to dissipate into the surrounding spiritual ether. John Hawkins, director of the Caldwell Heritage Museum, says that when Powell built his second house, in 1818, he not only built it of brick to diminish the fire hazard, but also provided a keyhole-shaped opening near the eave so that any dangerous or malevolent spirits could be encouraged to escape and not burn down the new place.

According to the *Autobiography* of the blind preacher Brantley York, born in 1805 in Randolph County, NC, a witch could "creep through a key-hole, [and] by the magic of a certain bridle called the witch's bridle—she could change any person on whom she could place it, into a horse; and then what is still more remarkable, both could come out through a key-hole, and, being mounted, she could ride this remarkable horse wherever she chose, nor could such an animal assume its identity till the bridle was removed." It's possible that George Powell made his keyhole oversized to avoid bumping his head or getting his sides scraped if some uninvited visitor turned him into a horse.

The Keyhole House (which stood roughly where the church is now) was finally torn down, but the keyhole itself was saved and remounted intact. However, the opening in the hole seems to have been bricked up. We suppose that means it's up to the Methodists to drive out any evil spirits themselves now.

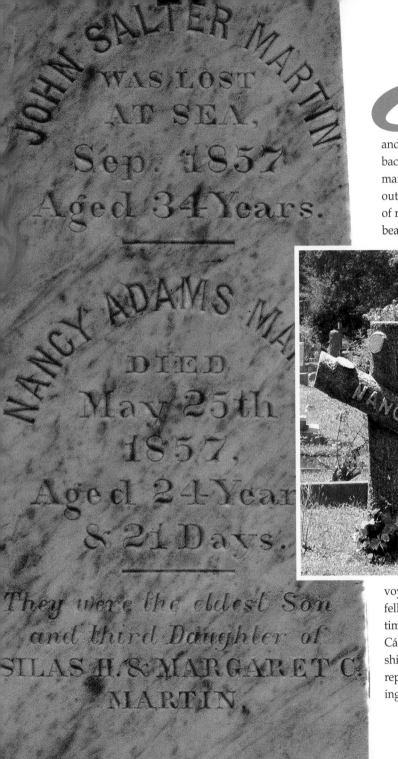

JOHN SALTER MARTIN
WAS LOST
AT SEA,
Sep. 1857
Aged 34 Years.

NANCY ADAMS MA...
DIED
May 25th
1857,
Aged 24 Year...
& 21 Days.

They were the eldest Son
and third Daughter of
SILAS H. & MARGARET C.
MARTIN.

Curse of the Martin House

Among a cluster of finely polished marble and granite tombstones found in a family plot at the back of Wilmington's old Oakdale Cemetery is one marker that, though smaller than all the others, stands out among them. Carved of stone to replicate the look of rustic logs and notched together to form a cross, it bears a single word—the nickname of the girl it memorializes—NANCE.

In the spring of 1857, Nancy Martin and her older brother John set out to help their father, Captain Silas Martin, attempt a major family investment venture. For a captain to take family members along on a trading voyage was not uncommon in those days. It helped assuage the loneliness that set in after months at sea and meant having crew members who could be counted on, since they'd want the venture to succeed as much as the captain himself would.

This was not to be one of those lucky fortune-making voyages, though. Not long out of Wilmington, Nancy fell ill and spent the next few weeks groaning every time the ship pitched as it slowly made its way to Cárdenas, Cuba, its first port of call. The moment the ship docked, Captain Martin sent for a doctor, who reported that the girl was too far gone. There was nothing he could do.

A few days later, the fever took her. Captain

Martin couldn't bear the idea of leaving his daughter on foreign soil, and he knew his wife would never forgive him if he buried her at sea. So he did the only thing he could to preserve her body before refrigeration—he and John put her into a barrel that could be filled with liquor, topped it up with whisky and rum, and then sealed the barrel and lashed it down to keep it from rolling.

This wasn't the last disaster on the journey. Four months later, the ship encountered a storm. The following morning, young John was nowhere to be found. The crew presumed that he had been washed overboard.

Though Captain Martin finally made it back to Wilmington, no amount of profit could make up for his losses. He and his wife, Margaret, buried Nance, still in her barrel, and erected the cross beside her. The experience had taken a huge toll on the captain himself, and within four more years, he too would die.

Some say that the home where Nance and her family once lived seems to be cursed.

The house still stands on Ann Street in Wilmington. It was built in stages between 1784 and 1830, and Captain William Cooke was the first to live in it. In 1791, George Washington commissioned Cooke as captain of the revenue cutter *Diligence*. Forerunners of coast guard ships, vessels like the *Diligence* patrolled the coast for pirates and smugglers. Cooke was highly successful at the job and confiscated a great deal of gold and contraband, which then went into the U.S. treasury.

But around 1796, Cooke disappeared. Perhaps he pursued his job a little too eagerly, as some say, and crossed the wrong wrongdoer? Or was it something to do with the house? Tradition says there was a tunnel from it to another location in Wilmington, but now the tunnel is

caved in and only the entrance remains. So where did it lead, and what purpose did it really serve? At this point, it's anybody's guess.

After Captain Cooke vanished and Mrs. Cooke passed on, the Martins moved in and the terrible things that happened to them followed.

Next was William Anderson, a jeweler and silversmith, who moved in around 1860. He was not a good businessman and eventually fell so heavily into debt that he hanged himself from a tree that still stands behind the house.

In 1886, the house was sold to E. H. Keathley, a watchmaker. He, too, came to an untimely end.

What is it about this place? All its former occupants have come to a bad end. The current owners say they hope to figure out how to make peace with the house before it strikes again.

Tut's Curse Comes to Carolina

Within weeks of the opening of King Tutankhamen's tomb in Egypt's Valley of the Kings, on February 17, 1923, the international press was buzzing with the possibility that the tomb had been protected by some kind of "mummy's curse," and that evil would befall those who had defiled the ancient pharaoh's

remains. Sure enough, on March 6, Lord Carnarvon, who had underwritten archaeologist Howard Carter's excavations and was the second person to gaze into the burial chamber, was bitten on the cheek by a mosquito and soon died. By 1929, eleven people who knew or were related to Carnarvon or Carter had died young or unexpectedly.

Those who downplayed the curse pointed out that of the twenty-six people who had actually been present when the tomb was opened, only six had died within the following decade, and given their ages, this was statistically normal. Nearly everyone, in fact, lived to a ripe old age. But the legend refused to go away. And a few years later, the curse seemed to have spread to America, more specifically to Winnsboro, SC.

One of the major local industries in Winnsboro was the quarrying of a premier building material called Winnsboro Blue Granite, America's densest, strongest,

and most flawless granite. It is the stone used in the building of, among others, the Washington Monument, and is actually mostly gray. The source of the granite is a series of pits about eight miles west of the town, locally known as The Rock, or the Old Anderson Quarry, after one of its former owners.

In the mid-1920s, Ben Huger Heyward and his wife, who then owned the quarry, took a trip to Egypt to see the newly discovered wonders of King Tut and the ancient ruins of Egypt for themselves. They came back from their trip with marvelous stories of the incredible sights they'd seen and the experiences they'd had.

One of the favorite treasures they'd picked up on their journey was a small funerary statuette called a *shabti*, which an unscrupulous guide had sold them on the sly while they were in the Valley of the Kings. Mrs. Heyward liked to regale her friends with the story of how the guide had spoken in whispers, asking them to pocket it quickly and keep it out of sight until they were safely out of Egypt. When she imitated his furtive Egyptian accent the whole room would burst into laughter, and then inevitably someone would jokingly mention the Mummy's Curse. It made a good story.

But before long, people began whispering that maybe the Mummy's Curse wasn't such a joke after all. Things started to go wrong at the quarry. A series of labor disputes interrupted the workflow at the big pits. Strange fires broke out from time to time. Finally, on July 18, 1930, tragedy struck when a chain broke and five tons of granite fell onto Ben Heyward, killing him instantly.

The Mummy apparently wasn't finished. In 1941, Ben's son Dan was killed in a fiery automobile crash. Several years later Dan's wife, Nancy, was found in the basement of the family home, where she'd committed suicide. Not long after Dan's death, the quarry closed for the next six decades, its pits filling with water.

A young couple eventually acquired the property and began selling some of the stone, and the mysterious misfortunes began again when a piece of machinery killed the husband. Locals whisper that the man's wife, now a well-known Charleston artist, continues to sell the stone but is careful to keep a wide distance between herself and the pits, rarely visiting the area at all. She may know all too well that the angry spirit of the Pharaoh might be waiting to claim his next victim.

Nïkwäsï' Mound, Home of the Fighting Nûñnĕ'hï

On East Main Street in Franklin, NC, there is a strange little park almost wholly dominated by an artificial hill covered in carefully maintained grass. Traffic whizzes by, and no one seems to pay the mound much attention. Which is just as well, since something about it seems to want to keep a low profile and repel visitors. No one knows what that might be.

Known as Nïkwäsï' Mound, it is at least 1,000 years old and may be a great deal older than that. It's one of the few ancient sites that have never been excavated. Mounds in other places have contained things like human burials, stone sculptures, and artifacts made of copper or mica, but this one continues to keep its secrets.

It is a good deal smaller than it once was. A few centuries of erosion and neglect have worn it down since the time it was surrounded by a Cherokee town of the same name as the mound here (sometimes spelled Nequassee, Nucassee, or Noucassih). The Cherokees never claimed to have built the mound, but said they only maintained and used it. It was probably built by an earlier people usually called the Mississippians. According to legend, it may contain an *ulunsu'ti* crystal from the forehead of an *uktena,* the giant snakes that live in deep holes or in caves near high mountain passes. It is also said to contain the Cherokees' most powerful allies.

The Cherokees considered the mound to be inhabited by a race of powerful spirit-beings called the Nûñnĕ'hï, who also had other "townhouses" inside Pilot Mountain in Surry County, and at the head of the Tugaloo River in Oconee County, SC. According to folklorist Gary Carden, Nûñnĕ'hï means "those who live anywhere." "In ancient times," he says, "smoke from their underground town-house could be seen emerging from the top of the mound. (They also fished in the sky and hunted deer on the bottoms of rivers.) Since they were favorably disposed towards the Cherokees, they often gave them advice, socialized with them (they loved to dance) and even came to their rescue in a battle fought near the mound."

Anthropologist James Mooney recorded the story of this battle when he visited among the Cherokees in the 1890s. According to what the Cherokees told him, the warriors of the old town of Nïkwäsï' kept scouts constantly on guard, looking for danger. One morning before daybreak, their lookouts saw an enemy approaching and at once gave the alarm. The Nïkwäsï' men rushed out to meet the attack, but after a long, hard fight they found themselves overpowered and began to retreat. Suddenly a stranger stood among them and shouted to the chief to call off his men. He himself would drive back the enemy.

The Nïkwäsï' fell back along the trail, and as they came near the townhouse, they saw a great company of warriors coming out from the side of the mound as through an open doorway. Then they knew that their friends were the Nûñnë'hï, the Immortals, although no one had ever heard before that they lived under Nïkwäsï' Mound.

The Nûñnë'hï poured out by the hundreds, armed and painted for the fight. But the most curious thing was that they became invisible as soon as they were outside the settlement, so that although the enemy saw the glancing arrow or felt the rushing tomahawk, they could not see who sent it. The invaders tried to retreat and hide, but the Nûñnë'hï arrows went around the rocks and killed them from the other side, and they were defeated.

When the battle was over, the fighting Nûñnë'hï went back into the mound.

And they may still be there. In the Civil War, when a strong party of Federal troops came to surprise a handful of Confederates posted in Franklin, they saw so many soldiers guarding the town that they retreated without making an attack.

Today, some people believe that it is possible to hear drumbeats from deep within the ancient mound, where the Nûñnë'hï are said to have their living quarters. We hope no one ever digs into the place to find out if they are really there. Some things need to remain a mystery.

Ancient Mysteries

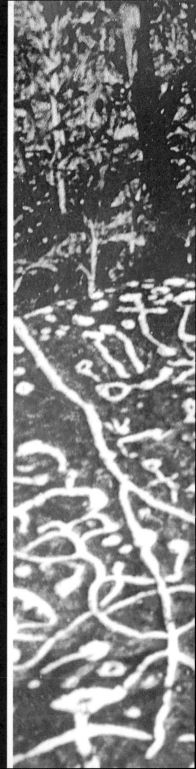

What kind of world would we have without mysteries? Without unknowns that hang in the shadows around us, we'd be trapped in a kind of *Truman Show* existence, with nothing waiting to be discovered beyond the horizon. Mysteries hint that there is more to our world than we can see. That it is all much bigger, more complicated, more *interesting* than we may have imagined.

Some of the most intriguing mysteries are the ones from the past, things that actually happened and left some kind of evidence behind. It might be a mysteriously carved stone, an empty ship drifting in the sea, a mound of earth. Each of these had some reason for being at the time, but its purpose and significance have been lost. What happened in the ages that came before us to create these things? What do they mean to us today? Let's visit a few of the thousands of Carolina mysteries that, to date, remain unsolved.

Sand River

In Aiken, SC, it's possible to walk on a river and not get your feet wet—because this river is made of quartz sand. In many ways it's like an ordinary waterway; its tributaries are several narrow and crooked sand creeks that widen into a broader streambed. It performs like any other river, except that it is white, silent, dry, and, from ordinary human perspective, immobile. Geologists maintain, however, that it *does* move, though so slowly you can't see it.

Emerald City

Well, "Emerald Town," anyway. Hiddenite, NC, is the home of Jamie Hill, a.k.a. the Rockhound with the Green Thumb. Hill owns a tract of less than fifty acres on which he has discovered some of the world's largest emeralds, both in terms of size (a ten-inch twin crystal discovered in 2006) and weight (an 1,861.9 carat "hog's leg" he found in 2003). Hill had already found the previous record holder in the 1980s (1,686 carats), as well as some of the most valuable emeralds ever mined in North America—the 858-carat Empress Caroline and another 71-carat stone that was subsequently cut into two stones, the 7.85-carat Carolina Prince (which sold for $500,000), and the 18.88-carat Carolina Queen, valued at a million dollars. And there may be more to come. Hill has recently discovered and begun exploring a crystal-lined cavern on his mining property that he calls Aladdin's Cave. He's convinced it will hold yet more amazing treasures.

Hiddenite itself is named for another green gemstone, named in turn for mineralogist W. E. Hidden, who discovered it while hunting for platinum. Hidden had been hired by inventor Thomas Edison to survey various mineral locales for rare metals to be used in Edison's incandescent light manufactures. The mineral hiddenite is one of the rarest gems on earth, and has been found only on two acres in North Carolina and in extremely small deposits in Madagascar and Brazil.

North Carolina is also the home of the world's largest sapphire, which weighs 385 pounds. It is located in Franklin, an area famous for rubies.

Healing Springs

North of Blackville, SC, is the tiny community of Healing Springs, named for a cluster of artesian wells where water gushes up out of the ground under natural pressure at the edge of a small swamp. Not exactly a mystery, the water is said to have remarkable healing powers, and people come from all over the region to fill up containers and lug it home. There's no charge, since paying the owner would be somewhat difficult, at least in this world. The springs are the legal property of God, left to Him in the last will and testament of Mr. L. P. Boylston on July 21, 1944.

The waters have been known since ancient times for their miraculous powers. They first came to the attention of European settlers when Native Americans used the bounty of the springs to treat four wounded Tory loyalists given up for dead by British general Banastre "the Butcher" Tarleton in 1781. (Native Americans were frequently allied with Redcoats during the Revolutionary War.) After a few months drinking the waters, the men were raring to get back to the job of shooting patriots.

GOD'S ACRE HEALING SPRINGS

ACCORDING TO TRADITION THE INDIANS REVERENCED THE WATER FOR ITS HEALING PROPERTIES AS A GIFT FROM THE GREAT SPIRIT. THEY LED THE BRITISH WOUNDED TO THEIR SECRET WATERS DURING THE AMERICAN REVOLUTION AND THE WOUNDED WERE HEALED. THIS HISTORICAL PROPERTY HAS BEEN DEEDED TO GOD FOR PUBLIC USE. PLEASE REVERE GOD BY KEEPING IT CLEAN.

Great Hickory Sinkhole

On August 17, 2002, heavy rains fell in the Hickory, NC, area. Customers dining in the new Buffalo's Southwest Café on Highway 70 were feeling glad to be dry and safe inside, when someone happened to look out and notice that a sizable portion of the parking lot had just sunk out of sight in two places. Those who could, quickly moved their cars, but not before one man saw his brand-new Chevy Corvette plunge into one of the holes. The car was soon crushed as the sides of the holes continued to collapse and eventually join to form one gigantic pit. Exposed water mains and drainage pipes ruptured as the pit kept growing.

As of the publication of this book, the sinkhole still exists, despite four years of ongoing efforts to slow its destructive expansion and refill it. Multiple lawsuits are now threatening further progress toward repairing the humongous hole.
—*Thanks to Barry Huffman*

Ancient Submarine Cities

Angela Michol of Newton and Concord, NC, runs a Web site at www.satellitediscoveries.com that documents earth-surface anomalies observed from satellites orbiting our planet. These anomalies include underwater features that seem to be artificial, whether made by humans, extraterrestrials, or some other (subsurface, marine?) intelligent life forms.

For example, Michol has found rows of aligned circles off the coast near the Outer Banks, areas of extremely straight parallel lines both on land and underwater, and submarine features that seem to mimic the Carolina Bays. As she points out, the "discovery of the ancient city of Akroteri on the island of Santorini [a part of Greece] was made by a local landowner who noticed numerous circular sink holes on his land. One day while inspecting his land, he fell into one of the sinkholes and discovered the lost city of Akroteri below. The smaller circular features in Florida, the Bahamas, the Keys, Cuba, the Caycos Islands, the Carolinas and [elsewhere] along the East Coast may not be evidence of meteor strikes, but they could be evidence of something below ground. This is a possibility that has been overlooked by researchers and theorists as to how the Carolina Bays and similar circular features were formed. Perhaps they could be artificial in origin. The jury is still out."

Michol looks forward to a time when alternative archaeology like the kind she pursues will become more accepted, but meanwhile she's used to listening to others ridicule her theories. "People accept what's in books too much," she says. "They should try to figure stuff out on their own."

We couldn't agree more.

Headless Bodies of Folly Beach

In an October 27, 2005, article in The Journal of James Island and Folly Beach, SC, Sally Watts described how fourteen bodies were found in May 1987 when foundations for a construction site at the west end of Folly Beach were excavated. Construction was halted for a month while authorities investigated the remains.

According to Watts, "All of the bodies except one had been buried with shoulders directed to the west. Twelve of the bodies were missing skulls and other major body parts. Some of the burials had coffins; others had only ponchos. With the bodies were found Union Army eagle buttons, one '#5' insignia from a cap, and Enfield Rifle .57 caliber Mini Balls." State archaeologists finally decided the men were from the Union Army's 55th Massachusetts Volunteer Regiment. "Because the bodies had no injuries, the possibility of death in battle was eliminated. That left only the possibility of death by illness, head injury, or beheading.

"There are several (unproven) opinions as to why the remains were minus [their] skulls. One theory is that bounty hunters sought the skulls of buried Union soldiers when the federal government offered rewards for retrieval of bodies. But the odd thing was that while the skulls were missing, the rest of the bones were undisturbed. . . . It's not likely bounty hunters would be so respectful when 'collecting' their prizes. Another opinion was that the skulls were removed by local islanders for voodoo rituals."

A final, even scarier, and perhaps more likely theory imagined a scene in which a deranged Confederate commander took things into his own hands, dispensed with official military regulations regarding the proper treatment of his prisoners, and ordered their heads cut off.

Pardo Stone

One day in 1934, Bryson Hammett was plowing on his farm near Inman, SC, when he struck a rock with strange markings carved into it: the date 1567, an arrow, a sun, and a parallelogram.

In 1566, Juan Pardo had led a group of Spanish conquistadors into the interior of the Carolinas. They left their fort at St. Elena (today's Parris Island) and made it as far as an Indian village called Joara, about fifty miles east of Asheville. They built a small fort they named Fort San Juan. The hope was that this

fort would become a way station on a land route from Mexico to the Atlantic, so that the Spanish treasure caravans could transport gold without having to risk losing their galleons to pirates or storms.

Unfortunately, they didn't realize how far away Mexico City is from the Low Country (roughly 3,000 miles), and were hopelessly undermanned to set up a series of forts to cover that distance. But what really messed things up was something that happened while Pardo was away from his troops.

He had been ordered back to St. Elena, because French forces were threatening the fort there. While he was gone, he left about thirty men in the charge of a Sergeant Boyano. Boyano led an unprovoked attack on a group of Indians in eastern Tennessee. By the time Pardo returned, word had spread among native communities that the Spanish were vicious killers. A large group of Native Americans gathered near the village of Coosa, in northern Georgia, preparing to ambush the Spanish. Pardo learned about this and was forced to abandon the plans for a string of forts. They beat a retreat to St. Elena and never returned.

The stone farmer Hammett plowed up seems to have something to do with Pardo's exploits, but the meaning of its symbols remains a mystery.

Judaculla Rock

Around Cullowhee, NC, a strange greenish-brown outcrop of soapstone jutting up at an angle has long been called Judaculla Rock. That's a corruption of Tsul`kälû', the Cherokee name for the "slant-eyed" giant they believed placed it there. The weird markings on it are between 1,000 and 10,000 years old, according to some archaeologists. No one knows what all the peculiar images in its surface mean. Some think it is a history of the local people, some think it records a treaty with the Catawba tribe, and some people think it's just a giant doodle.

It's a mystery that not even the Cherokees can solve. In their own legends, the markings were left after Tsul`kälû' used the rock as a stepping-stone while leap-

ing from his mountain home eight miles away down to the Caney Fork creek that runs below here. Since the Cherokees don't remember what the markings mean, the field is wide open for any other explanation.

One Asheville-based paranormal group has advanced the hypothesis that the rock is evidence of a visitation by ancient astronauts from another planet. These aliens had microscopes thousands of years before that device was invented. To support this notion, the group points to similarities between some of the peculiar shapes visible on the rock and infinitesimal amoebas, hydras, and certain forms of bacteria.

On the other hand, many of the shapes also bear an uncanny resemblance to 1950s linoleum patterns, but we're not willing to conclude that this means the rock was carved by a prehistoric Ozzie and Harriet.

We're more inclined to think Judaculla Rock is covered with some kind of archaic pictograms. The Cherokees are among the first Native Americans to have a written language, after Sequoyah developed the Cherokee syllabary between 1809 and 1823. But maybe a much earlier individual who lived in this valley gave written language a shot a few thousand years before that. If so, he or she would have been a real giant, but in the intellectual sense of the word.

To visit Judaculla Rock, go about four miles south of Cullowhee on Highway 107, and then turn east for three miles on Caney Fork Road and follow the signs. The road fizzles out in a private driveway, but park just before that and walk downhill.

Carroll A. Deering—Ghost Ship

The ocean waters just off the Outer Banks of North Carolina are often called the Graveyard of the Atlantic. They earned that ghastly nickname because more than 2,000 known maritime disasters have left the remains of more than 600 ships on the ocean floor, one of the highest densities of sunken ships in the world.

One of the reasons the area is such a maritime danger zone is that two currents meet just offshore, at Cape Hatteras. The southbound arctic waters of the chilly Labrador Current collide there with the northbound warm waters of the Gulf Stream in a violent confrontation that creates tossing whitecaps on even the calmest of days. At the same time, both currents slow down just enough to deposit particles of silt, seashells, and sand that have created a shallow, turbulent zone called Diamond Shoals that extends some fourteen miles out to sea.

The strange fate of one ship that sailed these treacherous waters is one of maritime history's greatest mysteries. On the morning of January 31, 1921, a lookout at the Cape Hatteras Coast Guard Station spotted a five-masted schooner stranded on Diamond Shoals, with all its sails set, almost as if it had intentionally run aground. Two rescue boats were immediately dispatched, but the freezing swells were running so high that they were unable to approach it. Through binoculars, however, they could make out the vessel's name, *Carroll A. Deering*.

They could see no crew aboard, but the fact that the *Deering*'s lifeboats were missing was possibly a good sign. At least it suggested that the rescuers could wait until conditions improved before attempting to go aboard her. Four days later, the wind and waves had abated enough to make it worth the risk.

What they found was unsettling. Nautical charts were scattered about in the captain's cabin and toilet, but the log, chronometer, and sextant were missing. Food had been set out on the crew table in the galley but never eaten, as if something had happened just before they sat down to a meal. There was no sign of a violent struggle. The ship's anchors, however, were missing. The steering cables had also been severed intentionally and the binnacle compass had been smashed with a hammer. Since this would render the ship unsteerable, no one could think of why this might have been done. Even if the crew had

mutinied, they'd probably want to keep the ship functional. Three different sets of boots found in the captain's cabin suggested that he hadn't been the only one to use it. The spare bed had been slept in. The only living thing aboard the *Deering* was the ship's tabby cat.

After saving the cat and gathering up whatever other evidence they could, the rescuers headed back to shore. There they put out word to other stations in the region to keep an eye out for her lifeboats and crew, whether alive or dead. Every inlet and bay and every inch of beach was searched. Weeks passed, however, and no clues were found to explain why the *Deering* had been abandoned as it was. As the days passed, the ship began to fall to pieces under the blows of the waves, and it was becoming a hazard to other ships. After three weeks, it was dynamited into pieces small enough to wash away.

Meanwhile, the investigation continued. During the first leg of this particular voyage, the *Deering* had been hauling coal from Newport News, Virginia, to Brazil. The original captain had fallen sick and been replaced at a port in Delaware. The trip down to Brazil had been uneventful, and then the ship had sailed to Barbados for another cargo. When this didn't materialize, it began the trip back to Newport News, empty.

Besides the fact that the ship had failed to make the return leg pay by hauling anything, that part of the trip started off with a sour incident when the first mate got boisterously drunk and was arrested the night before the ship got under way. The captain told a friend that he expected trouble and wasn't particularly confident in his crew either.

The ship was seen off the coast at Cape Fear on January 29. Six days later, she was noted at Cape Lookout, just seventy miles north—a trip that should have taken only a day. As she passed the Cape Lookout Lightship, someone on board shouted through a megaphone that the lightship crew should spread the word to stay clear of the *Deering*, since she had lost her anchors in a storm. Only after she had sailed on did the lightship crew sort out that there had been no serious storms on the coast for several weeks. They also realized that the crew had been seen milling around on the poop deck, an area normally off-limits to common seamen. Something looked suspicious.

The next time the ship was seen, she was empty and aground. All eight members of her crew, along with the mate and captain, were gone. To this date, the mystery of what happened has never been solved, though there are many theories: That Barbadian rumrunners had taken over the *Deering* and used it for a run, then scuttled it. But if so, what happened to the rumrunners? That the crew had staged a mutiny or that there had been some kind of crime on board. That it had simply foundered on the shoals and everyone had perished trying to get ashore. But how does that explain the severed cables and the lost anchors? And since the ship hadn't sunk immediately, why didn't the crew just stay aboard it a bit longer and wait for the Coast Guard to rescue them?

We may never know the answers to any of these questions. According to Edward Snow, the mysterious incident remains "the greatest mystery of the seas during the first half of the 20th century." *—Thanks to Terrance Zepke and Richard Walser*

Where Did This Junk Come From?

One of the most daunting pieces of real estate in North America is the immense region of soggy, largely impenetrable territory straddling the North Carolina-Virginia line called the Great Dismal Swamp. Despite centuries of exploiting its trees for lumber, carving canals through it for commerce, and draining parts of it for agriculture, some six hundred square miles of the thickest junglelike growth of the swamp still remain. And in this zone, there are not only places no human eye has seen, but also things that have been found but for which no explanation has been forthcoming.

Among these was, remarkably, a Chinese junk. Many decades ago, the government took over the Great Dismal Swamp for forestry management and dredged some of the old canals that had gradually become silted-in. In 1928, while enlarging one of the canals, the Army Corps of Engineers found that its dredging machinery had cut through the hulls of several strange ships, one of which was reportedly a junk of Chinese origin.

In his controversial book *1421: The Year China Discovered the World*, Gavin Menzies discusses his theory that Chinese sailors may have explored much of North and South America long before Columbus arrived in the New World. While that book has come under criticism for its inaccuracies, the Dismal Swamp junk does make one wonder. But even if Chinese explorers were sailing up the East Coast at some point in the distant past, how would a junk have wound up in the swamp itself, when it is difficult even for canoes to pass through parts of it?

We may never know. During World War II, much of the swamp became off-limits or restricted, since it was being used for bombing and jungle-warfare training. During that period, all records of the discovery of the junk seem to have been misplaced—or covered up.

Revolving Rock

A lone, strangely shaped rock in the pinewoods near Winnsboro, SC, seems so peculiar that it would be a surprise if there were no legends associated with it. But there are, of course. According to local lore, the Anvil Rock can *hear*; and loud sounds, such as the

honking of cars or the crowing of roosters, are said to so upset its equilibrium that the rock will begin to swivel around on its pedestal, usually three times. The outcrop's recorded history goes back to the early colonial period, when its owner, the Regulator Thomas Woodward, named his spread the Anvil Rock Plantation. You can find it in the woods on the south side of Highway 34, about one mile east of the SC Railroad Museum at Rockton. Be very quiet as you approach, though. It may be listening. *—Thanks to Pelham Lyles*

Steepletop Mystery

Sometimes the best mysteries are the ones that hide in plain sight. That was the case with St. Joseph's African Methodist Episcopal Church in Durham. The grand church was built in 1891, complete with a buttressed tower, Art Nouveau chandelier, and twenty-four stained-glass windows. The church was at the center of a vibrant neighborhood called Hayti,which included some of the largest black-owned companies in the world.

Unfortunately, decisions made in the 1960s to route four-lane highways through this part of town all but destroyed the community. Whole blocks were razed and businesses folded. The congregation moved out and the area turned into a wasteland.

In the 1970s, efforts began to reclaim the original energy of the place. The church building became the Hayti Heritage Center and extensive restoration efforts got under way. While workmen were repairing the steeple, they made a strange discovery. Everyone had assumed the ornament atop the steeple was a weather vane or lightning rod. But it turned out to be a Haitian voodoo symbol for Erzulie Freda Dahome, an African goddess of love. No one knows how it came to be atop the church.

Was one of the builders a former slave who remembered enough of the old beliefs to install it without anyone else knowing what it meant? If so, he must have smiled to himself when he walked by, until the secret died with him—almost.

Mystery of the Sewee Shell Ring

About three miles due south of Awendaw, SC, on Salt Pond Road (off Doar Road) there's a trail leading through the woods to the edge of the marshes surrounding Bulls Bay. Here is what looks at first like the remains of the world's largest and longest-lasting oyster party. Imagine a few hundred truly die-hard oyster lovers standing together making small talk while slurping down oysters like there's no tomorrow. As they finish each oyster, they pitch it and reach for another one. Eventually, they've tossed enough of the leftover shells over their shoulders to form a big ring around the whole group. A really big ring that is, more than head-high and about 160 feet in diameter.

Did it happen? No one knows. Archaeologists have been trying to come up with an explanation for the shell ring for years. (Everyone calls it a mound, but it is really shaped more like a ring or a crater.) Some have thought it was built as a kind of fish trap, but recent measurements prove it has always been high and dry. Some archaeologists pushed a kind of "Levittown theory," claiming that it was once a ring of little huts built all the same size and the same distance apart atop the shells from the oysters they ate all the time. Others have insisted it was a ceremonial structure, intentionally built in a circle for some religious ceremonial purpose.

We're not convinced by any of those theories. We were at a poorly maintained campground frequented by bikers and other rowdy types not too long ago and noticed how around every picnic table there was a perfect ring of beer cans about ankle-high and thirty feet in diameter. That picnic area has only been around since the 1980s. The carbon-14 dates on the Sewee Shell Mound suggest it's about 4,000 years old. We think that's *plenty* of time to account for our oyster-party theory. Everyone knows you can toss an oyster shell a whole lot farther than an empty beer can, especially if you're a muscular, native-type guy.

The oyster-party hypothesis makes even more sense when you find out what happened to the people

who used to live here. In 1600 the Sewees (or Xoxi, according to the Spanish explorers) had a village of about eight hundred people, but by 1700 the tribe had dwindled down to fewer than sixty. Diseases like smallpox had killed some of them, but many others had been wiped out in a depressingly simpleminded get-rich-quick scheme. Tired of dealing with English fur traders who drove such hard bargains, they decided to cut out these annoying middlemen and take their products straight to the consumer. So a group of them loaded down their dugout canoes with furs and hides and headed off into the ocean, planning to paddle all the way to England. They were never seen again. After that happened, the folks who had stayed behind probably didn't much feel like partying anymore. A few years later, they had all gone.

−Thanks to Robert Welch and Bud Hill

Mysteries of the Lost Colonies

It's impossible to write about the Carolinas without mentioning the famous Lost Colony. Most of us know the bare bones of it: Walter Raleigh got the franchise from Queen Elizabeth I to open a sure-fire moneymaker on land that didn't quite belong to either one of them; how Raleigh's cousin Dick Grenville duped 108 gullible folks into getting on boats and heading to Roanoke Island with promises of land so loaded with corn, peas, and melons, and overflowing with wildlife and dripping with grapes that the living would be easy compared to living in England.

Once they got there, on June 26, 1585, the first batch of colonists began making the acquaintance of the locals. The Native Americans tried to be friendly at the outset—giving them seeds, showing them how to catch fish—but then one of them made the fatal mistake of borrowing a pretty cup from the colony. In response to this, the new arrivals destroyed their cornfields and burned their town. Later they attacked another community and killed its chief and all his counselors on the off chance that they might be thinking of attacking the colonists. After that, the local hospitality turned somewhat cooler.

In August, after spending just a few months in the colony, Grenville decided

to go back to England, promising to return in the spring. Meanwhile, the Brits realized they weren't prepared for the fast approaching cold weather. In fact, they had a pretty miserable time of it that winter. When Grenville didn't return in the spring, they were ready to get the heck out of there—and that they did, on the first boats that came along, Francis Drake's, in June 1586.

Two weeks later, in a classic case of "a day late and a dollar short," Grenville finally showed up. He had found fifteen additional chumps who hadn't had a chance to talk to the first outfit, so he was able to make them fall for the same line again: "You guys stay here, and I'll be back real soon, okay?" They were to hold the fort (and keep on claiming the land for England) till a third bunch could be rounded up and brought over to join them.

These fifteen didn't fare so well, and by the time the third gaggle of some 150 showed up a year later, on July 22, 1587, only the bleached bones of just one skeleton were left at the camp to greet them. The other fourteen had vanished.

Not surprisingly, this group were not so anxious to go ashore. But the captain of their tiny fleet (a Portuguese named Simon Fernandez) was so sick of his whining cargo that he insisted they get off. Before long,

their leader, John White, pulled the old "I'll be right back" ploy again. He stuck around long enough to see his daughter give birth to a daughter named Virginia (in honor of their Queen Elizabeth, the "Virgin Queen"), then promised to be back in six or eight months. Baby Virginia Dare was the first English baby born in the New World.

Instead of returning in the spring, however, White was gone for the next three years. Finally, on the stormy afternoon of August 17, 1590, he sailed back within sight of Roanoke Island. A rowboat was sent ashore, but it capsized in the rough surf kicked up by the storm, and the captain and six other men aboard it were drowned. Another rowboat, with White aboard, was sent ashore and made it. He stepped off and stumbled toward the woods, expecting to hear shouts of relieved greetings from the people he'd left behind.

But the colony wasn't there. It had vanished. There were no houses, no people, no skeletons, no livestock, nothing to indicate what had happened. On a tree near the entrance to the compound was a single word carved into the bark: CROATOAN. On another tree by the path back down to the mooring place were three more letters: CRO. That was all.

At this point, the storm was approaching gale force.

One of the two ships that had brought White and his men to the colony had torn loose from its moorings and was beginning to drift back out to sea. The men leaped into their rowboat and barely made it back in time to board the drifting ship and get it out into open water, which is much safer in a storm than staying close to shore. However, the wind was pushing them the wrong way and, helplessly, after only that brief time ashore, they found themselves on their way back to England. For the rest of his life, John White struggled to come back and search for his granddaughter Virginia and the rest of her community, but he was never able to muster the resources to return.

Where did the colonists go? It's a mystery that has taunted historians for hundreds of years. Some of the theories—that they were wiped out by disease, hurricanes, or drought (tree-ring records indicate that the worst drought in centuries occurred during John White's three-year absence)—seem unlikely, because even during that short survey, a few graves or bones should have been found.

Given the bad behavior of previous colonists on Roanoke, the possibility that they were simply killed by the local Indians and disposed of seems not at all likely. This would account for the total removal of bodies and houses, since among many Native American groups, even today, there is a taboo against corpses as well as against the places they once inhabited. During that three-year absence, killing everyone, burning their houses, and then tossing everything into the surf would have left little or no evidence, certainly none that could have been found on an extremely brief visit like John White's.

Or maybe they "went native," married into the local populations, and were absorbed into the country. The Lumbee tribe from Robeson County, NC, likes to point out that common Lumbee family names like Chavis, Dare, Lowry, Locklear, and Oxendine were among the last names of the colonists on Roanoke Island, and it seems unlikely that these names belonged to the Lumbees too—unless the colonists married into them.

Or perhaps they didn't go quite so far away. Croatan was the name of another island, south of Roanoke, with an Indian community. Perhaps the word on the tree was left as a clue to indicate that the colonists had headed that way.

Other historians claim that a Matchapungo settlement on the mainland, four miles south of the present village of East Lake, NC, was called Croatoean. Later a lumber mill settlement called Beechlands was established there, and a number of the men who worked there were of obvious Native American stock, but with blue eyes or fair hair, and with names like Culbert White, Thomas Coleman, Richard Taverner, and Henry Paine. Could it be coincidence that these were also names among the "lost" colonists?

Another local historian, Bill Colonna, probably answered that question in the mid-1980s. "I have come to learn that word of mouth, sometimes called unwritten history, usually proves out to be true. It's also clear to me that the people [currently living on] Roanoke Island, the Lost Colony [outdoor theater] group and the Dare County Historic Society want no part of any such talk, they want the colonists to remain lost, that's for sure."

Given the bad behavior of previous colonists on Roanoke, the possibility that they were simply killed by the local Indians and disposed of seems not at all unlikely.

Fabled People and Places

The Carolinas, with their marshlands and swamps, their craggy hollows, and trees dripping with moss, were a land of fables long before the first Europeans arrived on their shores. This is a place where the devil has been seen all too frequently, jumping from rock to rock or from mountaintop to valley, leaving his cloven footprints behind. The leaping Satan is seen so often, in fact, that some people wonder why he's so active here.

It's in the Carolinas that the devil himself has been spotted, leaving his, and his children's, footprints forever in stone for all who dare to find them. And who could forget, as much as we might want to, that it was a Carolina funeral home that kept an abandoned corpse hanging on its wall for decades, while the town cheered on. Or so the fable goes.

But that's only the beginning of the extraordinary people and places of these states. Read on for the whole story, or as much as we could fit into one chapter.

Old West Ways in Love Valley

By the early 1950s, Charlotte construction contractor Andy Barker had begun to cave in to his lifelong interest in horses, cowboys, and the Old West. In his childhood, western stories by writers like Zane Grey and weekly serials like the Lone Ranger had inculcated a deep feeling for a nearly forgotten time in which honor, loyalty, and the trust of friends took precedence over the scramble for success. But how to make it happen—how to bring back those old days?

In 1954, Barker heard about a large parcel of land for sale on Fox Mountain in northwest Iredell County, NC.

Convincing his wife Ellenora (a.k.a. Ma Barker) that this was their big chance, he bought it, named it Love Valley, and set about creating a community based on cowboy Christianity. A few basic rules set the tone—no cars allowed in the center of town, no weapons in public places, and a commitment to the "cowboy way." The rest would be provided by his own living example.

Barker's goal was to create a utopian community based on what he saw as a proven model, the 19th-century frontier village. The ways of the West were, he thought, a more sustaining and more genuinely American parable than any Hollywood fantasy. By recreating a place where it could be lived in reality, he thought he could reintroduce many of the small-town values that had been lost. Cars and televisions only promote connections to an "elsewhere" of other people doing other things. Requiring people to travel only by foot or on horseback—and making them slow down their pace of living at least for the duration of their time in the community—forced them to focus on a "here and now" that had gone missing for far too long.

The result is the only authentic western town east of St. Louis. Love Valley has a fluctuating population not unlike the boom-or-bust mining towns of the Rockies. There is a permanent population of less than a hundred that at times swells to thousands. It has a wide Main Street paved with dirt flanked by hitching rails for the horses, and on big rodeo weekends it can be hard to find somewhere to tie up. There are places to stay, places to eat, a couple of taverns to blow off steam, and plenty of places to go riding a horse. There are no tickets or entry fees, nor any performances of fake shoot-outs by actors. As one of the residents said, "We are not a tourist attraction. We're not a ghost town. We're a real Old West town." Though some have mocked it as a cowboy commune, it seems to be hanging in there far longer than any of the hippie hideouts of the 1960s and '70s and shows no signs of wasting away.

African Village of Oyotunji

If Love Valley is the only real eastern Western town, the only authentic African village in the U.S. is near Sheldon in Beaufort County, SC. Or rather, it *would* be in the U.S. except that it has declared its independence from the rest of the country. Its founder was Walter Eugene King, a native of Detroit and former dancer with the Katherine Dunham Dance Company of Chicago and New York. In the 1950s, King traveled extensively with Dunham's troupe, performing throughout Europe and East Asia. But it was the tours of North Africa and Haiti that had an especially profound effect on the young dancer. Long before Alex Haley began the explorations that would lead to the writing of *Roots*, King felt a spiritual attraction to the traditions and beliefs he encountered in places where African religious activities still thrived.

In 1959, shortly before Castro came to power, King traveled to the Matanzas region of Cuba to be initiated into the Yoruba priesthood.

He came home to the U.S. with a new name and a lifelong mission. As Efuntola Oseijeman Adefunmi, he organized a religious order based on African teachings that eventually became known as the Yoruba Temple, and tried to establish the precepts of the religion (a form of voodoo) in centers scattered around northeastern cities.

Adefunmi, like Andy Barker, eventually realized that the values he wanted to reintroduce from the past couldn't be accomplished in a modern setting. In 1970, he acquired property in Beaufort County on which he founded his experiment, an African village community that he called Oyotunji. Two years later, he visited Nigeria and was initiated into the Ifa Priesthood, which enabled him to be crowned Oba, or king, of Oyotunji on his return. A number of people moved to the village, began to build their own homes, took up subsistence farming with no running water or electricity, and settled in to stay.

Left, Oyotunji founder Oba Adefunmi I

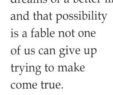

Or at least they stayed as long as they could. Facing sweltering summer heat and mosquitoes without air-conditioning or screens put a large dent in the number of residents who made the village a permanent home. Although Oyotunji reached a peak population of more than two hundred in the late 1970s, it is now the full-time home of only about a dozen individuals. Still, it sustains a surrounding population of some four hundred Yoruba-practicing people who decided to live outside the village itself.

Oba Adefunmi died in February 2005, leaving behind some fourteen wives, twenty-two children, and twenty-three grandchildren. One of his sons, Adelabu Adefunmi II, was crowned as the new king of Oyotunji in July 2005.

Like Love Valley, Oyotunji is a real place, and the people who live there are not reenactors. Religious activities at the ten temples and the multitude of shrines scat-tered around the site go on regardless of whether or not any visitors are there to watch them. And as in Love Valley, a first-time visitor feels a moment of surreal disconnection or transition that is missing from places that are as fake as a Disneyland set. Plywood and amateur construction techniques may set the standards in both communities, and both have a kind of ramshackle, ad-hoc feel about them—but then, so did towns in the Old West and so do villages in Africa today. Both places are built on dreams of a better life, and that possibility is a fable not one of us can give up trying to make come true.

At left, Devil's Head Rock overlooking Hickory Nut Gorge, NC; below, Whiteside Mountain

feature, legend, or firsthand account referring either to on-the-ground demonic activity or to the recognition of some correspondence between something local and something in the Bad Place. Hell's Half Acre was the old name of Providence, NC, in Caswell County—a name change obviously thought up by the image-improvement gang at the local chamber of commerce. The broken jumble of huge rocks they call the Devil's Kitchen, near Caesar's Head in Greenville County, SC, is said to emit smoke and the occasional smell of brimstone whenever Mr. S is cooking up for a dinner party. Speaking of dinner, the Devil's Fork is in Oconee County, while his evil Elbows are planted in southern Kershaw County and at a treacherously sharp railroad curve just south of Sharp, SC, north of Columbia.

For his day job, the devil holds court in not one but at least two courthouses in the Carolinas (not counting all the county, state, and federal judicial buildings, which probably *should* be included if pure deviltry alone provided enough criteria). Two peculiar rocky outcrops are both officially named Devil's Courthouse. The smaller one, which is often called the Lower Court, is on the Blue Ridge Parkway in North Carolina, near where Transylvania, Jackson, and Haywood Counties meet. The much larger formation, known in these parts as the Supreme Court of Pandemonium, stands on Whiteside Mountain, between Highlands and Cashiers. Not only the mountain

So Many Satans

It's a kind of chicken-or-egg question: Does the Bible Belt exist where it does because there was so much concentrated evil there to start with and all those churches sprang up to combat it? Or does Satan like a challenge? Was he particularly drawn, in other words, to the part of the country that had more than the usual share of pious people? In either case, one can certainly say this: If you're to judge by the sheer amount of physical evidence and eyewitness reports, the devil seems inordinately fond of the Carolinas.

From Hellhole Swamp in Berkeley County, SC, to Hell Pocosin (next to Purgatory Pocosin) in Onslow County, NC, there's scarcely any among the 146 counties in the Carolinas that doesn't have a place name, road, natural folks but also the Cherokees regarded these two spots as significantly sinister. They furthermore attributed the "balds" scattered irregularly among the mountaintops to "fire-scalds" caused when the Evil One used those particular hills as stepping-stones.

The Big Bad hasn't skittered around the two states without leaving plenty of evidence of his passing by, which means that any who doubt his existence can hop in their cars and go see for themselves.

Devil's Tramping Ground

We guess we have to mention the Devil's Tramping Ground in southwestern Chatham County, NC, since it's probably the most famous supernatural site in the two Carolina states. But we don't know why it's so famous. Our deepest suspicion is that some Force for Evil or other has hired some hotshot PR firm to secretly promote this place, because the general reaction of most first-time visitors who find it is, "Hunh? You mean that's *it?*"

If you, like so many other insatiably curious folks, decide to trek on out there, here's what you'll see: a firepit surrounded by a forty-foot-diameter circle of barren, ashy soil. Beyond the circle of soil, which may or may not have some broken bottles or empty beer cans scattered about in it, are scrubby woods that certainly do have broken glass and beer cans scattered in them. But don't expect to see much else, and if you go there and find yourself feeling a little let down, remember, we warned you.

Of course there's a legend, which is the reason people go. About 150 years ago, someone realized that anything left within this circle before dark will be gone by the next morning. The devil, they say, likes to drop by this particular spot at night to wander around in a circle while dreaming up new ways to tempt and trouble us mortals. Whenever he finds anything annoying in his path, he

gives it a swift kick. Supposedly, people have tested this on numerous occasions, heaping so much stuff in the circle that it looks like a garbage dump. By the next morning, all the items are gone—or at least launched into the surrounding woods.

Hardheaded nonbelievers in Satan have tried to come up with other explanations for why this circle exists, or at least why it ever existed in the first place. Now it mainly exists, if truth be known, because people come here to tramp around in it wondering why it exists. Some have claimed it was once a Native American ceremonial ground, or that it is the burial site of Croatan, a great chief, whose name also happened to appear on the tree at the "Lost Colony" site on Roanoke Island. Others say a salt lick was once maintained here, and over the years as cattle trampled around to get a lick at it, they compacted the earth and watered it with their unspeakable juices while the salt leached into the ground every time it rained. Those three things together rendered the spot relatively free of vegetation (though a little tough grass pokes up here and there) and more or less permanently circular. If these explanations don't do it for you, you're free to come up with your own.

Whatever it is, it's weird. Weird that a circle formed somehow, weird that people began coming to see it, and weird that it is *still* there after all this time.

To find it for yourself, head six miles south from Siler City, NC, on Highway 421, then turn west on Highway 902 to Harper's Crossroads. From here, go northwest on Devil's Tramping Ground Road (NC SR 1100). After about two miles, you'll cross an old railroad grade and see a place on the left (west) side of the road where other cars have pulled off. There's no sign or marker. Watch out for broken glass. If you step on any, avoid blaspheming, because someone may think you wish to avail yourself of the Evil One's services.

Devil's Tramping Ground II

You can avoid appending the royal roman numerals to this site by calling it by its more common South Carolina name, the Devil's *Stomping* Ground, or by the name you'll see on the map, Forty Acre Rock. In any case, it's all the same place, a 14.5-acre (not forty) stone surface that geologists have termed the largest diabase dike east

of the Mississippi. It is roughly 200 million years old by their calculations, and plenty weird for a variety of reasons. Certain rare species of plants grow here that grow almost nowhere else. Microclimates created because the rock reflects intense sunlight but absorbs enough moisture to sustain alpine plants make it a giant anomaly in the surrounding region.

There is an opening in it called the Endless Cave,

which sounds incredibly deep and from which running water can be heard. But it is impossible for a grown person to squeeze more than a short distance into it.

Supposedly it opens out into a sizable cavern at some point and connects to a series of other underground passages. According to local stories, a hunting dog chased a rabbit into it one day, after which its owner stood by the entrance for hours calling after it. He eventually gave up and was on his way home when he ran into a friend in a

Devil's Stomping Ground, far left

Devil's Track Rock, above, near Lexington, SC. The devil's permanent housewarming gift to the German immigrants who settled here. The locals thought their dialect to be witchcraft and here is proof that the devil himself came to welcome them.

Devil's Rock, left, near Afton, NC. The footprints are about 12 inches long and 1 inch deep.

pickup truck heading in the other direction. The missing dog was in the back of the truck, and the friend said he'd seen it run out of a hole about three miles away, had recognized the name on the collar, and was bringing it back to its rightful owner.

The rock is so odd and its features so unexpected that it all but cries out for legendary explanations, in disembodied voices, of course. Happily, there are a slew of legends connected to it. The enterable portion of Endless Cave was once the hermitage of a local Indian medicine man, they say. Later a Confederate deserter used the same cave as a hiding place during the Civil War. Later still, it was used by highwaymen resting up between stagecoach robberies.

Another cave here is called the House Rock Dungeon. The name seems peculiarly mismatched to the vestigial legend attached to it, which maintains that "Indian maidens and their braves spent their honeymoons there." Leaving aside the question as to whether or not Native Americans even had honeymoons, it still sounds a bit kinky.

The most persistent legend, of course, is connected to someone we all know perhaps a bit better than we should. Several enormous foot-shaped depressions in the rock are called the Devil's Footprints. Apparently, this is not a recent designation, because both the Waxhaw and Catawba tribes recognized these as potently evil spots and used them as places to stage executions of their captured prisoners. At the top of the rock is a flat space that almost looks like a theatrical set built for satanic rituals and is said to be the actual "stomping ground" of lore and legend. Once again, just as at the other Tramping Ground, any objects left there will be removed or destroyed. A quite recent legend insists that because of long millennia of experience with this kind of thing, Satan has been contracted to train airport security officials in the handling of suspicious passenger luggage. —*Thanks to Coy Bayne*

40-Acre Rock, SC

There is a place in South Carolina called 40-Acre Rock. It is said that the devil made his hoofprint in the rock. Also, if you sleep in his cave, when you wake in the morning you will find yourself outside of the cave with no idea how you got there. People say the devil moves you out. I have also heard not to go there at night, because a member of the family who owned the land, a very big and strange man, dances on the rock by firelight. Very weird. It is located on US 601 and the SC 903 North junction, close to I-77. It is in Lancaster County, SC, and is between Camden, SC, and Flat Creek. I have been there before and I saw the cave, but never noticed the hoofprints. —*Carla*

Devil's Pool

Mason Locke "Parson" Weems gave us a lasting belief in the honesty of our first President when he published *A History of the Life and Death, Virtues and Exploits of General George Washington*, in 1800. This is the book that told how as a child Washington fessed up to having chopped down the cherry tree by saying, "I cannot tell a lie, I did it with my little hatchet."

Before he died (in Beaufort, SC, in 1825), Weems wrote other uplifting, moralistic tracts about upright characters like Ben Franklin, William Penn, and Francis Marion. He also wrote a few pieces about people who didn't come across as such goody-goodies, although even these were intended to provide pointers for the improvement of readers' spiritual selves.

Weems's 1810 piece, "The Devil in Petticoats, or, God's Revenge Against Husband Killing" (he liked long titles), featured Becky Cotton, a real-life one-woman crime wave who lived in Edgefield, SC. Parson Weems didn't need to make up any stories about her; her deeds were real enough—and gory too. She was born in Edgefield, in 1780, and was widely considered one of the most beautiful females in the region. But she had a diabolical streak, which was at first interpreted as simple bad luck. Seems her husbands kept running off, though why anyone would leave such a lovely woman no one

could imagine. Until, that is, husband number three was found with his head split open by an axe.

That led to searches for the first two husbands. Dredging a pond in Edgefield that is still called Becky's Pool (or The Devil's Pool), authorities found them. The first had been killed by having a knitting needle shoved through his heart. The second had been poisoned.

The 1806 trial remains the most famous ever held at the Edgefield County Courthouse. The evidence was obvious, and Becky never denied it. But she turned the full force of her fatal beauty on the all-male judge and jury, and they melted. As Weems described the scene, "Mrs. Cotton came off clear—nay, more than clear—she came off the conqueror. For as she stood at the bar in tears—with cheeks like rosebuds wet with morning dew and rolling her eyes of sapphires, pleading for pity, their subtle glamour seized with ravishment the admiring bar—the stern features of justice were all relaxed, and both judge and jury hanging forward from their seats breathless, were heard to exclaim, 'Heavens! What a charming creature!'"

She got off Scot-free, and had so wooed the jurors that one of them even proposed marriage to her soon thereafter. But before she could work her wicked wiles yet again, her brother—one of the few men, apparently, who could see through her venomous act—shot her down in front of the courthouse.

Young Edgefielders still say the pond where Cotton dumped her spouses is a scary place at night. Tossing stones into its depths after dark is risky since, they say, you don't know who might turn up—one of the husbands or, worse, Becky herself.

Cheney's Treasure

The area south of Charlotte, where North Carolina's Mecklenburg and Union counties more or less meet up with South Carolina's York and Lancaster counties, has long been a bit confusing. The line that divides the two states makes a series of capricious zigs and zags, none of which run due north–south or east–west before they finally straighten out again in either direction. Long ago, continually changing land surveys and boundaries left settlers in the area no longer quite sure which state they lived in. The region became an administrative nightmare in which justice officials could rarely decide who had legal jurisdiction when a crime was committed.

Back in the 19th century, this governmental disorder made it possible for one Milt Cheney to run several scams of his own. Cheney operated out of a tavern located in the crossroads community of Hancock in Lancaster County, SC. One scam he was accused of consisted of going into cahoots with a black accomplice, whom Cheney would repeatedly sell as a slave to distant plantations, but who would then escape and make it back to Cheney's tavern (with free-passage papers Cheney provided) to take a portion of the loot and be resold again elsewhere.

The scam he was eventually caught for was trafficking in stolen slaves. Cheney was sentenced to hang on July 11, 1856. Then rumors of another crime came out. A disgruntled slave claimed that Cheney would sometimes kill his overnight guests and take their gold and bury it under a boulder near the tavern. But since the testimony was from a slave, since Cheney was already sentenced to death, and since neither gold nor bodies could be found, no second trial was held.

It did, however, draw a huge crowd to the hanging. As Cheney stepped up to the scaffold, everyone hoped he would reveal the location of the treasure. They were disappointed when instead he read a long poem to his family full of mysterious allusions.

The truth finally came to the surface thirty years later. When the railroad was extended through the community in the late 1880s, dozens of skeletons with blunt-object damage to their skulls were uncovered during construction, renewing interest in the story about buried gold.

Ever since, treasure hunters have scoured the area within a mile of that intersection and endlessly scrutinized the poem that Cheney read aloud at his hanging. If the treasure is still waiting to be found, you can bet that

whoever does find it will figure out which state has the more lenient tax laws before pointing to any particular hole and claiming it came from there. The weathered ruins of Cheney's tavern, shown above, stood until the 1970s, when they were finally torn down and the wood reused to build a shed. *–Thanks to Patricia Poland, Craig Faris, and* Ripley's Believe It or Not!

Witches of Fairfield, SC

Not everything about the good old days was so great. Our image of an imaginary golden past when everyone was upstanding and moral makes our ancestors look a lot more angelic than they really were. And it sometimes makes us seem far more degenerate today than we really are. Even if South Carolina and North Carolina now rank first and seventh respectively in highway deaths attributable to road rage, we hardly hold a candle to our forebears for downright meanness. It's fun to visit some historical reenactment sites and put your feet in stocks, but imagine the misery of sitting on the torturously sharp-edged seats they provided back then. Or trying to survive for days in the rain or snow.

In those times, it was completely normal to believe in curses and evil manifestations. To blame a "witch" for any misfortune that befell you was nothing out of the ordinary. And if you suspected some elderly female neighbor might be the cause of your bellyache or your milk cow going dry, you were expected to do something about it. After all, every Sunday your preacher reminded you of your duty to "stamp out the devil."

A widespread outbreak of witchcraft retribution took place in Fairfield County, SC, around 1792. Swiss-German settlers who had moved up into Fairfield from the Saxe-Gotha community near Lexington brought with them a form of faith healing that was often mistaken for witchcraft. As had happened in Salem, Massachusetts, exactly a hundred years earlier, the community's suspicions were aroused when teenage girls, and a few boys, began complaining of being attacked or put under spells by witches, and began pointing fingers at a number of the older women among their German-speaking neighbors.

Seventy-year-old Mary Ingleman, another woman named Sally Smith, and an elderly man named Mr. Harding and his wife were among the individuals tried and tortured as witches at the trials that took place in Thomas Hill's barn. Records of the testimony show that one woman claimed that Ingleman had made her vomit up hairballs full of pins. A man blamed a cow's seizure on her. Mary Ingleman's grandson, Jacob Free, was forced under threat of torture to testify against her, asserting that he'd been turned into a horse and that she had ridden him to coven meetings.

Finally, a man named Isaac Collins told a story about how he had gone hunting and tried to shoot a deer. When his gun refused to fire, he inserted a ball partially made of silver, since, as everyone knew even back then, silver bullets kill witches, demons, and vampires. This time the gun fired and managed to wound the deer, which immediately changed into a black cat and then limped off into the woods. A few days later, Mary Ingleman was seen with her hand in a sling. Therefore, her accusers insisted, she must have been the wounded black cat that had been the deer that had hexed Collins's rifle that day in the woods.

Naturally Ingleman and the others could offer no way to refute such bizarre testimony, and since their command of English wasn't good to start with, they may not even have understood their accusers very well. The trial concluded that of all the people who had been examined, four were definitely witches and punishment should be immediate and harsh. They were flogged and their feet

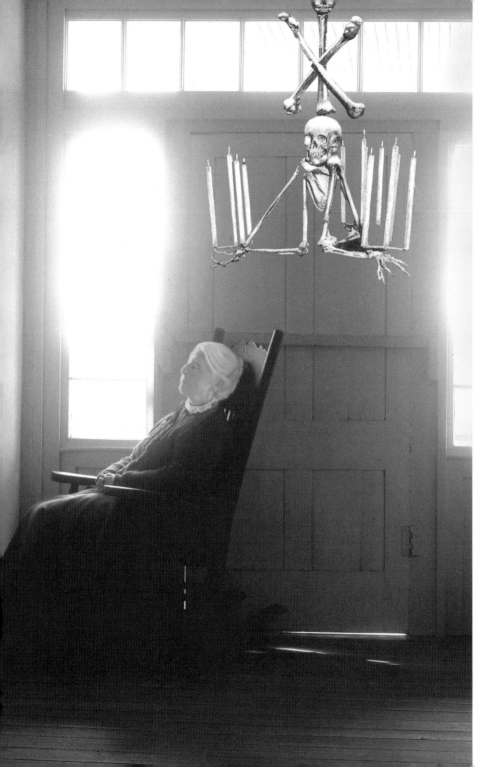

were burned to the bones over a bark fire.

Eventually, the accused sued for damages (which they were awarded, despite its being only a small amount), and that was the last of any allegations of witchcraft or wizardry.

"The great witch" Mary Ingleman was described long after she was dead by scholar Edward Pearson.

She was a remarkably neat, tidy and decent old lady. She was of German extraction and probably a native of Germany. Her conversation was pleasant, entertaining, instructive; her manners mild, simple and agreeable. Her knowledge of pharmacy was considerable and her application of simples [herbs] in the cure of country complaints was the result of much observation and gratuitous practice. . . .

Too bad that being a nice old lady who provided free medical care to her neighbors didn't count for all that much in those good old fabled days of yore! *−Thanks to the Fairfield County Historical Museum and Lee Gandee*

Spaghetti, the Mummy of Laurinburg

A young roustabout named Cancetto Farmica was little known in life. But in death he became one of the most fabled people to ever visit the town of Laurinburg, NC. Cancetto hung around McDougald Funeral Home, the oldest funeral home in North Carolina, for years and years, waiting for his father to show up. We mean he hung, literally, on the wall of the embalming room, dead as a doornail. Since he was of Italian descent, local wags soon nicknamed him Spaghetti. To most folks, he was known as the Laurinburg Mummy. Cancetto Farmica had arrived, living and breathing, with a traveling show that passed through the area in 1911. Still in his twenties, he was a hothead who apparently pushed one of his colleagues a little too far, because one of them brained him with a heavy tent stake. The blow killed the young worker, and he was taken to the nearby McDougald Funeral

Home, where his body was embalmed and prepared for burial. When Farmica's father arrived to claim his son's body, however, he didn't have enough money to cover even the cost of embalming, let alone a funeral. He would have to go back home to get the rest of the cash needed for the services.

But as months passed and the older man never returned, it began to dawn on them that they'd been left holding the bag, so to speak. They decided the easiest thing to do was just to keep on holding it. By then the body had completely dried out and stabilized, and had almost become a member of the family.

For the next twenty-eight years, Cancetto Farmica's dried corpse hung on the wall of the third-floor embalming room, gradually becoming a regional celebrity. As his gruesome fame spread, visitors passing through Laurinburg would pull over and ask for directions to "the mummy."

The morticians were happy to let tourists troop in for a look-see. After all, it was good advertising for their embalming skills (though his preservation probably had as much to do with the effects of simple desiccation), and also encouraged their other customers not to dawdle when it came time to settle their bill. In a way, Farmica was the equivalent of a bounced check taped to a cash register in a convenience store.

By 1939, the stream of visitors had increased so much that the work of embalming the regular clients was being impeded, so the McDougalds had a special glass-fronted case built in which "Spaghetti" could remain on permanent display elsewhere in the building. When they moved the business to a new location, he went with

them, repaying his initial cost many times over in the form of free publicity.

Eventually, the fact that an Italian American had gone unburied for nearly sixty years didn't sit so well with Italian communities elsewhere. Along with pleas from an Italian American Congressman from New York, the funeral home started getting threats from members of the Mafia, who expressed their annoyance at a *paisan* being treated with disrespect. By 1972, McDougald's decided that its mascot had become more of a liability than an asset, and made arrangements to have him laid to his well-earned rest. Several hundred people were on hand for the funeral as Farmica's casket was lowered into a grave at Laurinburg's Hillside Cemetery. It is said that two tons of concrete were then poured into the hole, but whether this was a tip of the hat to Mafia traditions or simply a strategy to keep him from ever going on display again is not known.

And who knows whether it will work in the long run? After all, the Great Pyramid of Cheops attempted to protect its mummy under *six million* tons of granite but stands empty today. Maybe you just can't keep a good mummy down.

Unexplained and Unnatural

The distinction between unexplained (or anomalous) phenomena and supernatural events is often a little hazy. Sometimes it depends on matters of belief and degrees of intrusion. Some people, for instance, might hear a weird sound or see something zoom across the sky and attribute it to something normal, since it didn't intrude on their reality enough to force them to confront it. But when something like a half-ton ice ball falls out of the sky and smashes into your car, there's no "belief"involved. It is there. You can see it and touch it, even if you can't explain it.

UFOs, mystery lights, blood, and other strange objects falling from the sky—they've all been witnessed, recorded, photographed, and described, by both die-hard anomalists and skeptics. Weird stuff really does happen, and keeps on happening—and not "even in" but "especially in" the Carolinas. So keep your ears alert and your eyes peeled—and most of all, keep your mind open. Who knows what you might encounter?

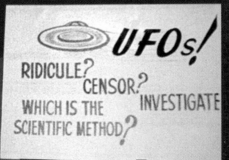

UFOs!

RIDICULE? CENSOR? INVESTIGATE

WHICH IS THE SCIENTIFIC METHOD?

Dr. Venable and the Great Shower of Blood

We begin with a few facts about our chief investigator, lest anyone be tempted to dismiss outright the bizarre facts described below. Professor Francis Preston Venable was one of the most accomplished scientists of his day. He excelled in chemistry and held multiple degrees from the University of Virginia and the German universities of Berlin and Göttingen. He authored major scientific books on atoms (1904) and radioactivity (1917), and is credited with having perfected the Bunsen burner. Dr. Venable retired in 1930 after serving fifty years on the University of North Carolina faculty. Venable Hall, one of the main science buildings on the U.N.C. campus, is named for him.

So this is not the kind of guy who would risk his reputation on a trifling subject. But in 1884, he filed a serious scientific paper on a very strange topic indeed, namely, that a large quantity of blood seemed to have fallen out of the sky onto a small plot of land in Chatham County, NC, less than fifteen miles from Chapel Hill. The event was first brought to the public's attention in the March 6, 1884, issue of the *Chatham Record* newspaper.

"The wife of Kit Lasater . . . who lives on the farm of Mr. Silas Beckwith in the New Hope Township, states that, about 2 o'clock on Monday the 25th of February . . . a shower of blood fell around her from a sun-bright sky! Many of the neighbors, after hearing of her statement, visited the spot and they all say that the ground—embracing an area about 60 feet in circumference—was covered with splotches of something like blood, and an examination of the trees in this space showed blood on the branches."

Upon hearing about the strange event, Venable visited the spot himself and did a very detailed analysis of the samples he obtained. His extensive tests revealed the presence of hematine, a component of blood. His conclusion in the *Journal* of the Elisha Mitchell Scientific Society:

[t]his leaves little or no reasonable doubt then that the samples examined had blood upon them. The question arises, were they carefully taken; had no animal ever bled on the same ground; had pigs ever been slaughtered in the quarter of the field? etc. As to theories accounting for so singular a material falling from a cloudless sky, I have no plausible ones to offer. It may have been some bird of prey passing over, carrying a bleeding animal, but a good deal of blood must have fallen to cover so large a space. If a hoax has been perpetrated on the people of that neighborhood it has certainly been very cleverly done and an object seems to be lacking."

Similar observations had occurred from time to time, and Venable's decision to submit his report may have been encouraged by intriguing articles that had appeared many years earlier in other scientific journals. In 1841, the *American Journal of Science* described a rain of muscle tissue, fat, and blood that landed in a tobacco field near Lebanon, Tennessee. The incident created fear among people who saw biblical portent in it.

Fears were reinforced when an article in *The North Carolinian* several years later headlined "GREAT FALL OF FLESH & BLOOD, EXTRAORDINARY PHENOMENON IN SAMPSON COUNTY" and described the "astonishing particulars" of a shower of gore that occurred on February 15, 1850, on the property of Thomas Clarkson, near Clinton, NC.

The shower fell in a roughly rectangular pattern and covered a zone about thirty feet wide by nearly three hundred yards long. It also included many large pieces of flesh—meat, liver, lungs, and brains—along with gobs of blood. The blood fell in enough quantity to run down the leaves of the trees and splash on the ground like a heavy rain. A lawyer who lived nearby reported that it came from "a cloud overhead, having a red appearance, like a wind cloud. There was no rain." He took samples of the fallen materials, which were later confirmed to be putrefied flesh.

The site of the old Beckwith farm in Chatham County is thought to have been along Parker's Creek, about a mile east of Mount Gilead Church (a few miles northeast of Pittsboro), while the Clarkson farm in Sampson County was thirteen miles southwest of Clinton. —*Special thanks to Tom Maxwell*

Summerville Light

Most "ghost lights" are likely to be benign, but not so the Summerville Light. We don't know if it's because the location—out Sheep Island Road, just north of Summerville, SC—feels so desolate or what, but there's definitely a bad vibe here. Maybe it's a matter of contrast. One minute you're at a busy shopping center with lots of other cars and people all around, and then the road dips around behind the center and the pavement ends. There, it quickly turns ugly. In fact, if it's been raining, we recommend four-wheel drive, or better yet staying home.

The story about the light begins with the usual beheaded railroad worker, but this time there's a twist. The light is supposedly that of the wife of the dead guy, out looking for him after he didn't return home for dinner. She stalks up and down the road, mad as a hornet—but whether she's mad at him, mad at the railroad company for not looking after its workers better, or just mad in general isn't so clear. What *is* clear is that the light isn't friendly. Observers have reported dents and burn marks on their cars, shorted electrical systems, mysterious stalls (you *really* don't want this to happen while you're out there at night), and damage to iPods and digital camera gear. People who have encountered the light say metal objects, including zippers and the rivets on jeans, sometimes become uncomfortably hot to the touch. We say look, but keep a safe distance. And don't go by yourself after dark.

Vander Light

Mysterious lights have been seen in the vicinity of Vander, NC, since the mid-1700s. Whenever they've been encountered, the experience has been roughly the same: A light glows like a lantern in the distance. You try to approach it, but at some point it disappears. If you keep going in the same direction and then look back over your shoulder, you'll discover that it has somehow gotten past you (whether around, over, or through, we can't say) and is now glowing just as merrily in the other direction. Like the proverbial pot of gold at the end of the rainbow, the Vander Light manages to elude its pursuers every time.

Of course, once the railroad came through the area in the 19th century, some joker couldn't wait to get his head lopped off so he could become the Vander Light. And sure enough, a railroad worker lost it yet again. This time it was a switchman who averted disaster by throwing a switch just in time to keep two trains from having a head-on, but not quite quick enough to avoid being run over by the train himself. Oh well. At least now there's some kind of explanation for that slippery light.

Land's End Light

Undoubtedly the most well-known mystery light in South Carolina is the one that appears along old Land's End Road on St. Helena Island, near Beaufort. This light has been seen since the Civil War. There are no railroad tracks on the island, so in this case the beheaded with the lantern is said to be a Confederate soldier who was jumped by some Yankee ne'er-do-wells and suffered the loss of his thinker in the melee that erupted. Other stories say it was a Federal soldier who was ambushed by brave Rebels who lopped off his head when he besmirched their family honor. Or else it was an escaped slave. Or a Spaniard. Or a lost lover. In the end, perhaps it doesn't matter—*something* is out there at night throwing a glow and causing a stir.

If you want to see the Land's End Light, go to the village of Frogmore on St. Helena Island and turn south on Land's End Road. Not too long after you pass the campus of the Penn Center, you'll come to the ghostly ruins of the 1740s Chapel of Ease. After darkness falls, this is a good place to stop and look for strange lights. Orb watchers will find plenty of activity to keep them occupied, both in the ruins of the chapel and around a sadly vandalized mausoleum that looks like a miniature Egyptian temple.

If you don't have any luck here, head on past Adam Street Baptist Church and then pull off the road. You won't be able to see the old Hanging Tree from here if it's really dark—it's even farther down the road—but this is the most likely place to encounter the Light. You have to be patient and quiet. In the summer, be sure to bring some mosquito repellant.

We should add a word of warning. If you do see the Light looming down the road, just stay put and enjoy it. Don't make the same mistake as some folks who have attempted to drive toward it or through it. Several years ago, some off-duty marines from nearby Parris Island were killed when they tried this and slammed into a tree.

Brown Mountain Lights

It's amazing how something can take place in plain sight, within easy reach, on a regular basis over hundreds of years and *still* remain a total mystery. So it is with the Brown Mountain Lights. People have been seeing them for centuries. Cherokee legends say they are the glow of hovering spirits searching for lost wives and husbands.

A German engineer named Gerard Will de Brahm was the first European to write about them. In 1771, he said he thought they were caused by "nitrous vapors" seeping out of cracks in the ground and spontaneously igniting. It's an interesting idea, but wrong. While there actually are places where this kind of thing can happen (usually above coal seams, volcanic activity, or natural gas deposits), Brown Mountain isn't one of them. As mountains go, it's about as ordinary as could be: just a long granite ridge only 2,600 feet high, covered with the same kinds of trees as the surrounding terrain.

Ordinary, except for those peculiar lights. From any of several vantage points, and under the right conditions, you can see brightly glowing balls of light that seem to begin below the crest of the ridge, lift upward above it, waver in the air for perhaps ten seconds or so, and then vanish. You can photograph them, and even hike around the mountain to look at their presumed point of origin, but no one is completely sure what they are.

One idea proposed by the U.S. Geological Survey in 1913—that the lights were a kind of mirage, reflecting the lights of locomotives down in the Catawba Valley—lost credence when a flood washed out all the railroad bridges in 1916 and the lights continued appearing anyway. Not to mention that the lights had been there long before locomotives had even been invented. Arguments that the lights are reflections of the streetlights of nearby towns don't hold water for the same reason. They predate both the founding of the towns *and* the invention of light bulbs.

So what are they? No one knows. Go see for yourself and come up with your own theory. And even if they don't appear, it's a fine way to spend an evening. All you have to do is wait until it gets really dark atop Jonas Ridge (at milepost 20 on Highway 181 north of Morganton, NC), or else at Wiseman's View (get off Highway 183 near Linville Falls) and look off to the east toward the long, low ridge in the far distance. Ideal conditions are between 8:00 p.m. and midnight on cool, clear fall evenings with no moon. They do not always appear on every favorable night, and no one knows why that is, either. Be sure to take a few dependable flashlights with you on any of these nighttime outings, and stick to the marked trails; many of these viewpoints overlook sheer cliffs with fatal drop-offs. —*Thanks to Nancy Roberts, John Harden, Terrance Zepke, and www.FarShores.org*

Flying Fire of Rattlesnake Knob

It's a safe bet that few, if any, of the guests who check into the new Harrah's Cherokee Casino Hotel at North Carolina's Cherokee Reservation are aware that the small mountain looming behind the hotel has a strange legend attached to it. The mountain, sometimes referred to as Rattlesnake Knob, is also known

as *Atsi'la-Wa'ï*, Cherokee for "Fire's Relative." According to the old legend, a ball of fire was once seen to fly through the air from the direction of Highlands, in Macon County, and alight upon this mountain. The Indians believe it to have been an *ulûñsû'tï*, a magic crystal stolen from the forehead of an *uktena* monster. Or so reports James Mooney in the *Nineteenth Annual Report of the Bureau of American Ethnology 1897–98*. Maybe the casino's owners are counting on its burning a hole in the pockets of their visitors?

Seneca Guns

For reasons that baffle scientists, every now and then a very loud percussive *whump* will rock the Carolina coast with enough sonic impact to rattle dishes, rock vehicles, or even cause picture windows to pop out of their frames. The booms are heard at irregular intervals from Morehead City, NC, to Beaufort, SC, but the highest concentration seems to occur in the stretch between Wilmington and Pawleys Island. They've been compared to the sound of bombs, plane crashes, trucks running into buildings, and thunder.

There are almost as many terms for these phenomena as theories for what causes them. "Carolina waterguns," "Barisal guns," and "shore booms" are just a few, but the most common is "Seneca guns," after an 1851 description by James Fenimore Cooper of remarkably similar sounds sometimes heard around Seneca Lake, in New York State. He wrote, "It is a sound resembling the explosion of a heavy piece of artillery, that can be accounted for by none of the known laws of nature. The report is deep, hollow, distant, and imposing. . . ."

Cooper goes on to say that "no satisfactory theory" had been developed to explain them. More than 150 years later, we're still no closer to understanding what they are than he was, though by now we know a bit more about what they are *not*. They aren't, for example, sonic booms caused by aircraft flying faster than the speed of sound, since the sounds were heard long before airplanes were around. They aren't earthquakes, either. Nowadays, sensitive seismographs can detect even small tremors, but Seneca guns don't even jiggle their needles. Besides, earthquakes themselves don't really make noise. Things like collapsing buildings or cracking pavement make the sounds associated with them.

A few folks have pointed to a peculiar feature of the Carolina coastline itself that might have something to do

We may be unknowingly walking along the rim of the world's largest natural loudspeaker system.

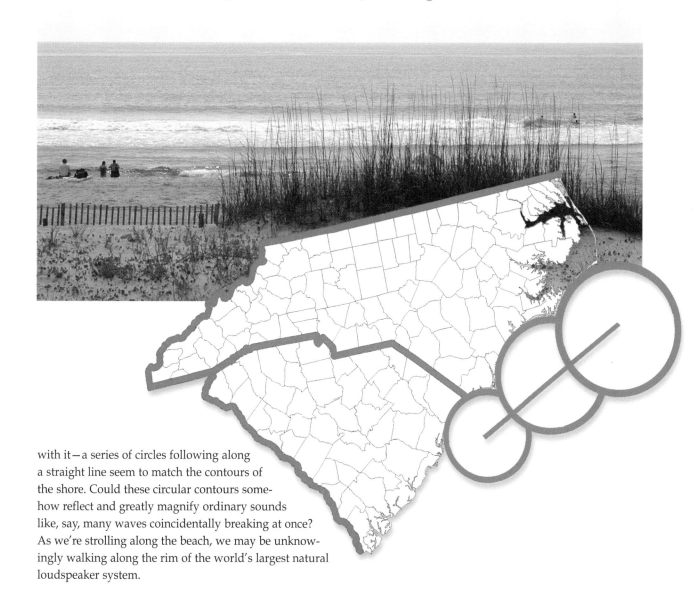

with it—a series of circles following along a straight line seem to match the contours of the shore. Could these circular contours somehow reflect and greatly magnify ordinary sounds like, say, many waves coincidentally breaking at once? As we're strolling along the beach, we may be unknowingly walking along the rim of the world's largest natural loudspeaker system.

Mystery of the Carolina Bays

One of the strangest and least understood natural phenomena on earth is right under our noses in the Carolina coastal plains, yet somehow they went completely undetected until about seventy-five years ago. Even now, few Carolinians are aware of them, though millions drive through them, work in them, and live among them every day.

In the early 1930s, soil and water conservationists with the Department of Agriculture, trying to solve Dust Bowl conditions caused by erosion, drought, and poor farming techniques, began making use of a relatively new tool: aerial photography. By patching together photos shot from low-flying airplanes, they created soil conservation maps that helped identify areas needing attention. But in 1933, when a number of photos taken just west of Myrtle Beach were spliced together, the researchers were startled to find something they hadn't expected.

Scattered over the landscape were thousands of strange elliptical shapes; some filled with water, others choked with swamps or thick stands of trees, and still others visible only as rings of lighter soil or shorter vegetation. Roads had been cut directly through many of them, and farmers had plowed across them for years without discerning their almost mathematically precise shapes. Even stranger, nearly all of them seemed to be aligned in the same direction.

As adjacent areas were photographed and mapped, tens of thousands more of the big ovals were discovered—estimates now say that there are between 300,000 and half a million of them. They have been detected in scattered locations along the eastern coast of the United States, but the greatest concentration is in the Carolina coastal plains. They're called the Carolina Bays, after the bay trees that predominate in them. What in the world are they, and how did they get there?

Amazingly enough, we're still not sure. One of the earliest theories suggested that they were created by a swarm of meteorites, or by an asteroid-size hunk of space rock that shattered into thousands of pieces. Other elliptical craters, like Sudbury Crater in Ontario or some oval craters on the moon, seemed to suggest this was possible—except that core samples taken from inside the Bays show neither bits of meteorites, nor that the rock layers below them were crushed or fused due to impact, the way they should have been.

After this, the theorists went wild. Some surmised they could have been caused by high-intensity winds during the ice age, blowing in the same direction for up to 12,000 years, or created by melting glaciers, stranded icebergs, or peat fires. Some blamed sandbar dams, artesian springs, underwater eddies, whales wallowing in shallow water, fish nests created by the simultaneous waving in unison of zillions of fish fins over submarine springs while they were spawning (back when the seas were deeper and the coastal plains were under water), or giant prehistoric beavers. The latest theory is that an icy comet exploded over the earth's surface as it skipped off the atmosphere like a stone skipping over a pond, creating the Bays. Who knows? Anything seems possible at this point. The Bays will stick around till someone eventually figures them out.

If you want to visit them, there are plenty to be found around Bladen Lakes, Lake Waccamaw (at 9,000 acres, the largest of the water-filled Bays), or anywhere east of Fayetteville or west of Myrtle Beach. —*Thanks to Roy Campbell and George Howard*

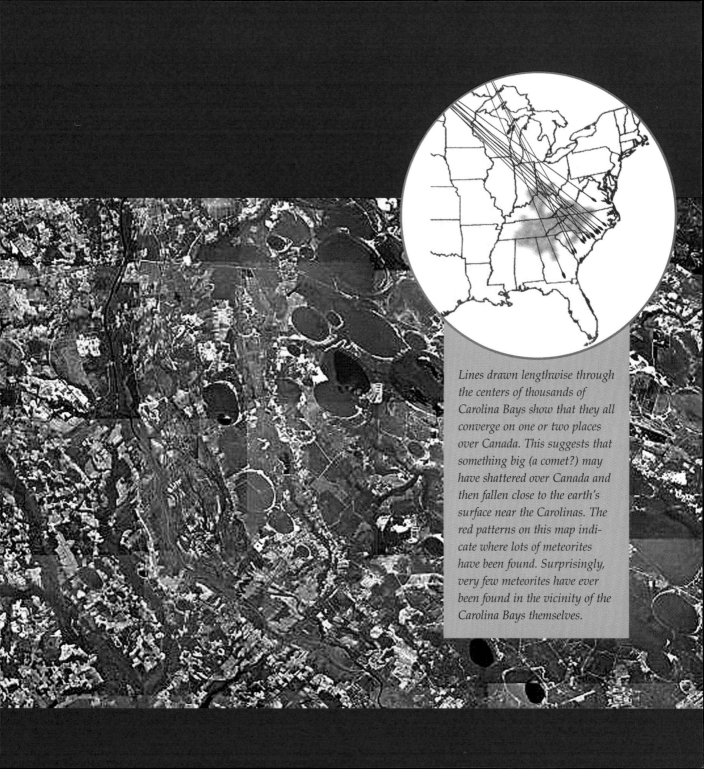

Lines drawn lengthwise through the centers of thousands of Carolina Bays show that they all converge on one or two places over Canada. This suggests that something big (a comet?) may have shattered over Canada and then fallen close to the earth's surface near the Carolinas. The red patterns on this map indicate where lots of meteorites have been found. Surprisingly, very few meteorites have ever been found in the vicinity of the Carolina Bays themselves.

It's Not a Bird. It's Not a Plane!

Aliens from other planets must be uncommonly fond of basketball, barbecue, beach music, or some combination of the above, because they certainly do flock to the Carolinas. Whatever the attraction is, we rank among the top UFO-spotting sites in the world. There have been upward of 3,000 reported sightings in the Carolinas, and researchers suspect that the number unreported may be ten times as high. We include only a tiny sampling here.

April 8, 1897, Wilmington, NC

Hundreds of Wilmingtonians saw a kind of airship with many colored lights and a searchlight, which shone its beam over the city. It came in from over the ocean, moving west at high speed. It could have been an early kind of dirigible (an aluminum airship was patented in 1897, and a zeppelin prototype was built in 1896), but the reported high speed and the fact that no attempt was ever made to publicize or profit from the event make this seem unlikely. There were dozens of airship sightings in 1896–97, which prompted H. G. Wells to write *The War of the Worlds*, published in 1898.

July 11, 1947, 7:20 p.m., High Point, NC

According to the *Wilmington Morning Star*, two pilots flying a plane at a thousand feet just south of High Point saw a "ball of fire . . . a huge red object traveling at a rapid rate of speed." Glancing to their side, the pilots described the object as "round on top with a black band through the center, flying in a northerly direction at a rapid rate of speed." The bottom part of the object was revolving, and periodically a burst of fire came from underneath as if from some sort of exhaust.

April 3–5, 1975, Lumberton, NC

The largest concentrated cluster of UFO sightings in the Carolinas took place over three days, when eight separate sightings occurred on April 3, eleven on April 4, and three on April 5. Area papers referred to it as a "UFO Attack," although no injuries or property damage occurred.

Abducted by Aliens

Between 1978 and 1983, diesel mechanic Bill Herrmann became a regular guest of a group of alien beings who frequented the South Carolina Low Country. He first spotted their ships when he, his wife, and some neighbors (including some cops) noticed UFOs flitting to and fro among the power lines near Charleston Air Force Base and the city airport. On November 27, 1977, Herrmann got a few snapshots before the craft disappeared, and when the film was developed, the images seemed to show a silver-colored disk about sixty feet in diameter flying some 1,500 feet above him.

In January 1978 he got a few more pictures of one of the disks. When they were mentioned in an article in the *Charleston News & Courier*, an intelligence officer from the base contacted him and asked to see the images. Herrmann lent the air force copies of his prints, and a week later was told he'd only photographed an F-4 Phantom military jet. A senior officer told him to "forget what he'd seen."

After this, according to Herrmann, mysterious vehicles tried to run his car off the road. Threatening phone calls became a routine event. Undeterred, Hermann continued trying to prove the presence of UFOs. On March 18, 1978, he looked across the Ashley River and saw the disk zipping back and forth above the power lines. When he walked out near the river the object abruptly appeared just in front of him above the marshes. As it got closer and closer, Herrmann found he could no longer speak, then fell to the ground and lost consciousness.

When he woke up, he was standing in an open field with no idea where he was. He made his way to a nearby road, flagged down a passing car, and called the sheriff's department. Deputies found Herrmann in a dazed state. They informed him that several hours had passed since he had left his house and that he was now fifteen miles away from home.

In the following months, Herrmann was plagued with migraines, during which he had a sensation of being watched by huge eyes in a room with bright blinking lights. Tormented, he contacted a UFO group in Tucson, Arizona, called the Aerial Phenomena Research Organization (APRO). APRO sent its director of research, Dr. James Harder, to Charleston to meet with Herrmann. He put Herrmann through a series of hypnotic sessions in order to discover what had happened to him during those missing hours on the night of March 18. Over several hypnosis sessions, the story began to unfold.

After being knocked unconscious by a blue-green ray, Herrmann had awakened on a table in what he thought was a spotlessly clean hospital room, lighted with a "red brilliance."

Suddenly he became aware of several other beings watching him. They were about three feet tall and dressed in little red leather coverall outfits with their pants tucked down into their boots. Their faces were classic post-*Close Encounters* aliens with large, bulbous, earless heads, black "wrap-around" pupil-less eyes, dinky mouths, and pasty complexions. When one of them touched him, Herrmann felt only a boneless arm with the consistency of a sponge.

In perfect English, they explained that they were from Zeta 1 and Zeta 2 Reticulum, a double star system near Orion, thirty-two light-years away. They were part of a network of similar vehicles, which had come to Earth to conduct experiments in hydrodynamics and osmosis.

The Zeta Reticuli also gave Herrmann a ride on their ship. They first took him up to view a larger "mother ship" and then headed out on a little spin around the Charleston area. Finally they dropped him off where he was found dazed, disoriented, and far from home.

Over the next few years, Herrmann had several more interactions with the Zeta Reticuli, and he appeared on television a number of times, eventually inspiring or coauthoring several books and a film.

Ultimately, though, Hermann's attitude toward UFOs changed. He was fired from his position as a Sunday school teacher when he announced that he had committed "evil acts" by speaking about the UFOs on television. In the end, he would disavow all of his claims to alien contact, finally writing to film reviewer Nathan Shumate in 2005. "I have destroyed everything connected with my UFO experience because I believe that the entire Phenomena is based on Satanic deception. I have had absolutely nothing to do with the Phenomena for over 25 Years of my life."

UFO Hunter

Nothing about the unassuming gray ranchette on Battleground Road in Lincolnton, NC, seems unusual until you notice that the welcome mat reads WELCOME UFOs AND CREWS. You are now at the home of one of the nation's most renowned UFOlogists, George D. Fawcett.

Now in his late seventies, Fawcett has been fascinated by the possibility of alien life forms visiting Earth since 1944, when as a Boy Scout he began making a scrapbook of items related to the war and found an article headlined "Silver Balls Floating in Air [Are] Nazis' Newest War Device." The article described the unexplained sighting of the balls but never, in fact, said where they originated.

Fawcett had his own first sighting in the summer of 1951. He was running late to class at Lynchburg College in Virginia when he saw a hemispherical orange-colored object ("just like half an orange") floating over Hopwood Hall. He stopped and watched for several minutes before it lifted up and tilted out of view. From then on, he was a changed man. He'd found his calling in life, a pursuit that would ultimately lead him to amass one of the world's largest collections of "sauceriana." Fawcett has written several books and founded the North Carolina chapter of MUFON (Mutual UFO Network).

In his investigations of UFO sightings, Fawcett's experience has taught him that most sightings of UFOs can be explained by ordinary phenomena—weather conditions, airplanes, raindrops on a lens filter. But there are enough "possibles" left over to keep his mind open to the prospect of intelligent life elsewhere in the universe.

Here are just a few of the thousands of reported UFO encounters from Fawcett's files.

May 10, 1952, Ellenton, SC

Four employees of the DuPont Company who worked at the Savannah River nuclear bomb facility saw eight "disc-shaped" objects approaching the plant. These objects varied from yellow to gold in color, and approached at such a low altitude that they had to lift up to pass over some tall tanks in the area. The noiseless craft weaved from left to right and moved from side to side before they departed at a 90-degree angle.

January 29, 1953, 11:15 p.m., Conway, SC

Drawn outside by a commotion among his livestock, Lloyd C. Booth saw a streamlined object, twenty-four-to-twenty-six-feet long and shaped like "an egg, cut end-to-end" hovering at a low altitude over his farm. He shot at it with a pistol and the bullet hit something that made a metallic sound. He fired again but heard nothing because the craft increased its noise, "like a stepped up electric motor . . . As soon as the [first] shot hit the object," Booth wrote. "It seemed to tilt upward just a bit and soared into the air at about a 65-degree angle. It continued this upward move at about 600 m.p.h. until it vanished."

August 1968, 2:30 a.m., Mount Airy, NC

Mrs. Harold Eggers went to her front door to see why her dog was barking frantically and saw a dome-shaped flying object with a short lone occupant inside wearing a silver helmet and skintight uniform. The object hovered about ninety feet away from her home, making a sound "like a swarm of bees." Mrs. Eggers closed her bedroom curtains, hoping it would go away. She peeped from behind the curtains from time to time to see if it was still there, and noted that it remained nearby at a Duke Power substation for almost forty-five minutes. In the morning, she discovered that all three of her electric clocks had lost an hour.

October 19, 1973, Copeland, NC

David Doby and his wife spotted a large blue object flying over their home, then discovered a three-and-a-half-foot-tall being in their front yard, dressed in a golden metallic suit and a helmet. Terrified, the couple grabbed their son, jumped into their car, and drove off to spend the night in the company of relatives. Their dog also fled the property and was not seen until the following day.

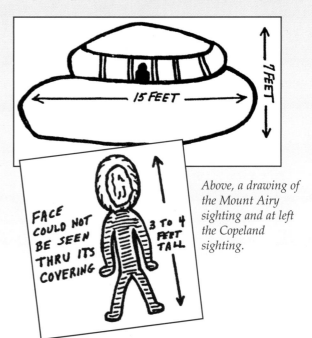

Above, a drawing of the Mount Airy sighting and at left the Copeland sighting.

Bizarre Beasts

With the highest mountains, largest virgin forests, biggest intercoastal sounds, and some of the deepest lakes and most forbidding swamps found anywhere east of the Mississippi, the Carolinas offer plenty of hiding places for frightening creatures of every stripe and slither. We're not talking just alligators or black bears. There are credible reports of other, more ominous beings hiding out in our backwoods—and in some other not-so-remote places.

In fact, there are so many weird beasts in the Carolinas, we can't cover them all in just one chapter. By mounting your own investigations you may be able to track down others, like the Non-Human Entity that's been seen near Sidney, NC. The Entity should be easy to recognize. He has red glowing eyes, a grayish face with long pointed ears, and a hooked nose. And he's known to wear a medallion, which he uses for communication. So unlike most monsters, you can actually talk to him. Just ask him first if it's okay to snap a picture.

The Thing of Clarendon County

In early 1972, two events shook Clarendon County, SC, one literally, the other emotionally. A series of earthquake tremors frightened residents already worried about a mysterious series of pet and livestock deaths. A creature one newspaper dubbed the Spook of Summerton but that was referred to locally simply as the Thing roamed at loose in the area, seemingly able to perform feats no ordinary animal could. Bill DuBose, for instance, had kept seven goats in a pen surrounded by an eight-foot wire fence topped by three strands of barbed wire. One morning he went to feed his animals and found six of them dead—each with two deep fang marks in its throat. The seventh goat was gone altogether.

Clarendon County Sheriff T. J. Jackson was baffled. "I don't know what it is," he said. "Some folks say it's a giant bobcat or lion, but I can't see how even a mighty big cat could get over a fence that high and carry off an entire goat." When two witnesses caught a glimpse of something clearing a ditch and a fence in a single leap, a distance of nearly forty feet, the leap seemed almost supernatural. A skeptical article in the *Charlotte Observer* joked that perhaps the Thing was a mythological beast with wings, but Clarendon County locals stood by what they'd seen—the ditch and the fence were there, and they could be measured. For a while, anytime a pet failed to show up for its food bowl, its owners worried.

Gradually the mysterious deaths tapered off, and the community returned to normal. The Thing itself faded into the stuff of legend, something to frighten teenagers with, to keep them from staying out too late at night.

But what was it? State wildlife officials remain as puzzled as anyone. Large native cats like pumas or mountain lions, while extremely rare, are still thought to

exist in the most remote pockets of the eastern swamplands. But they almost never venture near humans, steer completely clear of dogs, and usually eat their prey at or near where they kill it. Sick or injured wild animals will sometimes break these general rules out of desperation, but the Thing hardly seemed to be impaired. Instead, it seemed to kill easily, mercilessly, and for the sheer pleasure of killing—almost a human trait, some might say. From time to time, local people still wonder if it might come back out of hiding and strike once more. Perhaps the next time the earth shakes in Clarendon?

I Don't Know What It Was, But It Was SomeTHING!

On the way back from Florida, driving through North Carolina around one in the morning, we came across a thing crossing the road. It was gray-brown and looked a bit bigger than a large Great Dane. However, it was very thin and sickly looking. It had long straight ears laid back by its head and a long skinny tail. I would have thought it to be a sick dog, no question; but as we approached, the animal raced away in a catlike manner unlike a dog. We had a strange feeling about it, and wondered what this creature might be. We thought maybe a panther, but it was too large. Weird—I'm still spooked about it to this day.
—Elvis Barsczewski

Bigfoot, or the Carolina Woollybooger

What book on weird stuff would be complete without mentioning the world's most popular boogeyman? And yes, whether you call him Yeti, Sasquatch, the Abominable Snowman, or just plain Bigfoot, it seems that he not only wanders through exotic lands like Nepal and Tibet, but also tramps barefoot through the Carolina woods and pocosins—the upland swamps—in all that fur, no matter how hot or buggy it may get. He's been spotted in the Blue Ridge, been seen trudging through the coastal swamplands, and left his size-28 footprints at various scattered points in between. Although there have been a few photos and bits of film footage that seem to show a big hairy, humanoid creature running through the woods, no confirmed skeletons exist in any public collections anywhere. Because of all this, many scientists doubt that he exists at all. Still, there have been enough reports of encounters to keep the doors of possibility open.

Unfortunately, most sightings don't result in close encounters. A loner, Bigfoot is about the least confrontational big bruiser you're ever likely to meet. As soon as anyone from our relatively runty human race shows up, he's more likely to run than fight. Most of the evidence we have is based on glimpses, footprints, and odors.

According to most descriptions, a typical Bigfoot is six to ten feet tall (some say up to fifteen feet), covered with hair except on its face, hands, and feet, has a somewhat pointy head, walks upright, and smells absolutely awful. While Carolina mountain folks like to call him the Woollybooger or the Boojum, in the flatlands Down East the term of choice is Skunk Ape. This not only refers to a silvery or grayish stripe of lighter-colored fur often observed on the creatures' backs but reflects their pungent smell.

Woollyboogers, Boojums, or Skunk Apes have been seen by scores of Carolinians, including law enforcement officers, librarians, schoolteachers, and members of the clergy—by people, in other words, who usually tell the truth. A guy from Mechanicsville, SC, named Cal is among the many people who have been lucky enough to catch a glimpse of one of them in the Carolina swamps, back in the mid-1980s. As he told us, "Me, my cousin and my father were idling up the Great Pee Dee River in a small boat. I was shooting a 22 pistol at some things

Bizarre Critters

In Dovesville, SC, a dog belonging to Barney Odom named Flat Nose could shimmy up trees like a cat and preferred chewing on empty Pepsi bottles instead of bones. He appeared twice on *The Tonight Show* with Johnny Carson in the late 1980s. Flat Nose Road is named for him. *—Ripley's!*

and while I was looking toward the left bank I saw something that did not look right, but could not tell what it was. Then all in a split second the thing stood up and dove into the river with his arms stretched out, just like a man would dive, and it never was seen again. We went over and looked for tracks but only found slide marks on the hard muddy surface. . . . When I first saw it, it was on its feet with knees bent, kneeling down like it was doing something between his legs. As I said, 'Look!' it was already going into the water. My father saw it as it was going in, but it all happened in about two seconds. I don't 'think' I saw a Skunk Ape, I know I saw one."

Bizarre Critters

During a flood in Pitt County, NC, in July 1886, huge sturgeon were able to swim through cornfields and gobble up as much corn as they could swallow. One 328-pound fish was captured and found to have eaten enough corn to fill two barrels. *–Roger Kammerer*

Most of those who come forward say that the vast majority of sightings probably go unreported for fear of ridicule by those who haven't seen the creature themselves. Meanwhile, outfits like the Bigfoot Field Research Organization (BFRO) continue gathering ever more evidence that indeed something mighty big and hairy is really out there. They like to remind us that despite hundreds of reports by witnesses, many scientists refused to believe in the existence of the giant panda or giant squid, until hard evidence finally proved them real. The irrefutable proof just hasn't been found yet, that's all. As former Defense Secretary Donald Rumsfeld so often repeated, "The absence of evidence isn't the evidence of absence."

Don't Shoot the Woollybooger

Want to go in search of Woollyboogers yourself? By far the most Bigfoot sightings in the Carolinas have occurred in the South Mountains region of North Carolina where Burke and Cleveland counties touch, with scattered encounters in adjacent parts of Rutherford, Lincoln, and Catawba counties. However, do the responsible thing and leave your guns at home. While Woollyboogers have not yet been listed on any federal endangered species list, they are undoubtedly extremely rare. Even if you don't end up going to jail, bagging one for your trophy wall is more likely to make you a societal outcast yourself than earn you any real glory. So take pictures, not lives. And maybe take some plaster too, in case you find only footprints.

The human foot to the right demonstrates how Bigfoot got his name.

The Lizard Man of Lee County

Scape Ore Swamp was known only as a haven for snakes and mosquitoes and the occasional moonshiner until it gained nationwide notoriety as the home of South Carolina's celebrity swamp monster. Its rise to fame began the day Lee County Sheriff Liston Truesdale drove into the tiny community of Browntown at the edge of the swamp to investigate what he thought was an act of simple vandalism.

Tom and Mary Waye had phoned to say that their 1985 Ford sedan had been "chewed up." Truesdale assumed they were just using slang until he saw the car covered with dirt and tooth marks, and with part of its chrome ripped off. "I knew right away that whatever did it was way stronger than me," he said. "My deputy and I tried pulling on that chrome ourselves and we couldn't even wiggle it." A bundle of chewed wires and huge tracks on the hood were further evidence that something out of the ordinary had happened here.

While Truesdale was looking for clues, bystanders mentioned that several of their neighbors had recently seen a strange creature in the area. A few weeks earlier a man named George The First Hollomon and a friend had been chased by some kind of large beast

while they were getting water from an artesian spring over near the swamp. George The First had told his half-brother, George The Third Hollomon, about it when they got home. But it was the story of high school basketball star Chris Davis of Dalzell that convinced the sheriff that something truly weird might be afoot.

At first Davis hadn't come forward, for fear that other people would think he was crazy. In a sworn and taped witness report at the sheriff's office, however, he finally related his frightening experience. Driving home from his job, he had run over something sharp near the swamp, which caused a flat tire. Just as he finished changing the wheel, he suddenly heard a noise and looked across a moonlit butterbean field and saw something that stood more than seven feet tall.

According to Davis's report on the Associated Press wire service, the creature "was about 25 yards away and I saw red eyes glowing. I ran into the car and as I locked it, the thing grabbed the door handle. I could see him from the neck down—the three big fingers, long black nails and green rough skin. It was strong and angry. I looked in my mirror and saw a blur of green running. I could see his toes and then he jumped on the roof of my car. I thought I heard a grunt and then I could see his fingers through the front windshield, where they curled around on the roof. I sped up and swerved to shake the creature off."

Not long after, the strange man-beast was seen again. This time four people reported seeing a large, muscular creature jump a six-foot security fence and bound across Interstate 20. They went straight to the sheriff's office to report it. "It stood on its hind legs and was about seven feet tall, and its eyes glowed!" one of them said. Deputy Wayne Atkinson believed they were genuinely frightened. "I've been in law enforcement for ten years, which is long enough to know when people are faking being

scared," he said. "This was the real thing."

At this point Lizardmania set in with a vengeance. Reporters and TV news crews filled area motels as local merchants began hawking T-shirts, caps, and buttons featuring "The Lizard Man of Lee." Newspaper stories about Lee County's new celebrity began running nationwide. The *Charlotte Observer* staged a "name that lizard" contest. Among the suggestions were Newt Rockne, Sal Amander, the Lone Lee Lizard, and—in case it turned out to be a girl—Liz Erdman and Allie Gator.

Perhaps predictably, things finally got out of hand. An airman stationed at nearby Shaw AFB fired five shots from a .357 magnum at what he described as "a 5'6" creature" he saw running along U.S. 15. He claimed that one of the shots wounded it in the neck, and that it then stumbled, bleeding, off into the swamp. Up to this point, Sheriff Truesdale had mostly enjoyed the notoriety the Lizard Man had brought his county (and of course area merchants were thrilled by the economic boom it generated), but enough was enough. Law officers charged the airman with illegally carrying an unregistered weapon and with shooting on a highway and hunting out of season, threatening him with up to a year in prison. This helped quash the enthusiasm of most of the local hunters. Not long afterward, another man reported hitting something with his car on Scape Ore Swamp Bridge that was "large, with an alligator face." Whether this car killed the creature, or the airman killed its (presumably smaller) mate with a gun, no one knows; but after that, the sightings ceased.

This all happened in 1988. The case remains open. Speaking out of his retirement, Truesdale still has lingering questions about the whole series of events. "Too many people saw something," he said. "But I still don't know what it was."

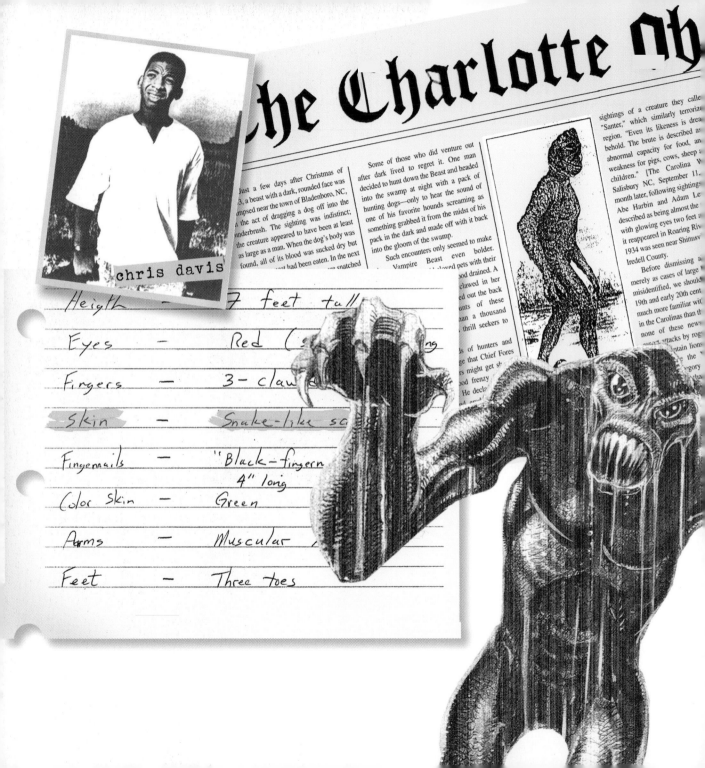

chris davis

Just a few days after Christmas of 3, a beast with a dark, rounded face was mped near the town of Bladenboro, NC, the act of dragging a dog off into the nderbrush. The sighting was indistinct; the creature appeared to have been at least as large as a man. When the dog's body was found, all of its blood was sucked dry but been eaten. In the next snatched

Some of those who did venture out after dark lived to regret it. One man decided to hunt down the Beast and headed into the swamp at night with a pack of hunting dogs—only to hear the sound of one of his favorite hounds screaming as something grabbed it from the midst of his pack in the dark and made off with it back into the gloom of the swamp.

Such encounters only seemed to make Vampire Beast even bolder.
loved pets with their od drained. A clawed in her ed out the back nts of these an a thousand thrill seekers to

ds of hunters and ge that Chief Fores rs might get sh od frenzy He decla

sightings of a creature they calle "Santer," which similarly terroriz region. "Even its likeness is drea behold. The brute is described as abnormal capacity for food, an weakness for pigs, cows, sheep children." [The Carolina V Salisbury NC, September 11, month later, following sightings Abe Harbin and Adam Le described as being almost the with glowing eyes two feet it reappeared in Roaring Riv 1934 was seen near Shinnsv Iredell County.

Before dismissing a merely as cases of large misidentified, we should 19th and early 20th cent much more familiar wit in the Carolinas than th none of these news attacks by ro tain lions the gory

Heigth — 7 feet tall

Eyes — Red

Fingers — 3-claw

Skin — Snake-like sc

Fingernails — "Black-fingern 4" long

Color Skin — Green

Arms — Muscular

Feet — Three toes

Lizard Man Ain't There to Change Tires

It was an unusually warm September night. We were driving down Joe Miller Road at about eight p.m. when my dad realized that we had a flat. He went out to replace the tire, and something large darted across the road. It was dark, so none of us saw exactly what it was.

My dad just shook it off and changed the tire. He placed the flat in the trunk and went to open the driver's-side door. All of a sudden, the creature darted back into the middle of the road and turned to look at the car. Then it froze, startled by the headlights, which were on so my dad could see what he was doing.

My mom and I got a clear look at it. I'd say that it was about 7 1/2 feet tall, with webbed feet and hands, RED eyes, sickly, brownish green skin, and scales covering every part of its body. It stood up like a man and walked on two feet. It ran really fast—it looked like a blur when it ran across the street the first time. Finally, it just turned and ran quickly back into the swamp. My dad jumped in the car and drove off as fast as the spare would let him.
–Tennisdog

Has the Lizard Man Gone North?

Myself and three buddies were riding around a local hang-out spot in St. Pauls [NC]. We were near a man-made pond called Five Points.

As we approached the pond, I saw a reflection in the woods. I stopped the truck to see a seven-foot-tall bipedal creature. He spotted us, then darted towards the woods near the truck. At this point we were already in reverse and tearing out of there. My friend Austin was crying. Many others have also spotted this creature. *–Nicholas J. Woodall*

White Monkeys of Kings Mountain

Near the town of Bethany, SC, between a pair of ridges that form part of the southeastern slopes of Kings Mountain, is a strange place called White Wolf Hollow that apparently abounds in odd creatures of various sorts. The white wolves from which the place took its name have almost undoubtedly been gone for a long time by now. Nowadays locals occasionally report seeing albino deer, large white panthers or wildcats, albino raccoons, and, strangest of all, white monkeys running across the road. The trouble is, while all these critters are often seen, they've yet to be captured or taken as a trophy.

Hunters say they're often especially startled when the white monkeys leap out of the underbrush in front of their pickup headlights at night. Though it looks like they can't avoid being run over, not one of their carcasses has been recovered after these sudden encounters.

Some researchers claim that the presence of all this oddly pale local fauna has to do with Kings Mountain itself, an ancient geological formation called a monadnock, which is reported to contain large deposits of lithium, quartz, and iron. They describe something called the Pinnacle Effect that makes magnetic compasses often wildly inaccurate in the vicinity of the mountain. Homing pigeons, which may depend on slight variations in magnetic fields to find their way, have been known to lose their bearings if their route takes them across the crest of the ridge.

Or perhaps it's not something as earthbound as magnetic fields. Kings Mountain has had more than its share of human phantoms too. One of the pivotal battles of the War of Independence was fought here, with animosity between the red-coated British loyalists and the American rebels running so high that after the battle was won, more than 150 loyalist corpses were left to rot on the battlefield, while nine men were hanged for switching sides during the fighting. Whether this grisly historic event has anything to do with all the nighttime appearances of ghostly pale animals is not known, but weird things are definitely afoot in White Wolf Hollow.

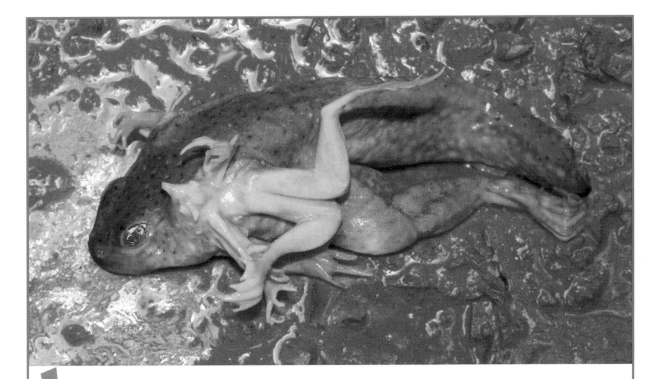

Lena the Fantastic Frog

In June 1937, Laird Harrington collected a frog—or, to be more accurate, a metamorphosing larva (tadpole, in common terminology) well on its way to becoming a full-grown North American bullfrog—with thirteen legs. Probably because he found it in Lee County, NC, and the genus name for bullfrogs is Rana, it was soon nicknamed Lena. Lena achieved nationwide celebrity after her appearance in Robert Ripley's syndicated weekly *"Believe It Or Not!"* cartoon feature. She is still in the collection of the North Carolina State Museum of Natural Sciences in Raleigh, but these days she's only to be found floating in formaldehyde. The curators sometimes refer to it jokingly as a "tadtoomanypole." *–Thanks to Roy Campbell*

Bizarre Critters

Mrs. W. Johnson of Badin, NC, owned a mouse that could sing like a canary. Many scientists are convinced that any talented mouse can sing, but they normally do it at such a high pitch we can't hear them. This probably means that Mrs. Johnson's mouse was a basso. Deer mice make the best singers, though they don't always feel any strong urge to do so. *–Ripley's!*

The Vampire Beast of Bladenboro

Just a few days after Christmas of 1953, a beast with a dark, rounded face was glimpsed near the town of Bladenboro, NC, in the act of dragging a dog off into the underbrush. The sighting was indistinct enough, but the creature appeared to have been at least as large as a man. When the dog's body was found, all of its blood was sucked dry but none of its meat had been eaten. In the next two days, several more dogs were snatched and found later, drained in a similar fashion. Word quickly spread that some kind of Vampire Beast was apparently on the loose.

Bladenboro police chief Roy Fores rounded up a posse of armed men to search through the nearby Big Swamp for the monster, but found nothing but huge footprints with the marks of inch-long claws or fingernails. As the days passed and more dead animals were found, fear spread throughout the region. Parents were cautioned to keep children and pets indoors, to avoid going out at night, and to use cars for even the shortest of emergency trips after the sun went down.

Some of those who did venture out after dark lived to regret it. One man decided to hunt down the Beast and headed into the swamp at night with a pack of hunting dogs—only to hear the sound of one of his favorite hounds screaming as something grabbed it from the pack and made off with it back into the gloom of the swamp. Newspaper accounts of this and other incidents drew more than a thousand professional hunters and thrill seekers to the area.

Finally the crowds grew so large that Chief Fores worried that bystanders might get shot in the frenzy that was feeding the hysteria. He declared a dusk-till-dawn curfew, and gradually the fear subsided along with the killings. Some stories say that a big game hunter from Asheville finally shot the Beast, but others maintain that the Vampire was never found at all, and just chooses to relocate from time to time.

There is evidence this is true. In 1890, newspapers in Statesville, Wilkesboro, and Salisbury reported sightings of a creature they called the Santer, which similarly terrorized the region. "Even its likeness is dreadful to behold," according to one report. The brute was described as having an abnormal capacity for food and a weakness for pigs, cows, and sheep. In 1897, it reappeared in Roaring River, and then in 1934 was seen near Shinnsville, in southern Iredell County.

Before dismissing these reports merely as cases of large bears or panthers misidentified, we should recall that in the 19th and early 20th centuries, hunters were very familiar with big game animals in the Carolinas, and none of these newspapers regularly reported attacks by rogue bears or large mountain lions. They placed the Santer—like the Vampire Beast—in a different category altogether. Which of course means that it could reappear.

Or perhaps it already has. In recent years, a creature closely fitting this description has begun making appearances in the vicinity of Shoals Creek, in Surry County.

—Thanks to Angelo Capparella III, Justin Lynn, and Abandoned NC

When the dog's body was found, all of its blood was sucked dry but none of its meat had been eaten.

The Lake Norman Monster

Over several decades, people spending time around Lake Norman in NC have caught sight of some kind of big creature in its waters. Some have attributed the sightings to giant catfish, sturgeon, or even alligators, since one of those was seen and videotaped just downriver in Lake Wylie. In any case, something big seems to be hiding within Lake Norman's 520 miles of shoreline.

Lake Norman has a coal-burning electricity-generating plant at one end and a hydroelectric dam and nuclear power station at the other. And it is subject to all kinds of domestic and agricultural runoff, from lawn fertilizers to treated sewage. Is it possible that some combination of territorial size, available biomass, chemical, and even nuclear factors has caused something unusual to start growing—and growing big?

Certainly a lot of people think so. Ordinary fish grow a lot larger in the lake than elsewhere. The state overall record for a freshwater fish was set at Lake Norman, a huge blue catfish. We know about this fish because it was caught. There's no telling what else is still living in the lake, growing bigger by the day.

Most of the indications are that the Lake Norman Monster is some kind of fish, not like the plesiosaur/sea serpent of Loch Ness in Scotland. The few photos that have been taken of the Monster so far seem to reveal rows of tough scales, fins instead of clawed feet, and glimpses of gills—all pointing to some kind of fish which, lacking any predators and finding plenty of food, has kept on gaining weight and size. Unlike most other creatures, fish don't have a set age or size limit. They just keep getting bigger till something eventually kills them.

Whether it is a fish or not, those who have encountered the Lake Norman Monster certainly found it more than memorable—and didn't much relish the idea of possibly becoming its bait. Hundreds of sightings have been recorded. Some recent samples follow.

Location: Queens Landing

My class went on the field trip from my school on the Catawba Queen. One guy was standing on the front and he saw it first. He yelled and we all saw it coming up along in the water between us and the side of the lake with stripes and spots all around it and really big eyes. It was the biggest fish I ever saw, and our teacher saw it too. Then it went away real fast, like a submarine on TV. —*R. Dickens, Mooresville*

Monster Likes Hot Dogs

My uncle and his brother bought a pontoon boat and we all got invited to spend the day on it. We were just going along for the ride, but they insisted we do some fishing. But I couldn't stand to put a worm on the line, so while my uncle wasn't looking I put a whole hot dog on mine. I wasn't really expecting to catch anything but at least I could pull on it and feel it. Then all of a sudden I felt a HUGE tug on my line and I almost let go, but it also grabbed my brother's bait and his pole was bending almost in half. All around the boat the water was whipping like something really BIG was under us, and then we felt it bump against the pontoons and almost fell over. We got only one quick look at it before our lines both broke, and it was like an alligator or something but it had a flat tail. After that, my uncle said we didn't have to fish any more; maybe we'd eat hot dogs. —*J. Sherrill, Statesville*

The Creature with a Big Mouth and Yellow Spots

Last year our family went to North Carolina with another family, which has a house next to Lake Norman. One day I went down by the lake and started throwing in rocks, to see if I could make them skip. Then the water almost like exploded right in front of me and I saw a big yellow head and spots and like a long mouth stick up in the air, but it was really, really big! I screamed and my family all came out running toward the lake. They all got a look at it too, but by then it was back down in the water so they didn't see it as good as me, though they could see how big it is. The guy that owns the house said he never saw anything like that, so I guess maybe I was lucky, if you want to call it that. —*M. Bradford, Cincinnati*

Lake Murray Monster

Unlike the relatively gentle (if frightening) fish-like monster of Lake Norman, "Messie," the monster in Lake Murray, SC, has been described as a classic prehistoric-looking lake serpent, who often comes across as hostile or downright aggressive. Whether it's a matter of too many water-skiers or just annoyance at having to spit out all those tiny fishing hooks, this monster has been known to attack people who are out on the lake in boats.

Gilbert Little of Ballentine, SC, first sighted Messie in 1933. Sightings have gradually increased over the years in proportion to the population settling around the lake. The beast gained even more notoriety in 1980 when it openly attacked Buddy and Shirley Browning, who had been out fishing with their friend Kord Brazell.

"It wasn't an illusion; it wasn't an eel or sturgeon," said Buddy Browning. "It was unlike anything I ever saw before, and I have been fishing Lake Murray for over 20 years. . . .

"It came towards the boat like it wanted us to leave. Whenever we came up to near where it was nesting or doing whatever it was doing, it just came up to us. It could've been mating. It was basically on top of the water where you could see it quite well. And leave is exactly what we did."

The few photographs that have been taken of the monster show it to be snakelike and long—according to some descriptions, up to sixty feet—and a variety of colors. Credible witnesses claim to have seen flippers, and many describe a long neck with a distinctive head, which is lifted out of the water. Army general Marvin B. Corder (Ret.) sent a letter to the South Carolina Fish, Wildlife & Parks Department saying he'd seen the creature on more than one occasion, and that it had a "head and body resembling a snake, with a tail of an eel."

Whatever's out there, it's probably best to play things safe until it's definitely identified. If you're on the lake, keep your arms well inside the boat and don't lean over too close to the water. And if you see a large wake or ripple headed your way, get outta there!

The Wilmington Sea Monster

At sea, the word of the ship captain is law. The logs he keeps are so respected that they are considered legal evidence if there is any need to refer to them. So when a log records the sighting of something unusual, we can be reasonably certain that something unusual at least seemed to be observed.

In 1947, a ship owned by the W. R. Grace Company was involved in an unusual incident off the coast of NC. The *Santa Clara III* was on its way to Colombia in South America. Third Officer John Axelson was on duty on the bridge when he observed what could only be described as a sea monster. As he

stared ahead, he suddenly saw "a snakelike head rear out of the sea about 30 feet off the starboard bow of the vessel." As he shouted, the other two mates on duty witnessed it as well. Unable to change the ship's course in time, they watched in horror as the *Santa Clara* apparently struck the creature. All three officers later provided descriptions, which included the following details: The head "appeared to be about 2¹/²' across, 2' thick, and 5' long. The cylindrically shaped body was about 3' thick, and the neck 1¹/²' in diameter. . . . The visible part of the body was about 35' long." It was dark in color, and after the ship struck, it fell astern and sank out of sight. Some reports say it was cut in two.

The sighting was recorded in the ship's log, and the ship sailed on without further incident.

What strange creature did this ship find in the treacherous seas off the Carolina coast? Some researchers have suggested it might have been an extremely unusual sighting of a giant squid. What was reported as the creature's head, they argue, might actually have been the widened club-end of one of the squid's two extra-long tentacles. But the dark color the seamen described, the fact that it was sighted during the day on the surface in the warm waters, and the size all cast doubt on the squid hypothesis.

A few paleontologists have suggested that it was a prehistoric basilosaurus instead. Basilosauri were distant cousins of the whale believed by most scientists to have died out about 37 million years ago. Much narrower and more elongated than today's whales, the Basilosaurus could have passed for a giant eel, though it was a mammal and breathed air and so hung out near the surface. But could some of these critters have survived, somehow, down through the millennia?

Maybe. This wasn't the only time a sea monster has been spotted off the Carolina coast. In fact, the city of

Wilmington has laid claim to a "sea serpent" which many citizens believe still lives in the zone where the Cape Fear River meets the sea—that is, if it survived the collision with the *Santa Clara*. Or else if it wasn't the only one out there. The Indians in the area had long maintained that a sea monster lived in the mouth of the river, and when the Italian explorer Giovanni da Verrazano passed through the area in 1524 he apparently described it in his ship's log. "We traveled to the mouth of the river and made camp," he wrote. "During the night one of the men saw a great snake resting upon the waves not far from shore."

In 1865, during the Civil War occupation of Wilmington, Yankee soldier James Calden described the numerous sightings of the beast by the locals. They "all seem to see the same thing," he noted in his nature journal. "A long snakelike creature that surfaces occasionally at the mouth of the Cape Fear River. It is described as being dull gray in color, approx. 4 feet wide and over 40 feet in total length. They have named it 'Willie' in honor of the town of Wilmington."

After the War Between the States, sightings tapered off for a while. Perhaps Wilmingtonians were too busy rebuilding their lives to look out for sea serpents. But then, on the 10th of May, 1903, Second Officer Joseph O. Grey penned a terse note in the log of the *SS Tresco*. South of Cape Hatteras and east of Wilmington, while in the same shipping lane where the *Santa Clara* would have its encounter decades later, he wrote: "10AM—Passed school of sharks followed by a huge sea monster."

His description almost matches John Axelson's, forty-four years later. A head lifting out of the water on a long neck. The head five feet long, a foot and a half in diameter. Dark in color, and almost dragonlike.

That day the creature—Willie? or some cousin?—came to no harm. Maybe it, or a descendant, still hangs around Kure Beach some days, to see what's for dinner.

Monkey Island

If the idea of ten-foot-tall Bigfoot-types stomping through the woods makes camping out sound off-putting, take heart. Most of the monsters of our swamps and forests are not only generally rather shy for their size, but these days they are also quite rare. You'll be lucky to see even a giant-sized footprint. But there's a place in South Carolina where hoards of hairy primates aren't at all difficult to catch a glimpse of. The trade-off is that they aren't all that big, and that you aren't allowed to chase after them. In fact, it's illegal to set your own relatively big feet on their territory without prior written permission and trained personnel to accompany you.

The place is Morgan Island, near Beaufort, SC. Shrouded in secrecy, it has been referred to by locals for nearly thirty years as Monkey Island, so-called because a private biomedical company developed it as a free-range breeding ground for rhesus macaques. Several years ago the state of South Carolina bought the island and now leases it to another company, which continues to breed primates for medical research. At any one time, some 6,000 monkeys roam wherever they like on the four-hundred-acre piece of land. On this island, the humans are the ones who live in cages, to protect them from raids by gangs of wandering monkeys. Like Alcatraz, the facility depends primarily on its water barrier to keep its population in place, and few have ever managed to escape. One monkey somehow crossed the Morgan River a couple of years ago and made it as far as the Lady's Island Golf Course seven miles away, but such incidents have been extremely rare.

Before the 9/11 terrorist attacks, there was talk of shutting down the strange facility. The out-of-state company that ran it had lost its lease, and animal-rights activists had nearly succeeded in convincing legislators that the island was more of a detriment than a resource. But Homeland Security concerns stirred by the new threats of terrorism convinced state government officials to do otherwise. The monkeys of Morgan Island, whether they like it or not, are now among those leading the charge against the possibility of chemical attacks and biological agents like anthrax and smallpox, as well as giving their lives for research directed at other potential global threats like the bird flu.

If you have access to a boat, it is possible to get close enough to the island to see the monkeys (bring binoculars), but approaching it or landing on it is strictly forbidden. Signs reading

**FEDERAL PROJECT
RESTRICTED ACCESS
NO TRESPASSING**

ring the shoreline, and security measures are in place. If that's not enough, keep in mind that the monkeys are agile, numerous, much stronger, and less cuddly than they look, and they are unafraid of humans. Many of them have extensive scars from biting one another in turf wars. If the fear of prosecution isn't enough to keep you at a safe distance, at least fear the sharp teeth.

Local Heroes and Villains

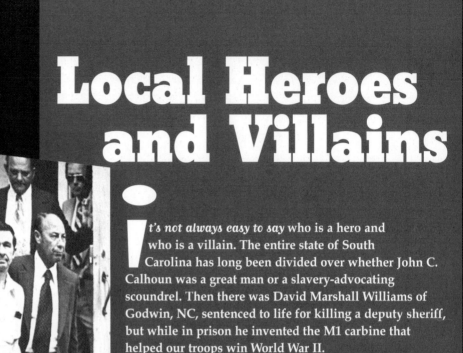

!

It's not always easy to say who is a hero and who is a villain. The entire state of South Carolina has long been divided over whether John C. Calhoun was a great man or a slavery-advocating scoundrel. Then there was David Marshall Williams of Godwin, NC, sentenced to life for killing a deputy sheriff, but while in prison he invented the M1 carbine that helped our troops win World War II.

We mention all this by way of saying that any presentation of heroes or villains is bound to seem incomplete and arbitrary, although some people, of course, come down definitely on the Heroic side of the fence, while others belong permanently on the side reserved for Villains. There is not room here to include all the interesting Carolinians who fall on either side of our porous divide, but at least this'll give you a good idea of the unique individuals who have become our sometimes awkward gifts to the rest of the world.

Osceola's Lost Skull

Just in front of the walls of Fort Moultrie, at the mouth of Charleston Harbor, is a tiny enclosure surrounded by a cast-iron fence. Here, beneath a misspelled marker and buried under tons of concrete, lies the headless skeleton of an Indian leader who was captured by treachery and brought to the Carolinas by force. It's quite a tale.

For many years, the Florida Seminoles, with their leader, Osceola, fought U.S. attempts to relocate them from their swampy home-land to the arid plains of Oklahoma. After spending nearly $50,000,000 and losing close to 2,000 soldiers, the army was ready to try anything. Under a white flag of truce, while negotiations were being held in St. Augustine, Florida, soldiers seized Osceola and his deputies and took them prisoner. They were hauled off to nearby Fort Marion, but after several managed to escape from there, the decision was made to ship them to South Carolina.

Here they were considered to be far enough away from their homeland so that the conditions of imprisonment could be a bit more relaxed than they had been in Florida. Osceola was allowed to wander about the fort, and could even have visitors. Many members of Charleston society made the trip out to see the famous rebel leader. He often spent mornings sitting for portrait painters (including George Catlin) and seemed to enjoy his notoriety. Half Scottish, Osceola was able to converse with his visitors in English (his English name was Billy Powell), although he firmly identified with the Native American ways of his mother's side of the family.

Despite Osceola's warm welcome, the fort itself was not quite warm enough in midwinter for a man used to living in central Florida. Osceola contracted an illness that a Florida doctor named Frederick Weedon (who had come along with the shipment of prisoners) diagnosed as a throat infection compounded by quinsy (suppurative tonsillitis). By mid-January 1838, the Indian leader had fallen gravely ill. Unable to speak, he painted half his body red, put on his full regalia, and then, in the presence of his people and his own medicine man, signaled farewell to everyone, and lay down and died. It was the evening of January 30, 1838.

Before the burial the next day, Dr. Weedon did a

Dr. Frederick Weedon

strange thing. He cut off Osceola's head and then arranged a scarf around the neck to hide the fact that the head was detached. Just before the coffin was sealed, he somehow managed to snatch the head off the body and conceal it, along with several other items that the leader's people had placed with the body to accompany it into the afterlife. For years afterward, Weedon kept these souvenirs in his home in St. Augustine, using the head to discipline his children by threatening to hang it over their beds if they misbehaved. At some point, he sold the head to a collector, and it eventually wound up as an anatomical specimen at the New York University Medical School. In 1866, a fire destroyed much of the collection, including, it was alleged, the head.

The activity around Osceola's burial wasn't over, however. For more than a century, Florida and South Carolina fought over the custody of the Indian leader's headless remains. Several Florida towns appropriated money for Osceola memorial gravesites to be erected in their city parks should they ever be granted custody of the bones, thinking that such a site would make a great tourist draw. Even North Carolina got in on the act, claiming that Osceola had been born in Columbus County and probably belonged back there.

Meanwhile, the *Charleston Evening Post* questioned whether Osceola was buried at Fort Moultrie at all, suggesting that the bones were really in a military graveyard in Beaufort. Scientists weighed in with the opinion that while he *might* have been buried in front of Fort Moultrie, by the 1950s (when most of this furor raged), no trace of the coffin or bones could possibly still be there. The marker covered only empty soil, they said.

Finally, in 1968, archaeologists decided to excavate the site. As it turned out, the fence and marker were almost but not quite directly over the grave. But the grave itself was there, and contrary to earlier conjecture, the coffin and headless skeleton were still quite visible. To everyone's surprise, an infant was found in a separate casket next to Osceola's bones, but who this was, no one knows. No trace of any artifacts was

found, which further damned Dr. Weedon as a thief.

After the excavation, the bones were placed in a new casket and reburied beneath tons of concrete to prevent any grave-robbing attempts. Then the original marker (with the name still misspelled as "Oceola") was repositioned in the correct location, directly over the casket.

One remaining piece of the puzzle may still be out there. For years, most references to Osceola's head have stated that it was destroyed when fire swept through the Medical College museum on 14th Street in New York in 1866. But recently discovered documents, including a reference that it was briefly on display at the Stuyvesant Institute at 659 Broadway sometime after the fire, call this version into question. It may yet turn up on eBay—or perhaps it already has.

Old Man Traffic

A remarkable intersection in Charlotte is the corner of Queens Road and Providence Road. The two streets meet here but don't actually cross—or at least their names don't. They kind of touch elbows at this point and then bounce off at right angles. It looks like an ordinary intersection but drive through it and a few seconds later you'll feel like you've entered the Twilight Zone: "Hey, where'd my street go?"

From the late 1950s until 1976, a man named Hugh Pharr McManaway took it upon himself to help the helpless travelers caught in this traffic nightmare. Hugh could be seen directing traffic here just about all day every day, standing on the median and waving a white dishtowel to guide vehicles toward their chosen destinations. He became a local fixture some people referred to as Boo Radley (after the benign outsider in Harper Lee's novel

To Kill a Mockingbird), but many just called him Old Man Traffic.

Directing traffic for the fun of it wasn't his only eccentricity. McManaway spoke in rhymed couplets, explaining, "I don't curse, I speak in verse." About his self-imposed traffic guardianship he said, "I see who will turn and who still stop, but I'm really not a traffic cop. Some play tennis, some play ball; I just direct traffic, that's all. I'm not serious. I'm delirious. I can't talk like you. I'm just crazy Hugh."

Though he called himself crazy, people who knew him better recognized him as a savant. Hugh had memorized the entire Bible and could recite randomly chosen passages word for word. He could also instantly replay almost any piece of music he heard—on a musical saw.

Growing up, Hugh and his mother sometimes staged concerts for neighborhood children, gathering them in the parlor of their twenty-room mansion at 1700 Queens Road. They all drank lemonade and sang hymns accompanied by Hugh on the musical saw and the McManaways' singing dog. But traffic was his real passion.

In 1976 Hugh had a mild epileptic seizure in a restaurant. After this, he decided he'd finally have to retire from his work as a human traffic signal. He died in 1989 and is buried in Charlotte's Elmwood Cemetery.

Several years later, Anne McKenna and her sister Kitty Gaston, who had both grown up thinking of Hugh McManaway as a permanent fixture at that intersection, realized that perhaps he *could* become a permanent feature there. With the help of hundreds of others, they began raising money to commission sculptor Elsie Shaw to create a statue. Bank of America Chairman and CEO Hugh McColl, Jr., and the Arts & Science Council provided the rest. As he himself might have said, "Old Hugh McManaway is really here to stay."

Giants Among Us

The Carolinas have produced some mighty big boys over the years. We mention the McCrary twins on page 220, but Peter Francisco and Mills Darden deserve mention too.

Francisco was a foundling discovered on the docks of City Point, Virginia, in 1765, when he seemed to be about five years old. An uncle of Patrick Henry's took him in as a foster son and raised him to adulthood. Peter grew to be a strapping young man, more than six feet tall and weighing more than 250 pounds, an amazing size in those days. Few people alive today could match him for strength, and that's probably why he projected an image even larger than he actually was.

Francisco was at the peak of his powers when the American Revolution began. He joined a Virginia militia in 1777 and fought on the Patriot side. Because he was so large and so strong, a special sword more than five feet long was made for him at the request of none other than George Washington himself.

Francisco quickly earned a reputation as a fierce fighter. At the Battle of Camden, SC, in which British forces under General Gates were defeated, he single-handedly pulled free a cannon that had become mired in mud. At the Battle of Guilford Courthouse, NC, he killed eleven men, including one who had earlier wounded him with a bayonet.

After the Revolution, Peter Francisco headed back to Virginia, where he raised a number of children. Although the veteran fighter was normally mild-mannered in the years after the war, he obviously hadn't lost his mighty touch when two men showed up one day and got him riled. He picked both of them up, *along with their horses*, and tossed them over the fence surrounding his property.

If Francisco was the strongest man of his times, his near contemporary Mills Darden wasn't far behind. Darden was one of the largest people in recorded history. He was born on October 7, 1799, near Rich Square, NC, and never stopped growing throughout his life (probably due to a pituitary gland malfunction). By the time he died, he stood seven feet nine inches tall and weighed roughly 1,080 pounds.

Peter Francisco

He wasn't merely a helpless fatty, however. Tales of his strength include the times he hefted a loaded wagon out of a mud hole, lifted a full (roughly thousand-pound) hogshead of tobacco onto an oxcart, and, for fun, lifted an entire table load of ten people at a family reunion by getting under the table and standing up.

According to Daniel Barefoot in his book *Seaside Spectres*, Darden was a prodigious eater as well. He once downed eleven watermelons at a sitting and typically ate a breakfast that included "several dozen buttered biscuits, eighteen eggs, two pounds of bacon, and at least two quarts of coffee." He traveled by walking or by oxcart since no horse or carriage could carry him.

Darden fathered eleven children by two wives, all of them of normal size. His bulk eventually killed him when, on January 23, 1857, his windpipe collapsed under the weight of flesh on his neck. More than five hundred board feet of lumber went into the construction of his coffin, which took seventeen men to carry. He is buried in Chapel Hill, Tennessee.

If We Can Help
This Man's Low Back
Pain, Probably We
Can Help Yours...

"Dr. Payne adjusted my aching lower back recently and relieved the strain and the pain. I highly recommend his treatments."

Joe Ponder
Love Valley, N.C.

I have had great success solving back problems! Find out if I can help you! In order to make your care affordable I will give you a spinal screening exam and 2 x-rays (if necessary) free of charge. I promise to do my best to solve your problem, or refer you to someone who can if I determine the problem is out of the scope of my care.

CHIROPRACTIC CENTER

Mighty Mouth Joe Ponder

Joe Ponder came to his true calling through illness. Ponder, who had worked as a truck driver, suffered a neck injury in a 1970 auto accident. As part of his recuperation therapy, his doctor told him to exercise his neck muscles as well as he could. So Ponder wrapped a towel around a bucket handle, clamped it in his teeth and began doing neck curls with the bucket, gradually adding a little more water to it each day. When that didn't provide enough weight, he threw a towel over a rafter and hung by his teeth.

It soon dawned on Ponder that not only was his neck getting stronger and stronger, but also his teeth and jaws seemed to have more than ordinary power—in fact, way more than ordinary. After discovering his great dental strength, he began pulling and lifting heavy objects to amaze audiences at circuses and rodeos. Joe would lift giant pumpkins, livestock, seminude models (among them, Miss Nude America and Miss Nude World—at the same time), and pulled a 55,000-pound tractor-trailer rig, a 92,200-pound boxcar, and a Mississippi riverboat. Billed as The Man with the World's Strongest Teeth, he received a Presidential Fitness Award from Jimmy Carter.

Ponder went on to attempt other feats of dental derring-do, including motorcycle stunts (smashing concrete blocks with a twenty-pound sledgehammer held in his mouth while riding nearly seventy mph), and bending half-inch bars of hot-rolled steel. Until he passed away in 2002, he also ran his own leather company in Love Valley, NC, making saddles, belts, and harnesses for his many cowboy neighbors.

Trotting Sally

George Mullins, a.k.a. Trotting Sally, was a fixture in Spartanburg County, SC, in the early 1900s. So-called for his trotting gait, Mullins, according to legend, would hand his hat to the engineer of a train in Spartanburg and beat the train on foot to Chesnee, twenty miles away, to retrieve his hat. He carried a violin he named *Rosalie* everywhere he went. As Ira Tucker of the Dixie Hummingbirds recalled in *Great God A'mighty*, "He was an excellent violinist. Nothing but strings and his fingers. He had that violin almost sounding like it was talking." Others recalled he could ask the violin questions and make it sound like it was answering back "yes"or "no."

Mullins was popular with children and was known to occasionally bark like a dog. But he was no fool. When faced with a group of white troops during the First World War, as the *Spartanburg Herald* rather proudly asserted, he made them look like "a bunch of nuts," saying, " 'Trotting Sally' had got their goat and gone off with it."

When he died at the age of seventy-six, in 1931, he received a full article in the *Herald*—an extreme rarity for African Americans at the time—with the article noting, "Trotting Sally's acquaintances were all friends."

— Thanks to Susan Thoms

Pee Wee Gaskins, a Mean Little Man

If anyone in the Carolinas deserved to be called evil, Donald Gaskins surely did. Small in stature, he was called Pee Wee for most of his life by nearly everyone. His diminutive size (five feet two inches) made him seem much younger and less threatening than he was, and that helped to mask his intensely cruel and vicious nature.

As South Carolina's worst (known) serial killer, Gaskins tortured and killed at least ten victims and, if his own confessions are to be believed, as many as ninety others. He often bragged about his exploits, including to law enforcers. He even drove a hearse around his community of Prospect Crossroads in Florence County with a

sign in its windows proclaiming "We Haul Anything, Dead Or Alive." If someone asked him what it meant, he would say, "Why, I kill people, so I gotta have some way to carry 'em around, right?" Nobody believed him.

Gaskins was born illegitimate and into an ugly home life. From a young age, he seemed to be a bad seed who took too well to the abuse and dysfunction around him. As a little boy, he tortured animals. By eleven, he had quit school and started a gang that abused other children, then graduated to crimes like house burglary. When he was thirteen, a girl caught him breaking into a house and chased him with an ax. He wrested the ax away from her and chopped into her head and arm before escaping. She lived, and he was arrested and sentenced to five years in a juvenile prison—but not without learning the lesson that it's better not to leave one's victims alive.

Gaskins was released from the reformatory in March 1951. Over the next two decades, he was in and out of jail for various crimes, and married several times. In fact, his fourth wife turned him in when she found out he was on the lam from a statutory rape charge of a twelve-year-old girl. For that crime, he was sentenced to six years.

In 1968, Pee Wee was released on parole—and began what he called his "serious crimes." Within a year, he picked up a hitchhiker in North Carolina and asked her for sex. She looked at the tiny man and laughed. For that, he raped and then murdered her by tying weights to her and throwing her into a swamp to drown.

When he did this, he

made a discovery that would prove to have awful consequences for his subsequent victims. Something about tormenting and killing another human being gave him satisfaction. From then on, Gaskins became a kind of connoisseur of pain and death. It was during this time (which eventually stretched to six years of near non-stop killing) that Gaskins bought the hearse and openly offered to take on contract killings for friends and neighbors. Everyone thought he was kidding.

Pee Wee normally committed his crimes by himself. But in 1975, now forty-two years old, he killed a van full of people who had broken down on the highway. Suddenly he realized he needed a little help to dispose of the victims and the van. An ex-con friend named Walter Neely agreed to drive the van so it could be repainted and sold, and soon the two of them were in business together. Gaskins later said that the two made good partners because, "I am as afraid of Walter as Walter is of me."

Taking on a partner ultimately proved his undoing, however. As Gaskins somehow managed to rack up two more wives (for a total of six marriages), the killings continued—contract killings, joy killings, killing people he knew (including Walter's ex-wife, Diane, who had threatened to expose them). Walter Neely learned about a private cemetery where Gaskins buried his victims, as well as the acid-filled tank where he disposed of other bodies.

A 1976 police investigation involving a missing thirteen-year-old girl finally unraveled a whole long list of unsolved crimes when it was determined that the girl had last been seen in the company of Gaskins and Neely. Neely was brought in for questioning, and soon cracked. In an attempt to save himself, he told police about the secret cemetery, where they quickly

discovered the bodies of eight more victims. In May of 1976, Gaskins was sentenced to face the South Carolina electric chair for one of the murders, before confessing to the other seven to avoid multiple death penalties. But in November of that year, Gaskins was saved. The U.S. Supreme Court declared the death penalty unconstitutional.

Gaskins's death sentence was reduced to life in prison, which he saw as a free ticket to keep doing what he enjoyed most: killing. He somehow managed to assemble a bomb rigged to an electrical device and to convince a fellow inmate named Rudolph Tyner that it was an intercom that would allow him to communicate with other prisoners. When Tyner held the "intercom" to his ear and plugged it in, it exploded and killed him.

Pee Wee Gaskins had been terrified that Satan worshippers would try to dig up his corpse and use it for ridiculous ritual purposes. The one thing he couldn't stand was ridicule.

Unfortunately for Gaskins, the Supreme Court had reversed its earlier decision and determined that capital punishment was legal once more. The state of South Carolina secured a new death sentence, and at 1:00 on the morning of September 6, 1991, Gaskins was put to death in the electric chair.

His one last request was honored. His body was cremated and the ashes scattered in an undisclosed location. Pee Wee Gaskins had been terrified that Satan worshippers would try to dig up his corpse and use it for ridiculous ritual purposes. The one thing he couldn't stand was ridicule.

Three Siamese Twins (Or Is It Six?)

Among the most peculiar of all sideshow freaks in old circus days were Siamese twins. Conjoined twins, as they are more sedately called these days, were intensely fascinating because they both shared and did not share the same issues as everyone else. What would life be like, to never ever be wholly one and only?

Siamese twins are among the rarest of all births. Only roughly one in five million births stands a chance of resulting in a living pair of conjoined twins, and only a relative handful of those have been recorded down through history as making it to full adulthood. It's all the more remarkable then that three Siamese twins wound up in North Carolina, including the pair that gave the unusual condition its common name.

Chang and Eng

Chang and Eng were born to a Chinese fisherman and his wife in 1811 in a small village in the tiny province of Samut Songkhram in the royal kingdom Siam, not far from present-day Bangkok, Thailand. The babies were born joined at the chest by a piece of connecting cartilage and blood vessels. Other than the fact that they had to coordinate their activities with extreme precision, their childhood was relatively normal. They learned to swim, handle boats, and play games like other children. From time to time, visitors were brought to the village to see them.

Among these visitors was Robert Hunter, a trader from Scotland, and Abel Coffin, a sea captain from New England, who heard about the amazing boys in 1829 while their ship was in port. They visited the village and paid the boys' parents a "reward" for being allowed to take the twins away with them, to be seen and admired by the rest of the world.

Chang and Eng traveled with the two entrepreneurs for several years, putting on public performances throughout Europe. The twins played games of badminton, danced, and did acrobatics to demonstrate their amazing coordination. Circus magnate P. T. Barnum eventually acquired the act and sent them on tours of the U.S. Barnum's relentless ballyhoo promoting "Chang and Eng, the Amazing Siamese Twins" firmly cemented the term in the public vocabulary.

By 1839, however, the two had grown tired of the circus life and felt ready to settle down. One of the towns they recalled fondly from their travels was Wilkesboro, NC. They bought a farm nearby in Traphill, where they happily raised pigs and farmed tobacco.

It took remarkably little time for the twins to be accepted by the local community. In 1843, Chang and Eng married the Yates sisters, who lived on another area farm. Chang married Adelaide Yates and Eng married Sarah Yates. Nine months later, they both had their first daughters, just six days apart. Chang and Adelaide eventually raised ten children, while Eng and Sarah had eleven.

In their later lives, the twins hoped to find a doctor willing to separate them, but no surgeons felt they had the requisite skills to risk the operation. Without X-rays, doctors were unable to tell if the twins shared any vital organs or critical blood vessels. (These days, it would be relatively easy to separate them.)

Over the next several years, Chang, who drank heavily, fell into ill health, and on January 17, 1874, he died in his sleep, of bronchitis. When Eng awakened in horror and discovered that his attached twin brother was dead, he very quickly died of fright. The twins' remains are now in the graveyard behind White Plains Baptist Church in Surry County, NC. Each year, a family reunion brings together all the descendants of this famous pair.

One Real McCoy

Unlike Chang and Eng, Mille-Christine McCoy (or McKoy, as it is often spelled) preferred to be referred to in the singular form, although she was essentially two women joined at the spine, with a shared nervous system. Either head could feel sensations from the other, and the two hearts beat in unison. Mille-Christine was born into slavery July 11, 1851, on the Welch's Creek plantation a few miles northeast of Whiteville, NC. She was the eighth offspring in her family and weighed seventeen pounds at birth.

Soon after her birth, the plantation owner took Mille-Christine away from her mother and sold her for $30,000 to a traveling circus operator named J. P. Smith. Smith and his wife saw to it that Mille-Christine was given an education, and she eventually learned to sing, play musical instruments, and speak five languages, including Russian and French. When she became a part of P. T. Barnum's show, she was billed as The Eighth Wonder of the World, The Carolina Twin, and the Two-Headed

Nightingale. Her two voices were different, one a contralto and the other a soprano, which enabled her to sing beautiful duets with herself.

In 1900, Mille-Christine retired from show business and returned to North Carolina to live with her vast extended family of brothers and sisters. On October 12, 1912, the side of her known as Mille died of tuberculosis, and Christine died just seventeen hours later. Her grave is located in a small family graveyard on the east side of Box High Road, Columbus County.

The Hilton Sisters

While Chang and Eng came to North Carolina by choice and Mille-Christine McCoy was born here, the Hilton Sisters ended up becoming Carolinians for a sadder reason. They got stranded.

Violet and Daisy Hilton were born in Brighton, England, on February 5, 1908, to Kate Skinner, an unwed barmaid. Their bodies were fused at the pelvis, and though they shared no major organs, blood circulated between them and each side could feel bodily sensations from the other. The midwife who helped with the difficult delivery was Mary Hilton, their mother's boss and landlady. Mrs. Hilton saw a chance to cash in on their rare condition and "adopted" them from her young employee. But it was an abusive situation from the start. As children, they were severely beaten whenever they failed to call her current husband (her fifth) Sir. The twins were kept hidden from the public and were taught a variety of show business skills, including singing, dancing, and playing musical instruments.

When the girls were three, Mrs. Hilton decided to take them on the road as The United Twins and toured them relentlessly through Europe, Australia, and the U.S. Hilton and her sixth husband, along with her daughter Edith and Edith's husband, Meyer Meyers, jointly managed the twins' career and split the money earned from their appearances. When Mary Hilton died in Birmingham, Alabama, she "willed" the children to the Meyerses, along with enough money for them to move into a luxury mansion in San Antonio, Texas.

The Meyerses booked their human "property" on the vaudeville circuit, where they soon made friends with other performers, including Bob Hope and Harry Houdini. Eventually, the twins broke away from the exploitive couple and went into show business for themselves as the Hilton Sisters' Revue. Free to be themselves at last, they began dressing in different clothes, dyeing their hair different colors, and doing everything possible to distinguish one from the other. In 1932, they played themselves in the Tod Browning movie *Freaks*.

They also engaged in a series of wild affairs, failed attempts to secure marriage licenses (to twenty-one different men in as many states), and even a few very brief marriages. The weddings were showbiz, too. Violet was wedded to dancer James Moore on the fifty-yard line of the Cotton Bowl during the Texas Centennial Exposition of 1936, and Daisy married dancer Buddy Sawyer in New York in 1941. Neither marriage lasted more than a few weeks.

As movies grew popular, Daisy and Violet headed to Hollywood, where they acted the role of Siamese twins Dorothy and Vivian Hamilton in the 1950 B-movie *Chained for Life*. But there were no other roles available to conjoined twins and the sisters had to find something else to stay afloat financially. They tried running a hamburger stand in Miami for a while, but that didn't work out. Then around 1960, they experienced a momentary windfall when *Freaks* was reissued and became a cult classic. They began touring with the film and signing autographs at intermission.

The last of these appearances was in 1962 at a drive-in movie theater in Charlotte. The next morning they waited for their manager to pick them up, but he never showed. Realizing that audiences were waning, the man had decided to skip town with the money from the gate the night before. The twins were stuck.

Fortunately, the manager at the Park and Shop grocery at Queen's Gate Shopping Center on Wilkinson Boulevard showed some southern hospitality and gave them a job as checkout girls. For the next seven years, the Hiltons worked a cash register at the Park and Shop.

When they failed to show up for work on the morning of January 6, 1969, the manager called the police. The Hiltons were found dead in their apartment, apparently killed by the Hong Kong flu. They were buried in Charlotte's Forest Lawn Cemetery in plot number M 313, next to one of their few friends, a man named Troy Thompson, who had been killed in Vietnam.

Darrel the Donut

Downstairs in the book-conservation department of U.N.C.-Greensboro's Jackson Library there is a celebrity donut that has recently celebrated "his" twenty-fifth year as the official departmental mascot. "Darrel the Donut" first proved his worth in the early 1980s after someone placed him on a radio antenna and he miraculously improved the reception. After many years in this capacity (for which he appeared in the nationally syndicated newspaper feature *Ripley's Believe It Or Not!*), he is now more often engaged in charity activities and human relations pursuits. An unpublished manuscript for an authorized biography is making the rounds, but at the moment he has no plans to retire.
—*Thanks to Jessica Beal*

Lee Roy Martin, the Gaffney Strangler

Although he was no Siamese twin, Lee Roy Martin did seem to have two personalities trapped in his brain. One side, the "dark Martin," was a murderer. The other side, the "good Martin," found the killings abhorrent but was helpless to prevent them. All he could do was phone in clues to the police and hope "they" got caught before more young women were killed or others were wrongfully accused of the crimes.

Lee Roy's bridge in Gaffney, under which some of Martin's victims were found.

Despite his pleas of innocence, a man named Roger Dedmond had been found guilty of the March 1, 1967, murder of his wife, Anne Lucille, and sentenced to life in prison at a Union County, SC, prison camp. Two months after his trial, *Gaffney Ledger* editor Bill Gibbons got a call from a man who claimed to be a murderer and gave detailed instructions on how to find two recent victims. The caller also said that he was the one who had killed Anne Lucille Dedmond.

Gibbons gave the information to the police, who quickly found the bodies of twenty-six-year-old Nancy Parris and fourteen-year-old Nancy Rhinehart.

Five days later, Gibbons received another call from the self-admitted killer. "If they don't catch me, there will be more deaths," he said. Gibbons tried to talk him into giving himself up. "It's no use," he said. "I'm psycho and I'd get the chair. They'll have to shoot me like the dog I am."

The next day, fifteen-year-old Opal Buckson was abducted within sight of her brother and sister. The siblings got a look at the car, a blue sedan, but were unable to stop the abduction before the man shoved Opal into the trunk and drove off with her.

Massive coverage of the abduction had everyone in the county on edge. Two days later, two men spotted a man standing beside a blue sedan. For some reason, the man aroused their suspicions; but before they could approach him, he jumped in his car and drove off at high speed. Not, however, before they got his license number. When police investigated the place where the man had been spotted, they found the strangled body of Opal Buckson. Police traced the vehicle to Lee Roy Martin, a mild-mannered man of thirty who didn't seem capable of such violent acts. But under questioning, Martin admitted to hearing voices and said that another Martin had committed the crimes. The "good Lee Roy" was almost relieved that he'd been caught.

Martin eventually got four life sentences. After serving a year for a crime he didn't commit, Roger Dedmond was released. Lee Roy Martin, both good and bad, was murdered in prison by a fellow inmate three years later.

Major Perry, the Sleeping Preacher

Major Perry was born into slavery in Fairfield County, SC, an uneducated farmhand unable to read or write. After the Civil War, he labored in South Carolina as a free man, making a living as best he could. Then in 1880, when he was in his late forties, Perry came down with a fever that put him in a coma for several days. When he awakened, he found that he had acquired a strange gift, but one that he apparently never got to experience firsthand himself.

On the night of June 16, 1880, a few days after recovering from his illness, Perry lay down, and started to talk in his sleep. The voice that came out of his mouth was nothing like his regular speaking voice. When awake, he spoke like the illiterate fieldworker he was; but in his sleep, he spoke perfect King James English, in full, measured sentences. And the words he spoke were beautifully formed sermons, exhorting his unseen audience to fear and praise the Lord. When he reawakened, Perry's normal voice returned and he had no recollection of the sermon.

As this continued to happen night after night, word of the "miracle" soon spread, and people began attending evenings at the Perry house. Soon the Perrys moved to Batesburg in Saluda County, where they bought a larger property that could accommodate the growing audiences that came to witness Major Perry's "mystery sleep sessions."

Visitors would be offered iced tea or water in the parlor while they waited for Preacher Perry to prepare for bed. Once his wife had given the signal, they'd troop into his bedroom and sit in chairs arranged around the walls. The curtains surrounding the canopied bed would then be pulled back, and they'd get to observe Major Perry lying flat on his back, delivering a sermon with his eyes closed. Amazed, they were only too glad to drop a few coins into the bowl in the hall on their way out.

In the early 1900s, Perry started taking his bedtime preaching on the road, giving sleep-trance sermons throughout Georgia and both Carolinas. As part of the "performance," witnesses were invited to test Perry's trance state by seeing if they could awaken him while he was sermonizing. Some took this to extremes by holding lighted matches against his skin or pinching him until bruises appeared, but nothing could awaken him until he'd reached the end of his lesson. Every night of the year from June 1880 until his death on November 8, 1925, he preached, and never repeated a sermon. He was still preaching on his deathbed, until the moment he finally passed away.
—Thanks to Gloria Caldwell

Personalized Properties

What would possess an otherwise sane person to erect a giant flying saucer in the middle of his hometown as a rest stop for visiting aliens? And why would an insomniac musician find comfort in attaching buttons to everything in and around his home, including the outhouse? And while we're at it, why would anyone choose to live in a concrete bunker hidden under sand dunes on the Carolina coast? What's the matter with these folks?

The Carolinas are sprinkled all over with sites like these. There are at least a few in every county, places where individuals decided to stretch the envelope by doing something a little different, and sometimes *really* different. Like building miniature versions of the world's great buildings, or an entire house out of bottles. They made places, in other words, where they could feel more comfortable just being themselves. And isn't this, after all, what we're all hoping to accomplish?

Haw River Animal Crossing

Anyone turning off the main road between Chapel Hill and Pittsboro, NC, and onto the little side road leading into the village of Bynum could be forgiven for thinking they'd entered the secret worldwide vortex of chain-saw art. Along both sides of the road, standing in front of almost every house and occupying nearly every yard along the way, are playful animals made from tree limbs and stumps and bits of what would otherwise probably be the waste products of industrial civilization. Deer with eyes made of tennis balls, porcupines covered with bed springs or artificial insemination tubes, rabbits outfitted with bottle caps for eyes, rhinos with hides made from old carpeting—all taking the places that might be occupied by ordinary dogs and cats in most towns. The whole town of Bynum is decorated year-round with a cavalcade of wooden beasts. It's all the work of one man, whose own home is surrounded by more than a thousand of what he calls his critters. Together they form an environment named The Haw River Animal Crossing or sometimes The Jungle Boy Zoo.

Clyde Jones, a.k.a. Jungle Boy, was born a few miles away on the Rocky River in 1938 but moved to Bynum, an old cotton-mill village on the Haw River, when he was a teenager.

Until the late 1970s, Jones supported

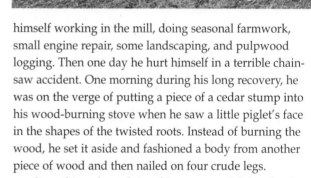

himself working in the mill, doing seasonal farmwork, small engine repair, some landscaping, and pulpwood logging. Then one day he hurt himself in a terrible chain-saw accident. One morning during his long recovery, he was on the verge of putting a piece of a cedar stump into his wood-burning stove when he saw a little piglet's face in the shapes of the twisted roots. Instead of burning the wood, he set it aside and fashioned a body from another piece of wood and then nailed on four crude legs.

Something about doing this was so satisfying that he soon made another little critter to keep the first one company. And before long, Jones was spending nearly all his time piecing together animals from every root and stump he could find. As they began overflowing his yard, he started giving them away to friends,

neighbors, and any children who happened to drop by to explore the yard.

These days, Clyde Jones is something of an art celebrity—his work has appeared in hundreds of exhibitions worldwide and been featured in publications ranging from the *New York Times* to the *New Art Examiner*. But all that hasn't gone to his head in the slightest. In fact, he almost never sells a piece, preferring to give his creations away. He still lives in the same simple (if by now highly embellished) house with the same wood-burning stove, and still mows his neighbors' lawns for his living. If you pass through Bynum, ask anyone there to point you toward his house. They all know where he lives. There's an annual Clyde Jones Day on the Bynum calendar, but one way or another they really celebrate every day in his honor.

Gotno Farm

After growing up in California, George Morris moved to North Carolina to work as a plasterer during the construction of the Sir Walter Raleigh Hotel in downtown Raleigh. After the hotel was finished, Morris decided to stay on in Raleigh and for many years found work as a cement and plaster man. During his long career, he nurtured a dream of buying a small farm, quitting work, and living out his retirement in idyllic daily pursuits as a gentleman farmer.

When he finally got that chance, however, farming turned out to require much more effort and many more skills than Morris had ever dreamed. In short, the farm he bought for his retirement was a disaster. Some of the animals ran off and others died. The harvests got consumed by bugs and diminished by drought. He soon found himself a laughingstock among those of his neighbors who were real farmers.

It was a tough decision, but Morris eventually decided that he'd better go back to the kind of activity he already understood, which was working with cement. But what could he do? While pondering this, he ran across a book called *The Wonders of Fungi*. This gave him an idea. He began making concrete fungi—mushrooms, puffballs, bracket fungus, stinkhorns—and attaching them to the trees in his yard. He liked the effect, and so he built a mushroom-inspired gazebo, and then various fungus-shaped planters and freestanding abstract

sculptures inspired by fungi and lichens.

Nothing seemed too odd to be converted into a concrete fungus. If Morris had been a Picasso, he might have inspired a movement called Fungism, such was his commitment to fungal reinterpretations of ordinary objects. Meanwhile, to burn the bridge with the unfortunate world of farming (and to get the local farmers off his back), he renamed his property. A sign at the entrance now proclaimed it GOTNO FARM.

Life on Gotno was good. Making fungus was fun, and visitors started dropping by to see it. But one day a particularly aggravating little kid happened to be among a group of folks visiting the property. The boy was unimpressed with all the concrete fungi. "Heck, anyone could make this stuff," he sneered. "It's just blobs, no real shapes at all." Morris was upset with the brat, and he snatched a little toy dog away from him. "I'll show you," he said. "Lemme have this for a week or two, and then you'll see."

When the family brought the boy back a few weeks later, they saw what Morris had accomplished. A giant concrete dog with the exact proportions of the toy loomed over them. After this, Gotno Farm saw the installation of a number of other large animals like frogs and deer—and even a concrete UFO or two to boot. Ultimately, Form triumphed over Fungi, but Time had the last word. Traces of Morris's creations still exist, but they're in bad shape these days. Still, what's left is a reminder of a man who lived out his dream, just not exactly as he'd planned.

Aunt Met's Indian Hill

Just outside the town of Highlands, NC, Almetta Pickelsimer (later known as Aunt Met Brooks) built a small environment she called Indian Hill. For years she ran a little grocery next to her husband's auto garage. Not long after World War II, she began converting the junked car lot next door to it into a sculpture garden.

Hauling quartz rocks in a surplus army jeep, Aunt Met built several dozen animal and human figures for the garden and even more for sprucing up the inside of her store. The store itself was further decorated with mosaics made from smaller stones, as well as painted jungle scenes, and foreign landscapes. It's still there. Stop by if you get a chance.

Charlie Yelton's Bottle Farm

In the early 1970s, Charlie Yelton saw a bottle house on a TV show about Knott's Berry Farm in California. After working in a textile mill for fifty years, Yelton had retired unexpectedly because of a leg injury, and he was bored. The bottle house on TV inspired him to begin building his own glassy structures. Stacking clear whiskey bottles, brown beer bottles, green 7-Up's, and blue Milk of Magnesia bottles in decorative patterns, he spent four years creating an entire bottle farm on the outskirts of Forest City, NC, including a full-size bottle house, along with sheds and outbuildings.

"There's 11,987 bottles that went into building up that house of mine," he told us. "And I set every last one of them in the mortar." We asked how he went about it. "Wellsir, I sure made a few mistakes at first, and then less and less as time went on."

Mistakes? "Yessir, that first place I started building, I reckon I had the bottles turned around the wrong way, and whenever that wind blew, I couldn't sleep! It was all a hootie-hoo, y'know! So I just had to start all over after that."

7 STEPS
TO
ETERNAL POWER
CHRIST SPIRIT
DIVINE LOVE.
HOLY THOUGHTS
JUSTICE.
FAITH.
LOYALTY
SINCERITY.
SEND HEAVENWARD

NOEL

Yvonne Leow's "Divine Sounds"

Yvonne Leow immigrated from Guyana in 1977, after voices told her to open a combination religious shrine/devotional supply shop she calls Divine Sounds, located near the state line separating the two Carolinas. She continually embellishes the site with brightly painted concrete statuary, Christmas ornaments, and artificial flowers. Found on the south side of NC highway 501 between Laurinburg and South of the Border (near Rowland), it's worth a stop.

Shangri-La in Prospect Hill

Let me live in a house by the side of the road/ and be a friend to man. The well-worn old line from Sam Walter Foss's deathless doggerel is embedded in cement at the entrance to a tiny village made of white quartz stones on a side road near Prospect Hill, NC. But the little buildings are what best reveal the daily concerns of Henry Warren, the fellow who made them with the

help of a neighbor named Junius Pennix. When Warren retired from running his White Rock Gas Station & Store, the Vietnam War dominated the nightly news along with the riots, assassinations, and social upheaval that marked the late 1960s.

Naming his small side yard Shangri-La after "the land that time forgot" in James Hilton's novel *Lost Horizon*, Warren began taking on the problems of the outside world by shrinking them down to more manageable size. President Lyndon Johnson's Great Society program had created the mammoth Department of Health, Education & Welfare, and its huge bureaucracy

became a symbol for Big Government. But in Shangri-La, the HEW building became a diminutive waist-high structure, which anyone could sit on and poke fun at.

Other famous structures—the IRS Office, which seemed to demand so much money to pay for the new social programs, the Supreme Court, which enforced them, and, eventually, the Watergate Hotel, which threatened to tear apart the fabric of democracy itself— all found their places among the little buildings.

Finally, walkways between the village and the house where the Warrens lived were paved with 11,000 arrowheads, set into the cement in decorative patterns. Were these intended as a reminder that all these accoutrements of society had been achieved at the expense of an even earlier people? We'll probably never know, since Warren died in 1978 without leaving any record of his goals or intentions. But the rest of the first stanza of Foss's poem, written in 1897 when Henry Warren was already 14 years old, may sum it up.

There are hermit souls that live withdrawn
In the place of their self-content;
There are souls like stars, that dwell apart,
In a fellowless firmament;
There are pioneer souls that blaze their paths
Where highways never ran;
But let me live by the side of the road
And be a friend to man.

Hardy Hodges was not particularly fond of children. In fact, from closer up you could see dolls with nooses around their necks, dangling from the bushes behind the fence.

perhaps because she stayed with her husband) she was blessed. One day she sawed a limb off one of the trees in the Kingdom and discovered the robed figure of an angel on the end of the stump. Wondering if it was just chance, she sawed another slice off the limb— and another angel appeared. She did it again to confirm the miracle, and lo, another angel emerged. Perhaps Someone Up There thought she deserved some recognition? Hodges's place is no longer there in Dillon, which probably makes the town kids feel a whole lot safer.

For years, one of the peculiar sights of Dillon, SC, was a block-long stretch of high chain-link fence surrounding a piece of property local folks called Hodges' Kingdom. Built by a cranky fellow named Hardy Hodges, on first sight it just seemed to be adorned with random junk—old toys and dolls and pieces of machinery. The more you studied it, though, the more it revealed Hodges' attitudes and personality.

Hodges was not particularly fond of children. In fact, from closer up you could see dolls with nooses around their necks, dangling from the bushes behind the fence. Or dolls riding tricycles, being run over by toy cars. Or being turned into little yapping dogs. Everything about it was geared to warn any kids to Stay Away.

Mrs. Hodges was a bit friendlier, and because of that (and

Pearl Fryar's Topiary Garden

Cruise into downtown Bishopville, SC, and you'll soon start to notice that, in addition to its classic small-town American Main Street, there are an unusual number of unusually well-pruned shrubs, trimmed in unusual shapes. Instead of the typical cheese-cubes and green meatballs you see everywhere else, here are spirals, pom-poms, abstracts, and weirdly tufted shrubbery. They're all either the direct creation or inspired brainchildren of one of the town's local celebrities, Pearl Fryar.

Actually, Fryar lives not in Bishopville but just outside it, and herein lies the source of the whole phenomenon. In the early 1980s, Fryar was the proud owner of a brand-new home. The son of a sharecropper, he was the first descendant of all his ancestors to earn a college degree, to achieve a fair wage with benefits (working for a beverage-can manufacturer), and to have his own house built on property he owned, a brick ranchette with a well-maintained lawn. Wanting to celebrate his achievement by drawing a little attention to the place, Fryar decided to enter the Bishopville Garden Club's "Yard of the Month" contest. However, he was told that he didn't qualify because his property was technically beyond city limits. "I realized then and there that I'd have to come up with something so much better than all the other yards that they'd have to make an exception!"

Fryar decided to add some nicer shrubs to his yard, and soon spotted a spiral-shaped plant at a nursery nearby. The owner declined to sell it, but he did show Fryar how to prune one like it for himself. "And once I got started," Fryar said later, "I couldn't stop." A talent that had lain dormant all his life suddenly emerged. The can-factory worker turned into a kind of real-life Edward Scissorhands who taught himself topiary — the art of sculpting plants.

Fryar quickly learned just how far he could bend, twist, or prune a plant without killing it, and before long he began pruning and clipping nearly everything green in sight. He clipped junipers two stories tall and twenty-five feet wide into massive abstract forms visitors now call "the ships." Other shrubs became hearts-within-hearts, mushrooms, loops, corkscrews, or individual standing letters. PEACE, LOVE & GOODWILL was carved into the lawn in words forty feet wide. Among thousands of shrubs, no two are quite alike.

Eventually the Bishopville Garden Club made the exception he'd counted on. Pearl Fryar easily won the competition—and kept on winning till he felt he'd reached his goal and decided to stop competing. By then serious garden enthusiasts had begun showing up from as far away as Europe and Japan, eager to find out how a self-taught gardener had accomplished so much in such a short time. World-famous topiary gardens, like the ones at Japan's Zen temples or in the courtyards of the châteaux of France, had taken generations of monks or gardeners centuries to accomplish what Fryar had achieved in just a few years. His weirdly beautiful garden is a living treasure. Don't miss it if you're in the area.

Kannapolis Castle

Henry James Sides brought his Belgian war bride back to Kannapolis, NC, after his stint in the army during World War II. He went to work in the weaving room of one of the Cannon towel mills, which dominated the town at the time. His bride was unhappy, though, and missed her life in Olde Europe. Sides wanted to cheer her up and thought he'd found a solution one day while listening to the radio.

It was a song called *"Every Man's Home Is His Castle,"* and a sale on brick inspired him to begin transforming his conventional brick ranch-style house into a castle, complete with crenellated ramparts, turrets, and bas-relief woodcarvings inside. When he'd first met his wife, he had promised to treat her like a princess if only she'd come back to the States with him, and this was his best effort to follow through on that promise. We don't know if building a castle proved enough to keep her happy, but it was enough to keep Henry busy for a long time.

A Brigade of Angels

For nearly forty years, a plain, well-maintained white clapboard house just across the street from the Buxton, NC, post office at Cape Hatteras concealed an amazing secret inside. There was no signpost, nothing strange about the yard, nothing peculiar about the carport or the curtains at the windows to indicate that anything other than the most ordinary contents lay inside. But a knock on the front door would bring a diminutive white-haired lady who would welcome you inside, and once your eyes had adjusted to the dimmed light, you'd see something that would boggle your mind.

Thousands of faces would be staring back at you. Every available bit of floor space throughout the house—every step on the stairs, every countertop in the kitchen and bathroom—was occupied by knee-high figures made of driftwood and concrete, painted in rich purples, reds, and burnished golds. With hair made of hardened putty and seashells for eyes, the sea of faces looked as endless and as solemn as a concert crowd who'd just been told that the main act had been detained at the airport.

The tiny lady had made them all, and over the course of forty years she had filled her entire house with the winsome figures. Annie Hooper had come from a very large family, including twelve natural siblings and fourteen foster children, and she had married into another large clan. Her husband was one of nine brothers. Growing up, she lived in the close presence of lots of other people.

But then World War II began, and all the able-bodied men, including her husband and her only son, left to join in the war effort. For the first time in her life, Annie found herself alone, and the solitude did not agree with her. Cut off from the rest of America (there were few phones in those days and only intermittent mail deliveries) and surrounded by wolf packs of German U-boats, which began sinking many merchant ships within sight of the shore, the Outer Banks had become what social psychologists later described as one of the most highly stressed communities in the nation. Facing this, Hooper had a nervous breakdown, collapsing and experiencing spells of amnesia. Her worried husband, who was working at the naval shipyards in Virginia, told her she could take in a few boarders to keep her company if she liked. She soon packed the house with thirty-five paying guests. Once she felt comfortably crowded again, her nervous problems ceased.

After the war, the boarders all left to return to their families. In a near-empty house once more, Hooper again began experiencing blackouts and memory lapses. These continued until one day she spontaneously began to replicate one of the scenes she saw in her old illustrated family Bible, using driftwood and twigs to create the figures of Adam and Eve. Over the next four decades, she refined her simple technique so she could mass-produce her figures—and did make masses of them. Constructing the figures not only filled the oppressive-feeling empty space around her, but as time went on and word about what she was doing got out, they drew hundreds of visitors to her house every year. After that, the loneliness and the blackouts were gone for good.

As the figures began to take over the house, Hooper started separating scenes with strands of tinsel and bunches of brightly colored artificial flowers. She inscribed Styrofoam meat trays with messages and placed them among the scenes. Some of the words were biblical quotes, while others were her own interpretations of Bible teachings. The colored lights, gold paint, and glittering tinsel combined to give the visitor a taste of the "supernatural"—the world in which she believed angels fought against the devil on behalf of humankind.

Annie Hooper died in early 1986, after having finished more than three thousand sculptures. These are now in safekeeping at NC State University in Raleigh, awaiting some future place to display them all permanently, as Miss Annie always envisioned her companions would be.

The Button King of Bishopville

One night, weary with chronic insomnia, bluegrass musician Dalton Stevens began passing the darkest hours by obsessively sewing some extra buttons on a pair of blue jeans. The next night, as the sleeplessness continued, he picked up needle and thread once again and added a few more buttons. After a few more nights, the parts between the buttons began to look a little too empty, so he kept at it,

adding more and more. Almost three years of sleep-deprived nights later, the outfit bore 16,333 buttons, and was about as heavy as a medieval suit of armor.

Something about this activity must have pushed Stevens's own buttons, because once he got started he found it hard to stop at just decorating his jeans. So next he covered his piano and his guitar (3,005 buttons), then his Chevrolet Chevette (149,000 buttons), his mailbox and an outhouse (with operating flush toilet, another 26,000 buttons), and—to go out in style as the self-declared Button King, two caskets (60,000 buttons each) and a hearse. The hearse is covered with some 600,000 buttons, all attached with contact cement.

In his heyday, Stevens appeared with Ralph Emery on *Nashville Now* and his button habit and quick wit earned him multiple invites from Johnny Carson, David Letterman, and a host of other shows. These days, the Button King runs a bluegrass music hall out in the rural countryside northwest of Bishopville, SC, where you can go hear a bluegrass jam session every Friday night. If you go, maybe you can cajole him into performing his own personal button song, which includes this refrain.

> *If you like the color of my clothes,*
> *would you give me buttons instead of a rose?*
> *Buttons can be square or round,*
> *they keep my pants from falling down.*

Joshua Samuel's Can City

Ask anyone around Can City Road in Colleton County, SC, how the road got its name, and you'll hear a tale that may be hard to believe. In 1942, they'll say, sharecropper "Jolly Joshua" Samuel encountered an angel out on that road, and the angel told him to build a city. Which he did. From tin cans.

We heard the story straight from the man himself. "It was hot and I was sitting on my porch taking a nap after a day out working in the sun. I looked up and I saw an eighteen-wheeler flying in the air. I went out to see what it was and it came down and stopped right here, and this man came out. I knew he was from heaven, but he had tattoos. . . . He was a truck-driving angel. He told me what to do. He said if I did it, he would come back and give me everything in the truck to give to the poor. It would be what they needed."

What Samuel believed the man had told him to do was to start building a city for the poor. There was enough room to begin constructing it in the abandoned field across the road from the house built long ago by his father, a former slave. Desperately poor himself, Joshua Samuel had little in the way of raw materials to work with except a heap of tin cans spilling out of the shallow gully where he and his sister had been tossing household garbage for years and years. The cans, then, would have to do. He began carting wheelbarrow loads of them to the field across the way and stacking and aligning them to create full-size buildings. A tin-can restaurant, a tin-can YMCA, and a "headquarters building" were among the structures he erected first. In time, even the huge pile of cans in the gully was exhausted, as well as thousands of quart oilcans from a nearby truck stop. "I wasn't done, so I prayed for what to do," Samuel said, "and that angel man answered and told me that if I needed more cans, all I had to do was plant some."

So he did. With the cans he had left, Samuel created a tin-can orchard, with stands of pine saplings loaded down with tin-can fruit, and then laid out a can garden with rows of stacked-can plants arranged along furrows like cotton bushes or tomatoes. "And he was right, too!" Samuel happily told us. "That field really produces!" It was of little matter to him that what had been happening was that local people, seeing all the cans piled in the field, began tossing their own empties into it whenever they drove by. From then on, there was a steady supply of cans to continue the construction.

Sadly, the place has now all but vanished. Soon after Samuel died in 1984 at the age of eighty-six, Can City was knocked down by a big windstorm. If you go there now, all you're likely to find are a few scattered cans rusting at the edge of the fields. But maybe someone nearby will tell you the story of the truck-driving angel and the city for the poor.

The Concrete City of Orangeburg

A snake slithered slowly through the entrance to a Greek temple where a Mayan deity awaited the sacrificial offerings of its worshippers. Tadpoles wiggled through the arches of London Bridge. A frog croaked near the Shrine of the Virgin of Guadalupe. A bird perched atop an Egyptian obelisk, then made a short hop onto Rachel's Tomb. Maybe it sounds like a scene from Hieronymus Bosch, but it was just another ordinary summer day in Concrete City.

Throughout his career as a building contractor, L. C. Carson of Orangeburg, SC, had dreamed of being asked to build at least one truly significant edifice—a vast church, a large government building, a railroad station. Something that would allow him to leave his mark on society. But as retirement approached, he realized that he was never going to get the chance, and that all he had to show for his years in the construction business was a string of ordinary residences.

Passing through Cullman, AL, on a vacation trip one year, he stopped off to visit the Ave Maria Grotto environment there.

Carson came home to Orangeburg inspired. He would go ahead and create all the structures down through history that he wished he'd had a part in building. He'd just make them somewhat smaller.

Concrete City ultimately comprised some thirty-five

waist-high versions of famous buildings, including such golden-age oldies as the Pyramids, the Sphinx, the Hanging Gardens of Babylon, Notre Dame Cathedral, and St. Peter's Basilica in Rome. Carson built them from heaps of surplus material gathered from his years in the building trade. Mostly he made it up as he went along, though he'd sometimes refer to a copy of an 1851 compendium entitled *The Complete Encyclopedia of*

Illustration for ideas about the details. "Sometimes I know where I'm going with it, and sometimes I don't," he liked to say. "It all depends on how hot it gets."

A few years before his death, when poor health made it impossible for him to continue building and maintaining Concrete City, the collection was donated to the SC State Museum in Columbia, where many of the little buildings can be seen today.

The Backyard Coast Guard

Jimmy Courson built a small fleet of ships representing Coast Guard vessels, which he would test for seaworthiness by floating them in one of the canals or creeks near his home in Belhaven, NC. In his backyard he constructed an elaborate layout of docks, lighthouses, and piers. His obsession with the Coast Guard and its equipment has gained him the recognition of the Coast Guard station nearby, which outfitted him with a uniform and made him an honorary member of the guard. Courson's fleet is still dry-docked in his backyard, so drop by and see him if you're in the neighborhood.

UFO Welcome Center

The sci-fi movie scene is all too familiar: A silvery flying saucer lands in Washington, DC. Surrounded by U.S. soldiers, the saucer hums and whirs as a ramp slowly descends. Then out of the depths of the saucer step the alien, Klaatu, and his giant silver robot, Gort. The terrified populace is stunned into silence. It's the beginning of the classic 1951 film *The Day the Earth Stood Still*.

While something like stunned silence could describe almost any day in Bowman, SC, a little crossroads community situated on the side road between Orangeburg and Charleston, the huge silver flying saucer that is parked in the heart of town is hardly a source of widespread panic. As far as most locals are concerned, the UFO is just where Jody Pendarvis lives. And if he wants to live in a giant saucer, well, that's his own business.

The saucer began to take shape in 1995, after Pendarvis decided to build a Christmas parade float using materials salvaged from tearing down his grandfather's old home. The intended float gradually evolved into a shed next to the mobile home where Pendarvis lived. But then he kept adding on to it. The shed became an office. Then the office became . . . well, for a while no one could tell what it was becoming. Pendarvis himself said he had no idea what he was doing. It was as if he were being guided by unseen hands, until finally a forty-two-foot-diameter silver-painted saucer emerged on the site.

Mounted on extendable columns, the saucer was intended to lift and tilt with the help of four electric motors. Inside is a maze of cast-off machinery distributed throughout several levels, fitted out with a bed, air-conditioning, toilet, and decontamination chamber, or what mere earthlings might call a shower. A control room allowed closed-circuit TV to monitor the exterior; completing the effect were flashing lights. And naturally, satellite TV was installed.

The big saucer—the Mother Ship—was never really intended to fly, though. It was to be a home-away-from-home for visiting aliens. On top of the main UFO Welcome Center is a smaller saucer, just twenty feet in diameter. "That's the Flight Unit," Pendarvis told us. "It's the part which eventually will separate and take off, or at least as soon as I can get the release mechanism worked out and then get it stocked with enough food for a trip." As he spoke, he interrupted his explanations in midsentence to glance quickly at the heavens as if he had just caught

sight of one of his competitors.

"I'm kind of an ambassador, I reckon," says Pendarvis, whose day job is at a lawn-mower factory in nearby Orangeburg. "Aliens are welcome to stay here as long as they like, if they behave okay. After all, most of them have been on some pretty long trips to come all the way here to the earth, so I want 'em to be comfortable. But I'll probably warn them not to stay too long—we've got a lot of F-14s flying around here which might try to shoot them down."

That's perhaps not as random a threat as it sounds. In late 2005, a big chunk of military aircraft used for launching missiles crashed into the ground just two blocks away. No one was hurt; but ever since then, Jody Pendarvis hasn't been the only person in Bowman keeping a wary eye toward the sky.

Sam Doyle's "Wallice Galery"

Anyone driving through the old Wallace Plantation community on St. Helena Island, SC, while Sam Doyle was still alive was in for a treat. Sam could not only dish out a good dose of island lore but would be happy to let you know what had been on his mind lately. In the yard and woods surrounding his house he maintained an outdoor painting gallery, which celebrated personal heroes, retold events in St. Helena history, and even offered admonishments to neighbors or acquaintances to mend their ways. Any locals caught engaging in acts he disapproved of risked being pilloried in paint in one of his public displays, which included images of men with their pants down and words like STOP THAT! Loose women might be labeled E-Z on their portrait panel, and women he thought too quick to change lovers might be called MISS DUMP SIR. At the same time, he memorialized island history—the first car, the first college graduate, and the Great Emancipation.

One of Doyle's most-feared fellow islanders was a root doctor called Doctor Buzzard. Doctor Buzzard wore purple sunglasses day and night, and was known for inflicting curses on his enemies. Among his magical gear was a seashell that he claimed was a telephone to Satan. He would sometimes extort money by picking up his seashell and threatening to call up the devil if his palms weren't "crossed with silver" quickly enough. Many

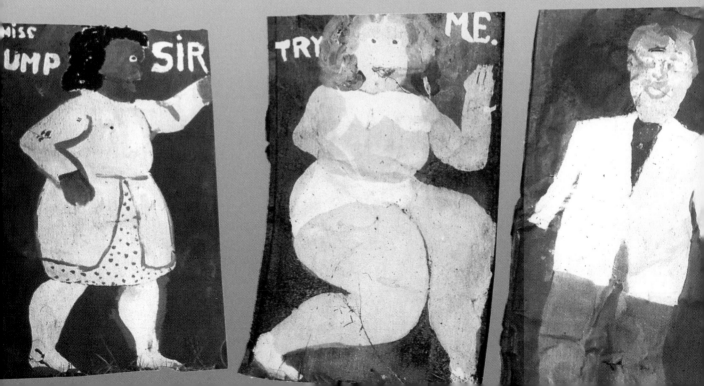

frightened islanders would pay the fee to get rid of him—but Doyle got even by memorializing the trick in many of his changing outdoor displays.

Doyle's preferred medium was enamel paint on sheet metal, which stood up to St. Helena's steamy tropical climate better than plywood or canvas. After every hurricane, he'd find loose pieces of tin roofing blown off nearby houses and would claim these for his artwork. Often when he found them, the metal pieces would be too bent or too corrugated to paint on easily, so he'd leave them out on the paved road and let cars and trucks drive over them for a few days. After that, they'd be plenty flat enough to paint on. Sam Doyle was nearly eighty when he died in 1985. His gallery passed away with him, but Sam's spirit is still alive on the island.

James Butt's Dream House

One of the weirdest and ultimately creepiest buildings ever constructed in the Carolinas was Butt's Dream House, erected in South Mills, NC, by an eccentric builder named James Butt. Originally covered with mirrors and embedded with found objects, seashells, and collages of magazine clippings protected under glass, it had become a dangerous ruin by the time we saw it. Several of the floors had collapsed and vegetation had begun to overgrow it like a Mayan temple in a lost city. Still, enough remained to make it one of the most intriguing sites we've ever visited.

Looming over the site is a multistory tower, reached by one of several twisting staircases. Inside and out, the Dream House was stamped with quotations from history books, the Bible, and writers ranging from Cicero to Edgar Allan Poe, John Steinbeck, and Ernest Hemingway. Surrounding himself with historical and literary references, Butt seems to have constructed the Dream House as some kind of projection of his jumbled thoughts and dreams.

Very little is known about the place or its maker, and what facts remain are not necessarily reliable. We are told that James Butt was born in New Hope, NC, in 1894. During his early years, he worked in various construction trades like carpentry and brick masonry. Shortly after World War II, and following some undisclosed illness, he began building a bizarre complex of interlocking rooms and towers next to his then rather ordinary house. At the same time, he stopped touching any electrical tools or appliances. Then, after years of working on the site, he suddenly abandoned the Dream House in 1968 and moved to Lone Star, SC, where he had family and where he is said to have died five years later.

It's hard to know what to make of the place. Certain images — owls, sailors, explorers, and the appearance of anomalies like crosses, fireballs, and other strange objects in the sky — turn up repeatedly. Certain events in history, from the arrival of the Pilgrims at Plymouth Rock to the repeal of local segregation laws, seem to have had a special significance, since they are referred to in so many of the quotes Butt pressed into the cement. It's all very mysterious. Unfortunately, by now it's a puzzle with too many key pieces missing. How all these thoughts and images may once have combined to mean something to James Butt is a secret he took with him to his grave.

Roadside Oddities

One of the crying shames of the late 20th and early 21st centuries (so far) is how the regional and very local peculiarities of so many American places have become standardized by what the poet Jonathan Williams irritably refers to as "the franchise people from beyond time and space." Blindfold any one of us and drop us off blinking in the bright daylight on the outskirts of almost any town in the country, and we'd be hard-pressed to say if we were standing in Cayce, Charlotte, or Kalamazoo. The same garish signs for the same cluster of nationwide outlets and burger joints are found everywhere there's a population for them to feed upon.

That's why, when you're driving along and see something remarkably different, it's worth paying attention. We call it the Oh Wow Factor, the places that make you crane your neck and swerve across five lanes of traffic to get a better look. They're increasingly rare, but they're still out there, mostly (but not always) lurking along the sides of our secondary roads and backcountry lanes. Here's a look at the ones we like best.

Shell Shape

A delightfully odd little building on the corner of Sprague and Peachtree streets in east Winston-Salem is the last of its species. At one time there were seven others like it, all built in 1930 by Quality Oil Company, which distributed Shell Oil products to central North Carolina. For a while the stations were a hit, though hard to maintain and prone to cracking in severe weather. Over the years, all the others were eventually torn down. In the days before widespread literacy, buildings whose shapes not so subtly suggested their purpose could be more successful than those depending wholly on signage, especially when the slogan was something like "seek super service at the shell-shaped service station." According to author Jerry Bledsoe, this is the only individual service station listed on the National Register of Historic Places.

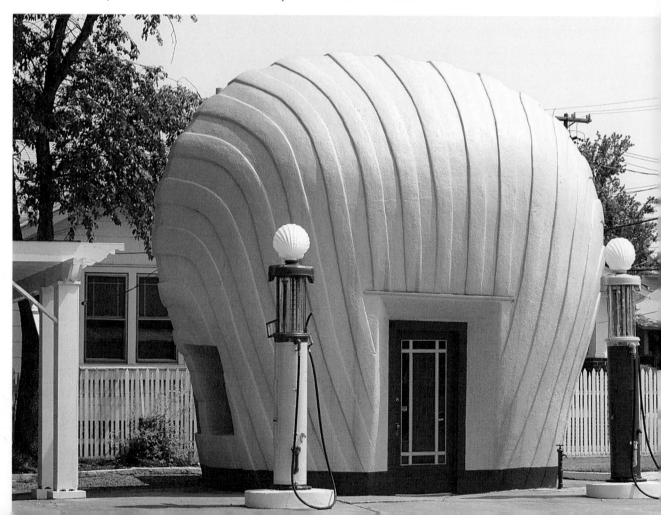

The House of Mugs

We came across The House of Mugs in Collettsville, NC. It is down a dirt road in the middle of nowhere. There is a guest book on the front porch for visitors to sign. The inside of the house is full of mugs also.

Since we moved from NJ six months ago, we have a lot of fun looking for weird places down here. This was the best so far!
—Tammy & Steve Levans

Paintings on Walls

No one knows for sure how long people have been painting on walls, but we know it goes back to Cro-Magnon times at least. That's 40,000 years ago. Those early paintings may have been a form of wishful thinking combined with a little magic. Say you wanted a nice tasty aurochs for dinner. Maybe you could encourage a hunt by painting you and your buddies successfully heaving a spear into one and then chowing down afterward. Then if you went out and did it, the painting would seem magical. What you wanted to have happen, you painted.

One of the most well-known works of wishful think-ing public art in the state is a trompe-l'oeil painting on the back of the Federal Land Bank at the corner of Taylor and Marion streets in downtown Columbia, SC. One of local artist Blue Sky's masterpieces, the Tunnelvision mural is what it says: a vision of pure escape, leading out of the mundane parking lot behind the bank and through a tunnel into the quintessentially American dream of heading off into the setting sun on the open road. The illusion is convincing enough that (they say) more than one drunk has tried to take this imaginary tunnel out of Columbia and driven straight into the substantial wall on which it's painted. Only in cartoons can you draw a door and then open it. And more's the pity.

Crenshaw's Store

Betty Jean Ireland put us onto this place, located in Cold Point, SC. "You can't miss it," she said. "The roof is covered with skulls." You can get things to eat there as well as things to tempt fish into attempting to eat.

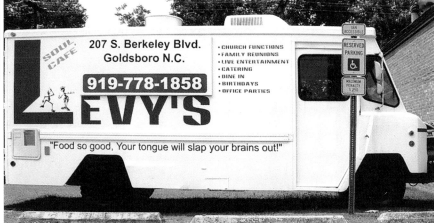

Levy's Soul Food

We've tried envisioning the claim made by Levy's Soul Food of Goldsboro, NC, and always find ourselves wishing we hadn't. But the food is tasty.

One-Day Church

The builders of the El Bethel United Methodist Church in Spartanburg, SC, probably didn't have enough time to think of anything so symbolically meaningful and its sign still calls it the "One-Day Church." According to the legend, the first bricks were set in place early in the morning, and by dark the congregation was ready to conduct the first services in it. Many hands make light work, etc. Sounds like the ancient Romans might have profited from having a few Spartanburgers on their side— maybe Rome really could have been built in a day. —*Ripley's!*

The Devil or the Dove?

Just as beauty is said to be in the eye of the beholder, when it comes to signs, the meaning is often in the mind as well. This church on Buchanan Avenue in Durham, NC, finally changed its signage after too many members of its congregation confessed that instead of looking like a dove fluttering over the Holy Grail of sacrifice, all they could see was a devil face in flames. Which version do you see?

The Bible's Big Here

All over the world, various religions revere the sites where their forebears experienced the visions and epiphanies that nourished their prophecies. Along with places like the Wailing Wall in Jerusalem, the cave of Hira near Mecca, or the Bodhi Tree in India, a well-manicured 110-acre biblical theme park in far western North Carolina takes its place as a starting point for a faith.

Fields of the Wood marks the spot where itinerant Indiana preacher and traveling Bible salesman Ambrose Jessup Tomlinson first found inspiration. Tomlinson had arrived in a small mountain valley community near Suit, NC, in 1902, and decided to stay. Before long, he gathered a group of followers and told them he wanted to start a new church but wasn't sure what form it should take. On the morning of June 13, 1903, after praying behind a neighbor's house, he came back down like Moses from the mountaintop and founded the Church of God of Prophecy (COGOP).

By the time of Tomlinson's death in 1943, COGOP had begun an ambitious project to create a focal point for

what had become an organization with over 500,000 in sixty countries. The land around the "Place of Prayer" where the founder had been inspired was cleared and construction began on the world's largest Ten Commandments. The Law of Moses was spelled out in King James's English in concrete letters five feet tall and arrayed across a mountainside in view of the site where Tomlinson had prayed.

Other acts of biblical gigantism include the world's largest altar (eighty feet long), the world's largest New Testament (a concrete Bible thirty feet tall and fifty feet wide with access to a rooftop viewing area), and the world's largest cross, which is 115 feet wide and 150 feet long and lies flat. There are also replicas of the crucifixion site at Golgotha (with creepy skull-like masonry to commemorate the "place of the skull"), the hauntingly "empty tomb" of Christ, and an outdoor pool with mass-baptismal capability, all complemented by picnic areas and a gift shop. Fields of the Wood is located on Highway 294, eighteen miles west of Murphy, NC. Admission is free.

Coburg Cow

For years, "riding the Coburg Cow" was a rite of passage for incoming Citadel cadets and local Charleston teenagers. It isn't hard to see why. The life-size cow, along with a giant carton of milk, revolves like a target in a shooting gallery or a one-note merry-go-round. Over the past forty years, the unfortunate ungulate has not only been ridden but shot at, repainted, lassoed, branded, outfitted with costumes and mustaches, and had its tail chopped off, sawn off, and rewelded in a different position. Coburg Dairy, which maintains the sign at the corner of Coburg Road and Savannah Highway, has often threatened to dismantle its vandal-attracting gyratory Jersey, but every time they've stopped the cow to repair it, so many people phoned up to ask if it was coming back that they've been reluctant to remove it altogether. But there's always that possibility. Meanwhile, the dairy is trying to beef up security around its famous sign.

Swan Quarter Sign

For most folks who only pass through, the tiny town of Swan Quarter, NC, is the jumping-off place for the ferry to Ocracoke Island on the Outer Banks. For the people who live here, though, it's a tight-knit community tough enough to deal with mosquitoes, hurricanes, isolation, a delicate economy, and incredible natural beauty. In the middle of the village is the News Sign, which gets repainted anytime anyone wants to make a general announcement. Births, deaths, illnesses, graduations, parties, promotions, accidents, and newborn babies are reported here. It's worth remembering that posting the news this way dates back almost to the invention of the written word. Newspapers have only been around for a few hundred years and broadcast media for only about ninety years, while online news is still in the process of being invented.

Stuff on Sticks

In olden times, when few people could read, advertising signage consisted only of an example of the available wares or services. For instance, a Roman bakery might have a wooden loaf of bread for a sign, or a medieval blacksmith shop might have a hammer and horseshoe hanging over the door instead of words. Some pure examples of this kind of thing still exist, often sitting high in the Carolina skies, attracting extra attention mostly because they seem so weirdly out of place.

Need a Lift?
TOMMIE'S TOWING

TOMMIE'S
AUTO & DIESEL
TOWING & REPAIR

Retirement Home for Senior Signage

Harry's and Piggy's are the Siamese Twins of roadside dining. Connected by a narrow hallway—Harry's is the grill and Piggy's specializes in ice cream—they have been a conjoined local eatery since the 1950s. The owners have been glomming onto classic fiberglass mascots

abandoned by other dining establishments for almost as long. Where does Big Boy go when he's looking ready for retirement? Where do Yogi and Booboo hang out once Pokemon, Hello Kitty, and Doraemon have run them out of Jellystone? Find them still out in the elements doing their thing on the rooftop of Harry's and Piggy's, on Duncan Hill Road off Highway 64 business route in Hendersonville, NC.

Strom Thurmond and the Rest of the Story

On the south-facing side of the South Carolina State House in Columbia stands the robust-looking statue of United States Senator Strom Thurmond. The pedestal below the statue enumerates his accomplishments, including setting records for both seniority and longevity in the U.S. Senate; he remained in office until his hundredth birthday. If Washington was the Father of Our Country, Thurmond could be called The Father of the State, at least for most of the 20th century.

He was also a father in the biological sense. Although his first marriage was childless (and ended with the death of his first wife), he married a second time, at age sixty-six, to twenty-three-year-old Nancy Janice Moore. He announced his first offspring, Nancy Moore Thurmond, in 1971 when he was sixty-eight. Three more children followed over the next five years, and all four were listed among his other lifetime triumphs on the stone pedestal. Having children at that age is indeed quite an achievement.

When the statue was first unveiled, however, it didn't mention another child. In 1925, when he was in his early twenties, Thurmond impregnated Carrie "Tunch" Butler, a sixteen-year-old African American maid who had worked in the Thurmond household. Sixteen years later, when Thurmond was thirty-eight, he met his illegitimate daughter, Essie Mae, for the first time. He thereafter secretly helped provide for her education and financial support, but never publicly recognized her relationship to him. Only after the Senator's death did Essie Mae come forward and claim him as her father, but by then the statue had already been mounted on the state capitol grounds. When the Thurmond family also acknowledged the relationship, her name was finally added to the pedestal. Instead of stating that Strom was "The Father of Four Children," it now says "Five." If you look closely, though, you can still make out the previous version of the facts.

Yankee in a Rebel Town

Speaking of mistakes, there's a whopper standing in the center of Kingstree, SC. According to Linda Brown, editor of *The News* there, the Confederate monument next to the Williamsburg County Courthouse really is a Yankee soldier. "The story we've always heard is that somehow it got mixed up with the monument that was to go to York, Maine. So York has Johnny Reb and we have the Yankee soldier. . . . Many Civil War buffs have stopped by my office to ask if we were aware of the Yankee soldier at the courthouse."

Eva Blount Way and the Belhaven Museum

The guest book at the old River Forest Manor in the little town of Belhaven, NC, includes such well-known names as James Cagney, Tallulah Bankhead, Twiggy, and Walter Cronkite. But the one that caught our attention was that of Robert Ripley, of *Ripley's Believe It or Not!* fame. We knew why he was there—for the same reason we were, to pay homage to a kindred spirit, Mrs. Eva Blount Way.

Somewhere in a parallel universe, one not quite like our own, popular tourist destinations must be enhanced by museums of the strange and wonderful called "Way's Believe It Or Not!" but here in our world there's only one, and it's called the Belhaven Museum. To step into its mazelike arrangement of cluttered shelves and jumbled displays is to step into a world of wonder. It's like Charles Dickens's Old Curiosity Shop, though nothing here is for sale. One can add to its marvels, but take nothing away.

And what mind-boggling marvels there are: a dress from a seven-hundred-pound woman; a pair of fleas dressed in itty-bitty bride and groom getups; a Cyclops pig; a giant tumor removed from a local woman at the Pungo hospital; a record-setting ingrown toenail; a necktie made from a diamondback rattlesnake skin; antique vegetables still floating in the old Mason jars from back when Mrs. Way canned them; petrified walrus tusks; a map of Vietnam made of plastic drinking straws; a German machine gun and swastika; a human skeleton; a whale skull; pieces of the square-rigged warship *Constitution*, of the walls of Jericho, of the White House, of the first transatlantic cable, and of a spacecraft that crashed in the Bahamas; a drill that electrocuted a local carpenter; collections of push mowers; and 7,000 more square feet crammed with other items equally peculiar but too numerous to keep listing here.

"Mrs. Eva," the wife of a lumber-company owner, lived on a medium-size farm a few miles outside town nearly all her adult life, and she obsessively gathered all this stuff. Here is what Tom Patterson wrote in *The Arts Journal* in July 1989.

> While her late husband once described her as "a child who found it virtually impossible to grow up," a 1951 entry in the Washington (NC, not DC) *Daily News* summed her up as "housewife, snakekiller, curator, trapper, dramatic actress, philosopher and preserver of all the riches of mankind."
> . . . Mrs. Way started Beaufort County's first country club and was president of the local D.A.R. chapter. She won more blue ribbons for canning homegrown fruits and vegetables than any other woman in the county. She was a poet. She beat 10 men in a hog-calling contest at the county fair. She hunted rattlesnakes with a garden hoe and made a point of killing four or five of them a year, always saving their skins and rattles. She trapped and killed a bear that had been eating her corn crop, then she canned and ate him, piece by piece, until all that was left was a claw that is still enshrined in her collection. And that, of course was the most remarkable thing . . . her constantly growing collection of the bizarre and the commonplace.

Mrs. Way opened her collection to the public at the outset of World War II in order to raise money for the war effort. There was no admission, but donations were accepted at the door and forwarded to the Red Cross and other organizations involved in relief work. The donation-only approach is how the museum still operates

A seven-hundred-pound-woman's dress on display at the Belhaven Museum.

one oy mrs Ways Rattlers
she had just killed

today, though the town of Belhaven has run it since her death (at age ninety-three) in the early 1960s. Donations of strange and interesting-enough items are still accepted, too.

The wacky hodgepodge of it all is part of the charm. We hope the Belhaven Museum never changes its display strategy. There are already enough museums that see their roles as primarily sorting and organizing, making clearly defined didactic points, and teaching their visitors cogent lessons. Surely a few like this should be allowed to remain as realms of surprise and wonder, where the visitor can realize meanings or find connections that the curators couldn't possibly have intended. The museum occupies the entire second floor of the Belhaven municipal building, above city hall and the police department, and is open every afternoon from 1:00 to 5:00.

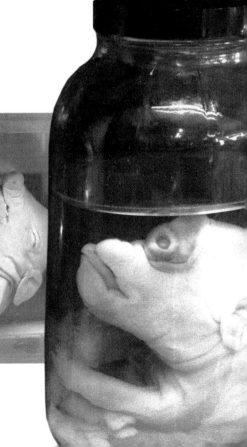

Bigger is always better, as everyone knows, right? Otherwise, what's the deal with all those humongous SUVs? It's not really about safety or economy, so it must be about attention getting. And that's exactly the point with all the Giant Stuff that's scattered around the highways and byways of the Carolinas, too. You can't ignore it if it's outlandishly Big. Here are a few of our favorite examples.

"World's Largest Strawberry"

this building proclaims itself. It sits on Highway 220 several miles north of Rockingham, NC. We have our doubts that it's really the biggest, but it's a pretty funny-looking building, anyway. It's the kind of place that would make our parents burst out singing the old Zeke Masters tune "Run for the Round House, Nellie, (He Can't Corner You There)."

The Pelion Peanut

The Great Goober stands next to the Citgo station on Highway 302 heading toward Columbia out of Pelion, SC. Pelion is home to the annual Peanut Party, a festival celebrating and advocating the primacy of the boiled peanut over the dry roasted as a true historic food. (The boiled peanut has been declared the Official State Snack by the government of South Carolina.) Pelion is also home to Cedar Creek Park, one of the Carolinas' more well-known "nudist colonies." Cedar Creek sponsors many family-oriented events, including "Running Bare," an annual 5K clothes-optional footrace to benefit the local library (entrants receive a free T-shirt suitable for framing), and "Nudestock," the Southeast's largest all-nude music festival.

Neverbust, in the 1500 block of Main Street, Columbia, SC, is another piece of art by local artist Blue Sky. It's a chain linking the Sylvan Bros. Building with the Kress Building. Blue Sky said he created it in 2000 because "one building looked like it was leaning a little bit."

The Giant Chair of Anderson, SC,

looks ready to rock. It's on Highway 29, heading toward the famous Anderson Jockey Lot Flea Market. If you're looking for something folksy, this might be it.

Smallest Police Station

Just to test the rule that bigger is better, we include its opposite. Until not too long ago, Ridgeway, SC, had the nation's smallest police station. The P.D. has now moved into a building twice the size of this, only a few yards away. Even so, it's still small enough that everything in it is literally within arm's reach.

Giant Acorn

Almost every town in the Carolinas has a moniker or motto. Charleston is The Holy City, because of all the steeples, or else Chucktown. Myrtle Beach is Sin City; Winston-Salem is Camel City, for all the cigarettes; Carrboro is The Paris of the Piedmont; and Goldsboro is The City with No Parking Meters.

Raleigh is The City of Oaks, a rather staid formulation which suggests that a political committee was tasked with coming up with something utterly noncontroversial. Even so, it gave artist David Benson a chance to make a really cool sculpture (privately commissioned, so a committee couldn't interfere with it): a giant copper acorn, which weighs about a thousand pounds and spends most of the year atop a pole in Moore Square. On New Year's Eve, the acorn leaves its plinth and gets "dropped" in synch with the dropping of the famous ball in Times Square, New York. The squirrels go wild.

The Durham Dinosaur

A ride along the bike path from near the old Durham Athletic Park north toward the Eno River parks could provide a startling experience for any newcomer pedaling this fine North Carolina byway. Around a bend in the path, and apparently poised to use its little herbivorean teeth to snag any unwary passersby, is a full-sized brontosaurus. It's a leftover from the old Life and Science Museum founded in 1946.

Giant Milk

Want to know how all those big people in our country got so darn large in the first place? Well, obviously, they had plenty of vitamins and always drank their milk—which comes, naturally, in giant cartons from big cattle. You can see giant milk in front of the Pet Dairy plants in Goldsboro, NC, and at exit 145 off I-85 near Burlington, NC. Champion cows are in front of Biltmore Dairy in Asheville, NC, and Coburg Dairy in Charleston, SC.

A Whole Lotta Coffee

At twelve feet high and sixteen feet in circumference, this pot could have held enough coffee to keep an entire town wired and wiggly. If it could have held any coffee at all, that is, which it couldn't. It was, in fact, a sign, ostensibly for Julius and Samuel Mickey's tinsmithing shop in

Salem, NC. In 1858, when the giant pot was built, tinsmiths made all kinds of handy household items, including candlesticks, kitchenware, and coffee pots, so mounting a giant example out in front of their shop was just good old-fashioned advertising.

The old coffee pot eventually became the symbol of Salem, which joined up with the adjacent tobacco town of Winston in 1913 to become a hyphenated city. Coffee and tobacco, ahh, now that's living.

Tea for Two (Thousand)

Though it does bear a certain family resemblance to the giant coffee pot of old Salem, the Giant Teapot of Stokesdale, NC, doesn't have quite the same colorful history behind it. It was originally created for the Cook Family Restaurant, and when that closed, it was moved and erected as part of the Countryside Manor Retirement Home's roadside sign. There doesn't seem to be any overarching purpose or philosophical reason behind this other than that it was too big and too fun to send off to the dump or the recyclers. It offers a (very) large element of eye-catching "country kitchen" nostalgia, too, and makes the location of the retirement home easy to describe. For once, "you can't miss it" is the right thing to say.

Bureaus of Biggism

High Point, NC, is not only the home of the world's largest furniture market, it's home to some of the world largest furniture. For example, there's the free-standing Goddard block-front chest nearly forty feet high, with a realistically not-quite-closed drawer with two pairs of socks casually dangling from it (to commemorate the local hosiery industry, though it isn't doing as well as furniture). It can be found at the intersection of Hamilton and Westwood streets in downtown High Point. The world's largest bureau is also located in High Point. And a highboy-style chest eight stories tall stands in front of the Furnitureland South Mart near I-85. Though you can't really rummage around in the drawers of any of these to see what's there besides giant socks, they make great photo ops for reenacting your favorite scenes from *Honey, I Shrunk the Kids*.

High Chair

Thomasville, NC, is home to the world's largest Duncan Phyfe chair. The chair itself is eighteen feet tall and sits on a twelve-foot-high base. Built in 1948, it is the second in Thomasville's history of huge chairs; the first was built in 1922 and decayed in the 1930s. The current chair is more durable, being constructed of steel and concrete. For a period, it was the largest chair in the world, but as competition got the better of them, Thomasville settled for being the world's largest Duncan Phyfe. The chair is located on the corner of Randolph and Main streets.

Gargantuan Gams

Not exactly a complete human figure but nonetheless eye-catching are the two giant gams on Welcome Road in Henderson, NC. Across the road is a pair of to-scale high-heeled shoes. The gate leading into the area between Ricky Pearce's excessive extremities is surmounted by the word REMINISCING but we're hard-put to put a meaning to it. All it made us think about were some moments when we felt, frankly, kind of little and inadequate.

S.O.B.

If Really Big Stuff is your bag, you can find a lot of it all at once at South of the Border, the ur-center of East Coast kitsch. A giant sombrero sits atop a twenty-story tower, a nine-story sign of the shop's politically incorrect symbol, Pedro the slow-witted Mexican (the "largest freestanding sign east of Las Vegas"). There's also a giant dachshund, a giant ape, a giant shark . . . more giant stuff than you ever saw in one place, probably, all right here in Dillon, SC.

You really have to like normal-sized critters of the *Turista americanus* species too, though, because you'll see plenty of those. S.O.B. is living proof of that old realtors' law—location, location, location. Look at a road map and you'll note that I-95 makes a small jog to the west as it crosses the state line here. S.O.B. mastermind and founder Alan Schafer, not without political clout, was able to get a small "adjustment" to the planned route so the new interstate would pass right by his property. In fact, the whole place got its start when Prohibition was lifted and Dillon County (SC) decided to allow the sale of liquor, while Robeson County (NC), just ten feet away, stayed "dry." Schafer's "Beer Depot" quickly metastasized into the "South of the Border Beer Depot," then just "South of the Border." And the rest is history.

Giant Peachoid

Ask just about anyone from either Carolina to name the weirdest things they've ever seen in the region and chances are they will mention SC's Gaffney Peach—or the Peachoid as it's now officially called. Towering some twelve stories above I-85 just northwest of town, the suggestively-shaped million-gallon water tower with its sixty-foot, seven-ton leaf is there to remind folks that although Georgia is known as the Peach State, South Carolina actually produces a lot more of the fuzzy fruits.

Designed and built in 1980–81 by Harold Beebe Engineering and Chicago Bridge & Iron Company, the fruit's oversize paint job is by artist Peter Freudenberg. By the time it won the 1981 Steel Tank of the Year Award, the Horton Waterspheroid, as it was named, had already acquired the Peachoid moniker.

It had also acquired quite a few other nicknames that probably hadn't occurred to the Gaffney Board of Public Works when they first cooked up the idea. Due to its gluteal cleavage, it's been called the Mighty Peach Butt, the Just Say No to Crack Memorial and several other less-savory epithets.

Traffic along this stretch of I-85 is relentless and unforgiving. Do not attempt to pull over here to get a good look. If you want more than a passing glance of the Peachoid's curvature, take exit 92 if you're headed toward Greenville or Atlanta, or exit 90 if you're headed toward Charlotte, then get over on the service road that parallels the north side of the interstate.

Weirdness on Wheels

"Spoonman" Elmer Fleming first earned his nickname as a teenager when his older brother taught him how to play the spoons for bluegrass and country 'n' western bands. But Fleming wanted more from his spoons, and the result is seen on his 1966 Chevy pickup. No two among the 1,480 spoons on the truck or in his far more vast Spoon Museum collection (next to the garage in his backyard) are the same. Look for the Spoon Truck on the streets of Newberry, SC.

Could Have Kicked Myself!

Maybe it has something to do with a talk-first, think-later attitude known as speaking one's mind, and known less positively as tactlessness, but it says something about North Carolina that it has not one but two machines designed to allow you to administer a swift kick to your own rear end. One is located in the parking lot behind the Angus Barn Restaurant near the Raleigh-Durham Airport, and the other (the original) is located next to an antique store called Martha's, near the town of Croatan on Highway 70, about ten miles east of New Bern. A sign above the Angus Barn's replica misattributes the creation of the original to Tom Watson (it was Tom Haywood). It also says the Croatan machine was retired—but if so, it's now back in service. Evidently, regret and the need for self-atonement are still found often enough in the state to keep two such service outlets as these in regular demand.

The principle of the machines is simple. Turning a crank moves pulleys that drive four mounted boots into your backside. Angus Barn must be more worried about lawsuits from patrons muddled by jet lag, too much beef, or some combination of the two, because their machine's sign includes not only a disclaimer but a practical rule stating that one should not stand facing the whirling boots. Ooof!

Roads Less Traveled

Ah, the open road. The quick spin. Tooling around. As Americans, we've always taken real pleasure in getting out of our houses, hopping into the cars we're so attached to, and having the world unfold before us.

One of the real pleasures of driving around is discovering things like there really is a Tobacco Road (it's in Wilson, NC), or finding yourself heading down Bubba Boulevard in Greenville, NC, or cruising around with your baby on Pinchumslyly Road (north of Bishopville, SC). Other byways can be a little more sobering. Poverty Lane in Lexington, NC, is a place you don't want to wind up, nor do you especially want to stumble onto a Devil's Backbone (in Aiken or Leesville, SC) or a Devil's Racetrack (Eau Claire or Simpson, SC, or Seaboard or Bentonville, NC) without being in full control of your faculties. It's too easy to make mistakes in places like that, and the Dark Forces are waiting.

But it's being willing to take a few risks that makes it so tempting to get off the four-lanes and head toward the skinniest lines on the map. You're a lot more likely to see something that hasn't yet been packaged and price tagged for mass consumption. If you're on the hunt for a little strangeness of that sort, let us help you find it.

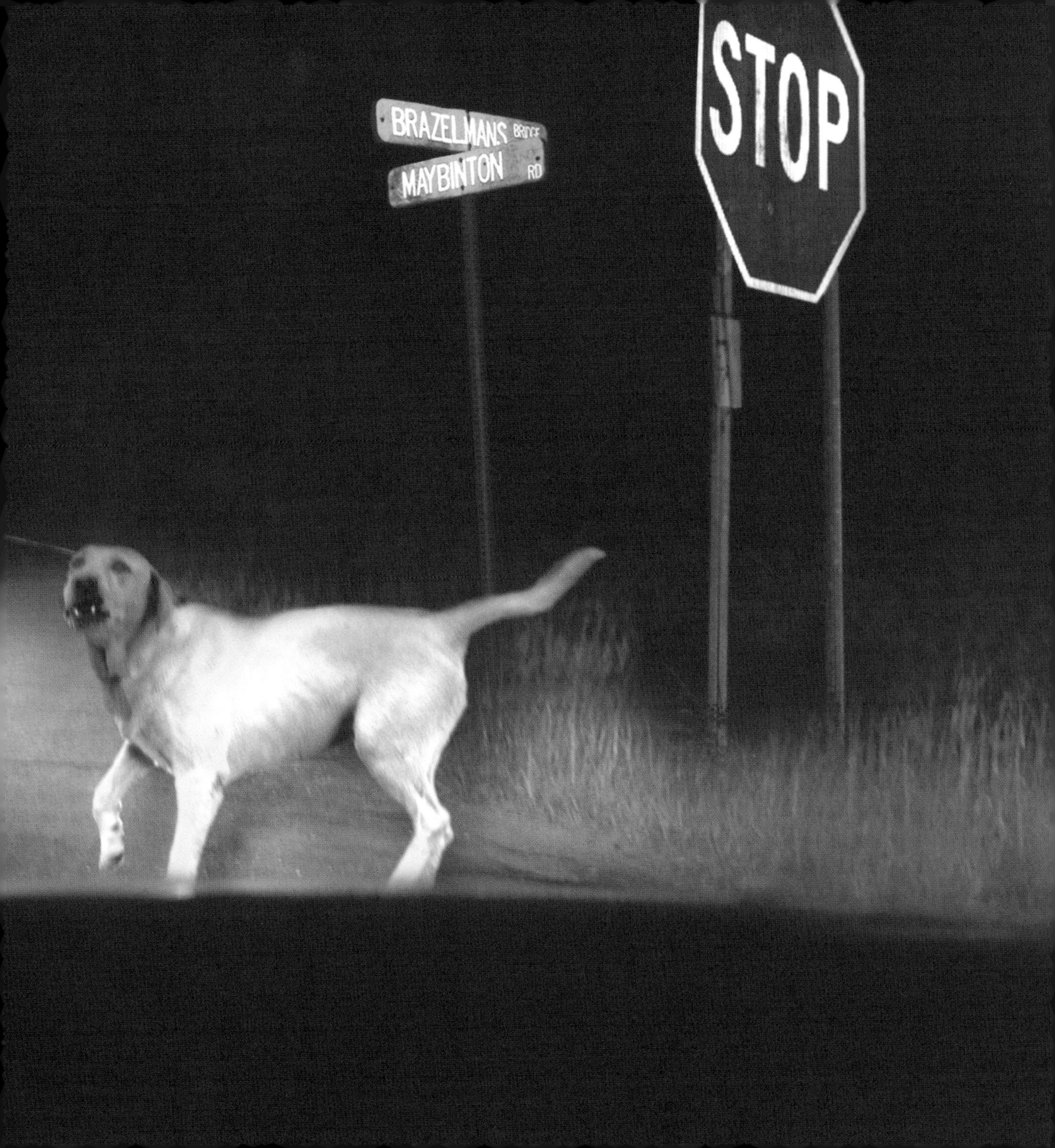
BRAZELMANS
MAYBINTON RD
STOP

Crybaby Bridge(s)

Bridges have always provided convenient places for getting rid of not only things you don't want anymore but things you don't want other people ever to find. Murder weapons, Mafia hits, wedding rings, kittens, Dave Matthews Band bus waste—it's all been dumped off bridges at one time or another. In most cases, no one ever discovers the evidence. But the one kind of discard that always seems to leave a lasting psychic stain on the site itself is a human baby.

Perhaps it's because the whole act of tossing a baby off a bridge is inevitably and inextricably a part of a larger tragic drama. A rape, an unwanted pregnancy, denying a fickle husband any living legacy, insanity—it has to be something mighty awful to cause a woman (or a jealous boyfriend) to take such an extreme step. And always, according to the stories, the event is followed by horrible heartbreaking regret.

All of this bad karma somehow seems to get stuck at the place where it happened. And in those places—for there are many, although every community thinks theirs is the only "real" Crybaby Bridge—the evidence keeps turning up again and again in the form of the excruciatingly plaintive sound of crying.

The Crybaby Bridge a mile or so north of Rose Hill Plantation in Union County, SC, is a classic example of the type. Sardis Road crosses the Tyger River on an old-style steel-truss bridge here. If you go almost any late afternoon or evening, pull over on either end of the bridge, then walk to the middle and hold very still, you will hear a baby crying. However, as soon as you toss a rock into the water, the sound stops. For some reason this seems to break the cycle, perhaps because, as some say, it "completes" the sound of the awful deed when it took place. The crying may start up again in an hour or it may not come back all evening.

According to the story, the original crime took place in the 1950s when, in a split second of insane rage, a woman threw her baby off the bridge to spite her husband. If you come back at midnight, they say you may also encounter the woman herself—or at least her ghost—reenacting the sudden realization of what she had done in her moment of insanity and now frantically searching for the baby she destroyed only a few hours earlier.

At other bridges, the tragedy was apparently more accidental. The baby of the

Crybaby Bridge near Pine Lake Golf Club, southeast of Anderson, SC, is said to date back to a wreck in which both mother and baby were killed. A similar story explains the crying sounds that can be heard at old Sally's Bridge, off Poplar Tent Road near Concord, NC. A young female driver and her newborn skidded at the bridge and wound up in the creek, where the baby, thrown from the car, drowned immediately. Young Sally survived the crash but then jumped into the creek to rescue her baby and followed it into the Hereafter. At this bridge, according to the stories, you might encounter

the figure of the young woman pounding on your car windows in a state of panic.

If meeting hysterically bereaved ghost mothers floats your boat, another place you could try is the Screaming Bridge on Holly Springs Church Road (near the junction with Williams Road) several miles southeast of Williamston, NC. Another girl, another baby, and another crash, but this one includes the detail that the girl was wearing a cat costume at the time. She was on her way back from a Halloween party when the tragedy happened, and the special cat-eye contact lenses she was wearing, with those vertical pupils, distorted her vision enough to cause the wreck. She screams, the baby cries, anyone who meets her ghost trembles in terror. In all, it sounds like a barrel of fun.

The old Morphus Bridge near Wendell, NC, provides yet one more variation on the tale. This time (in the 1940s), the whole family was together and actually getting along okay. They were on their way home from an evening church service and Dad was driving in the rain when the car went into a skid and drove off the bridge, to sink beneath the waters of the Little River. Late at night, they say, you can hear the screams and cries of the whole family, and sometimes even see the headlights of their sunken car still glowing down in the murky water.

Many such legends are what folklorists call "cautionary tales." They may or may not have happened, but they could have, and by retelling them, people point out common dangers in a memorable way. Bridge stories allow teenagers to warn each other about dangerous portions of the highway, but they also warn hotheaded younger people about the danger of acting rashly on any momentary angry impulses.

Moments of insanity have led to real-life horrors, too. Consider Susan Smith, who locked her two toddlers into seat belts and then rolled her 1990 Mazda Protege down a boat ramp into John D. Long Lake near Lockhart, SC, on October 25, 1994. She had done it, she admitted finally, because she had fallen in love with a man who didn't want to deal with her children from her previous relationship.

Not long after it happened, psychically sensitive people claimed they could detect the presence of the two boys near the lake, looking for other kids to play with, while visitors to the site often reported sighting two balls of light hovering near the dam. If indeed the boys were looking for others to join them in play, they didn't have to wait very long before they were answered in a tragic fashion. In September 1996, a vanload of people who had come to gawk at the site suddenly rolled down the very same ramp into the lake, drowning four more children along with three adults. We haven't heard whether anyone has begun seeing nine balls of light hovering around the lake, but if they ever do, that'll be the reason why. *–With thanks to Ola Jean Kelly and Tally Johnson*

Bleeding Stones at Teeter's Bridge

Four miles south of Mount Pleasant, NC, secondary road 1132 crosses Dutch Buffalo Creek over a span the local people still call Teeter's Bridge, after John Teeter, a wealthy landowner who lived in the area years ago. The first settler to build near the creek was a Swiss farmer named Heinrich Furrer, who bought 301 acres in 1763. His taxes each year came to just over twelve shillings, plus a tenth of any gold found on the land. This was weirdly prescient, for at the time no gold had ever been found in the American colonies. But when it finally was discovered—thirty-six years later—it happened just five miles away, on the Reed farm, sparking America's first gold rush. It's still possible to find gold in many of the local creeks, including Dutch Buffalo. However, there's something about the stones of this creek much rarer than gold. Historian James Dulin tells the story.

During World War Two, a young mother had driven into Concord to check the news of the war posted every day outside the Western Union Telegraph office on North Union Street. Her husband was serving in the European Theater. She took her infant daughter with her. After finishing her business, she headed back home with her baby on the front seat beside her—this was well before child car seats or even seat belts.

A sudden summer thunderstorm blew up, what we call down here a gullywasher. Visibility was poor. She had to cross Teeter's Bridge to get home. The bridge back then was not the one that exists today, but a rickety wooden structure. The rain was pouring. As she approached the bridge, she was momentarily distracted either by the baby or the storm, and she hit the wooden railing, flipping the car into the creek on its side. Her foot and ankle got caught under the gas pedal, so she was unable to free herself. She could only watch in horror as the car slowly filled with water, her precious child crying from the back seat where she had been thrown, just out of reach. Both mother and child drowned.

FURR

The old bridge is long gone, but the rocks and stones that lined the creek's bank that terrible night are still there, and to this day whenever there is a summer thunderstorm, they weep tears of blood for that unfortunate mother and her baby.

A granite stone sits close to the bridge, with the name FURR engraved in its surface. Many people mistake it for a memorial to that unfortunate mother and her baby. But it was erected almost two decades later, by the descendants of Heinrich Furrer, to mark the spot where his cabin once stood. (The family name was shortened after the American Revolution.) Now here's the weird part: although it had nothing to do with the accident, and although its granite came from a quarry far from the bridge, whenever a storm comes on, it too weeps tears of blood.

Hands Below the Bridge

An abandoned one-lane span that crosses Cane Creek in Lancaster, SC, has been known as the Green Hand Bridge ever since local men first spotted a hand emerging from the waters below it many years ago. The story goes that a small-scale but ferocious battle took place here during the American Revolution, during which a Redcoat's arm was lopped off by a saber slash and plummeted into the water. Now the hand emerges from the water from time to time, sometimes empty and sometimes wielding an old British officer's rapier. In either case, it's best not to get too close to it. It may not be ready to give up the fight.

The Green Hand Bridge is on Old Lansford Road,

between Memorial Park Road and the Highway 9 business route in Lancaster.

Meanwhile, the Greene Street Bridge in Greenville, NC, has some problem hands as well. Depending on who you talk to, they belong to a fisherman who drowned here years ago or to someone who committed suicide by jumping off the bridge. If you climb down along the riverbank and go up under the roadway and listen carefully, you can still hear dying gasps and screams echoing from the underside of the bridge.

However, if you do this, stay well away from the water's edge. Several years ago, some kids heard the screams and stepped a little too close to the Tar River to investigate, when a pair of "nasty, shriveled-up-looking hands" came up out of the water and grabbed one boy's ankles and snatched him under. His pals ran to get help, but the body was never recovered.

Several scuba divers have told Roger Kammerer that there is a headless statue of a Civil War soldier jammed into the mud beneath the bridge, but they haven't figured out how to free it and bring it to the surface safely. Whether it has anything to do with the pair of grasping hands that reach up out of the water from time to time nobody seems to know. Maybe he's really looking for a replacement head and keeps trying on for size anything he can reach.

Poinsett Bridge

A section of Callahan Mountain Road east of Old Highway 25 in northern Greenville County passes by the oldest stone bridge in the state and one of the few classic examples of Gothic architecture in upcountry South Carolina. Poinsett Bridge dates to 1820 but looks as if it could have been built by 13th-century Franks or Saxons. Instead, it was built by African slaves, a number of whom died during its construction, through either quarry accidents or sheer overwork. One particularly gruesome story we heard from a local man was about an incident that occurred during the placing of one of its massive foundation stones.

The stones—many of which weigh well over a ton—were dragged and rolled from the quarry to the construction site, and then were levered into place with stout logs hefted by slaves. As this particular stone was being shifted into place, one of the levers broke, leaving a chunk of wood wedged under it that prevented it from settling into the right position. Another lever was inserted to lift the stone just enough to remove the piece of wood. As the stone was lifted, two of the crew reached under it to pull out the broken stub of the first lever, and had almost freed it when the second lever slipped and let the stone fall on their hands, pinning them to the bridge. We'll never know whether their pitiful screams simply unnerved the overseer and made him want to put them out of their misery quickly, or whether he coldly calculated that their value as workers was now over and considered it a waste of time to expend any more of his crew's energy in freeing them. In either case, the outcome was the same. According to the story, the overseer ordered the rest of the slaves around to the opposite side of the bridge, then killed both of the pinned men and cut their trapped limbs even with the rest of the wall. Then he commanded that everyone get back to work.

By the use of such harsh measures, the bridge was finished on schedule, to the delight of Public Works president Joel R. Poinsett, who had the bridge named after himself. But it didn't come without a price. The bridge, along with the road that crossed a branch of the Saluda River here and the modern paved road that bypasses it now, are all said to be haunted by the men who died while constructing it. Screams are often heard in the woods around the site. Mysterious glowing lights appear near the bridge, and vehicles break down or refuse to restart after being parked here. Eventually the bridge and old roadway were abandoned, and now it sits like a ruin from an archaic civilization, one whose barbaric practices seem remote indeed from our own.

Covered Bridges

The two remaining covered bridges in North Carolina—Bunker Hill Bridge near Claremont and Pisgah Covered Bridge south of Asheboro—along with Campbell's Bridge near Gowensville, SC, are all known for dangling body apparitions. And no wonder. In the old days, if one really wanted to make a statement by hanging himself, the rafters inside a covered bridge would be a great place to do it. Not only could you be absolutely certain your body would be discovered at the earliest possible moment, but you could also guarantee maximum impact whenever it happened. During the daytime, any unsuspecting passersby would leave the bright, sunlit roadway and enter blinking into the dark, tunnel-like structure where a few seconds would pass before their eyes could adjust to the gloom and then blam!—there you'd be, scaring the heck out of everybody. And after dark, the casual traveler on foot or horseback might even smack into your cold flesh, which would be even better. Scaring the still living is pretty much guaranteed.

Maybe this is why nearly every covered bridge anywhere is known to have such a story—an apparition of a man or woman hanging overhead, who still haunts the place. And why wouldn't you want to hang around? As a ghost, once you've figured out how to maximize your impact, you'd probably want to keep capitalizing on the effect as long as possible.

Sadly, though, there's not much opportunity for haunting covered bridges now that the only three left have been spoken for. But back in the 19th century, there were hundreds of them in both states. Nearly all bridges were covered in those days to keep the heavy wooden beams of their trusses from rotting. Steel bridges, which required far less upkeep, eventually replaced nearly all of them by the early 1950s.

The Seven (or Is It Six?) Bridges

A road between Rocky Mount and Leggett, NC, is known by the street name Seven Bridges Road. If you drive down this creepy country road at night and count the bridges until the end of the road, there are seven bridges, but if you turn around and ride back down the road, you'll find to your shocked surprise there are only six bridges. Some people think it's an optical illusion. I believe there's more to it than that.
—*Mary Susan Kisner*

Legend of Sleepy Hollow, South Carolina Style

Sleepy Hollow Lane, southwest of Lockhart, SC, has one of those names that just cry out for a something that's missing something: a headless horseman, a legless demon—anything to suggest once again that less is more. As it turns out, you're in luck. It has an armless guy. The trouble is, no one quite seems to be able to settle on what kind of a guy he is.

Some stories say he's a Civil War soldier whose arm was cut off or shot off (or, most likely, hacked off by a battlefield surgeon). On the other hand, a woman we met in Lockhart told us he is of more recent vintage and lost his arm to a piece of machinery in the textile mill there, got laid off on a disability pension, and spent the rest of his life drinking himself into raging madness and wandering along that road. Apparently something about that activity was so satisfying that he didn't want to let a little thing like death slow him down. If you're lucky, you may still run into him raving by the road around midnight, when anyone with any sense would already be home snug in bed, or at least using their one remaining hand to surf the channels.

Ghost Hound of Goshen

If you glance at a map of South Carolina, you'll see four big patches of green. The one down near the coast indicates the land mostly set aside for Francis Marion National Forest. The other three make up Sumter National Forest, and the biggest and most cohesive chunk of this is the one north of Newberry. Its status as a protected forest has kept it from becoming as developed as all the land surrounding it; even now, roads through the area can seem a bit forlorn at night.

One place that seems particularly lonely is the stretch of secondary roads between the small communities of Maybinton and Cross Keys, centering on the even smaller cluster of houses at Goshen Hill. Maybinton Road and Old Buncombe Road change names at Goshen Hill, but neither one is a good place to have vehicle troubles after the sun sets. Here, locals say, a terrifying ghost is on patrol. Some call it the Hound of Goshen, though there's no indication that it was ever a breed of hound. Long ago it got saddled with the ironic misnomer of the Happy Dog. It's a canine, all right, but it's anything but happy, unless you accept the old saying that revenge is sweet.

The story goes that a traveling man passed through Goshen Hill sometime back in the early 1850s. He had a large white dog with him, not only for company but also for protection, since in those days fending off trouble was generally something people took care of for themselves. To his misfortune, however, he had just begun going from homestead to homestead selling his wares when a murder took place in the community.

An angry mob gathered when news of the killing spread. They hunted down the salesman, and despite his dog's best efforts to drive off his pursuers, the poor fellow was soon caught and quickly hanged, simply for the fact that he'd been in the wrong place at the wrong time. His dog managed to bite a few people during the lynch-ing, but one man aimed a rifle at it and wounded the brave pooch enough to send it whimpering off.

After that, the crowd dispersed and headed home, leaving the salesman's body where it hung. The next morning the dog was back, apparently still trying to protect the swinging corpse as it dangled from the tree. If it had been furious during the struggle the night before, now it seemed utterly ferocious. No one could get near enough

The House on Goshen Hill is widely considered haunted. It was the home of Doctor George Douglass, who in 1855 was the first person to document sightings of the Happy Dog, though slaves in the community had described seeing it weeks before he did.

to the tree to cut the body down and give it any kind of burial, decent or not. In a day or two, the smell of the rotting corpse cast an odor of injustice on the entire community, particularly after it became obvious that another man had actually committed the crime. Weeks passed as the salesman's body gradually shriveled to little more than a skeleton, but still the dog remained beside it. Nothing, it seemed, could lure it away from where its master dangled.

Finally, one day someone noticed that the body and the dog were both gone at last. A sigh of relief seemed to come from the entire community. They could put the mistake behind them. Or so they thought.

Not everyone was so lucky. One of the men who had participated in the lynch mob was driving a wagon of freshly harvested produce down the road toward Maybinton when he rounded a bend and suddenly spied the big white dog in front of him. His mules balked and reared in terror, and then twisted in their harness so sharply that the wagon overturned and spilled every-

The Happy Dog still shows up along Maybinton Road and Old Buncombe Road from time to time. Most people experience it as terrifying at the time and exhilarating afterward.

It wasn't too long before someone encountered the dog again. Slaves in the community had begun talking about a ghost dog, but no one believed them until Doctor George Douglass saw the dog for himself. Then another physician, Jim Cofield, saw it. Other sightings soon followed, usually accompanied by tales of how the dog would run beside the witness long enough to catch a scent and then disappear back into the woods.

thing on the ground. The dog started coming toward him with an evil snarl as the man barely managed to get his mules pointed back to Goshen Hill and took off at full gallop. Losing his harvest was a ruinous event, but he didn't dare go back to try to retrieve it.

Other people who had taken part in the lynching began reporting horrible attacks by the white dog. One man's hand was crippled by a bite that nearly severed it across the palm. Another was knocked into a creek and almost drowned when the dog stood atop him for several minutes. Still another had been riding as fast as his horse could run, yet the dog managed to lunge and bite him hard enough through his riding boots that he'd walk with a limp for the rest of his life. In time, the pattern became clear—the great white dog was bent on revenge. Another thing became clear as well. The beast was no ordinary animal. Shots fired at it had no effect and seemed to pass through the creature as if it were smoke.

Eventually, every man who had been there on the night of the lynching was somehow punished. But the worst punishment was meted out to the man who had fired the gun that had wounded—and perhaps killed—the dog. He himself was never attacked, and though he feared it terribly, he never saw the dog for the rest of his life. But his four-year-old son disappeared and was never seen again.

Sometime in the 1920s, the attacks ceased and tapered to only threats. They say it was because by then the last of the lynch mob had finally passed away. In 1936, a man named Berry Sanders reported being chased by the Happy Dog, though nothing came of it. The spirit vanished as soon as Sanders got near his home.

The Happy Dog still shows up along Maybinton Road and Old Buncombe Road from time to time. Most people experience it as terrifying at the time and exhilarating afterward. It's frightening when a large white dog lunges in front of you under any circumstances, and scary when it manages effortlessly to keep up with your vehicle at highway speeds. However, once it decides you're not the prey it's after and gives up the chase, there's a profound experience of relief. And that's always a good thing to feel.—*With thanks to Tally Johnson, Ola Jean Kelly, Terrance Zepke, and Daniel Garrett*

Dueling Down Philadelphia Alley

Philadelphia means brotherly love in ancient Greek, but the ancient Charleston alleyway that bears this name has a history that is anything but. Until recently, it was one of the roughest places in the city and was the last place in South Carolina in which dueling was openly tolerated. It's not entirely clear why this was, but one theory is that because both sides are lined with brick walls (in a city where wooden buildings predominate), nobody was much concerned about flying bullets, since only the duelists themselves were likely to get killed. Although Philadelphia Alley has become a bit gentrified in the last few years, many old-time Charleston people still avoid it. The street is still haunted, they say, by all the brothers who forgot what the name originally meant, walked in rashly, and were carried out dead.

Downed Aviator of Route 107

In the extreme northwestern corner of South Carolina, Highway 107, a narrow, twisting route, cuts through some very pretty but also pretty lonely mountains. Names of turnoffs like Winding Stairs and Moody Springs help convey the nature of the place. But if it seems forlorn now, back in the 1950s it was especially so. That's when a young pilot named

Larry Stephens crashed a small single-engine plane after venturing out in weather that turned foul before he could make it safely back to Greenville, his point of origin.

FAA investigators who attempted to reconstruct the final minutes of his flight based their report scenario in part on educated guesses combined with personal experience. However, given the position of the plane, the emptiness of its fuel tank, and the proximity of the wreckage to the road, it looked to them as if Stephens might have attempted to set it down on 107 but didn't quite make it.

Stephens is still trying to make it home safe, though. Whenever the weather conditions match those of that stormy night, motorists driving along Highway 107 are liable to see a handsome young man hitchhiking in an old-style leather flight jacket turned dark by the rain. It always occurs near where the plane went down, halfway between Moody Springs and Piedmont Overlook, and depending on which way you're headed, he'll ask you to let him out at either of those turnoffs. As soon as he gets out of the car, he disappears without saying another word, leaving only a damp spot on the upholstery to prove he was ever there.

A Tale of Three Dips

Almost anything that can be pointed to can be named. Medical doctors can tell you the name of the indentation down the middle of your back (it's the nuchal groove) and astronomers not only have names for the stars you can see but also for the dark, fuzzy areas in between. On Highway 763 in Sumter County between Wedgefield and Cane Savannah, SC, three successive dips in the road have their own distinct names: The Wreck, Hatchet Camp, and Drunken Dick. The last not only has the best name but is the most fun to drive through too.

Dead Man's Curve

Running around the perimeter of the old town cemetery of Manning, SC, is a sharply curving road with two blind turns. Although traffic is usually light, it's not always so, particularly on Halloween and on the nights after the prom and homecoming football game at Manning High School. Some years ago, the partying got out of hand and a young man left a car to walk home after he realized the driver of the vehicle he was riding in was too drunk to drive. As his friends continued to careen around the curved road, they accidentally ran over him just at the edge of the cemetery. His father had passed away only recently, and apparently his spirit still lingered in the area. When he realized that his son and only descendant had been killed so close by, he began lying in wait for the perpetrator. They say that you can see him still waiting beside the road on "big party" nights and nights of the full moon, which are, after all, associated with lunatics. He's hoping the driver who killed his son will be crazy enough to pass by again. That night, whenever it happens, will be his last time behind the wheel alive.

Carolina Ghosts

n days past, everyone accepted the existence of ghosts as undeniable fact. In modern times, however, more enlightened people struggle against the belief. Science tells us that ghosts can't be detected with any known machine or by way of some kind of experiment, therefore they must not exist. And yet, time and again, we will hear perfectly sensible people discussing what could be called their Conversion Experience. It usually has a preamble that goes something like "Well, I myself never believed in them, until one night . . ." which is followed by the revelation that the teller has run into something he or she simply can't explain. Maybe it was a ghostly light, some strange shape in the night, or the clearly seen spirit of a not-quite-departed. Whichever, it was weird, unexplained, and there.

Unless you've experienced the phenomenon yourself, you may be inclined to dismiss these stories as the result of overactive imaginations. But whether you're a believer or a naysayer, there's no doubting the power of a good ghost story. And lucky for us, the Carolinas are full of 'em.

Face in the Mirror

Many are the moralistic axioms about "making peace with the face in the mirror," all of them directed at browbeating us into becoming better human beings by coming to terms with ourselves. But what if the face you see in the mirror isn't even remotely your own?

When curator/director Pelham Lyles took a photo of the old mantel mirror in the building that is now the Fairfield County Museum in Winnsboro, SC, the image that appeared bore no resemblance to her at all. In fact, it looked like a woman from another century, lying horizontally, as if sick or perhaps even dying. The face certainly doesn't look happy, and anyone who knows Pelham Lyles knows that she likes to laugh. In ordinary room light, the image can't be seen at all.

There has been some speculation as to who it might be, or might have been, since the lady has presumably been long gone. Was it the wife of Richard Cathcart, the first owner of the home that later became the museum? Or could it be Catherine Ladd, who operated a girl's school here with her artist husband George in the mid-19th century? Or is it Priscilla Ketchin, who lived in the house with her family from the 1870s until her death in 1911?

In the years since then, the building served variously as a public school, hotel, and boardinghouse before finally becoming the county museum in 1976. In its time, it undoubtedly witnessed more than enough sickness, death, and unhappiness to generate the sad face that Lyles caught with her camera. But without more information, Lyles can only wonder who this woman was and why she might have been so sad.

Citadel Light

In February 1981, the *Charleston News and Courier* ran several articles about a mysterious light that cadets claimed to have seen in room 1123 of the First Battalion barracks at the Military College of South Carolina, a.k.a. The Citadel. Hardly the kind of place to accept any such tomfoolery from its corps of cadets, the school's top brass investigated the light as soon as they learned about it and found it to be a genuine mystery.

According to one of the articles, Lieutenant Colonel Dick Clarke said, "I don't believe in superstitions, but this might make a believer out of me." He said that the light appeared each evening around 12:10 a.m., showing up first as a spot on the ceiling and then moving around the room, seemingly in response to instructions or questions. Hundreds of cadets had seen it before word about the phenomenon reached the upper echelons of the administration. When it did, Lieutenant Colonel Clarke and six other witnesses came to the room of cadets Robert Grenko and Bruce Harding for a midnight inspection. "I went there fully expecting to see it, because so many others had," Clarke said, "and I wasn't disappointed."

The light seemed to want to communicate, and would appear on the ceiling if the answer to a question was positive and on the floor if negative. When told to do so, the light would move in a circular pattern, and it moved away if anyone tried to touch it. While probing the weird spectacle, Clarke suddenly turned on the room lights to see if anyone there might have been operating some device to cause it to happen, but "no one was touching anything," he said.

In the early 1960s, a cadet had died accidentally in a nearby area, but Clarke could offer no reason why, if that had anything to do with it, the spirit would wait nearly twenty years to manifest itself. A less otherworldly theory had to do with a new transformer that had been installed on the McAlister Field House at about the time the light first began appearing. Static electricity generated by the transformer could have made the light appear, according to this theory. But that didn't explain how the light seemed to respond to conversation.

Ultimately, General James A. Grimsley, Citadel president, issued an order that the mystery of the light would no longer be discussed, and that the cadets would go to sleep earlier and not try to see the light until it was no longer an issue. The next time anyone dared to stay up late enough to look at it, the light was gone.

Flags of Fort Sumter

The attack on Fort Sumter in the mouth of Charleston Harbor at 4:30 sharp on the morning of April 12, 1861, is usually said to be the start of the Civil War. In reality, civil war was in the air many years before it started, as the states increasingly disagreed over a number of issues, especially slavery. The fort, held by Union forces under the command of Major Robert Anderson, held out for thirty-four hours of intense Confederate bombardment before finally surrendering.

At the time of the surrender, the flag that usually flew over the fort had been damaged, and a smaller version of Old Glory, called the Storm Flag, was flying. Anderson had been given permission by his victors to lower the flag with one last hundred-gun salute. During the salute, a spark set off an explosion that killed Union Private Daniel Hough and seriously injured several other members of the gun crew. Hough was the only fatality of the Battle of Fort Sumter. Anderson called off the salute at fifty guns, the Storm Flag was lowered and folded, Hough was quickly buried, and the Union soldiers were taken off the island.

Soldiers from a militia unit called the Palmetto Guard immediately raised the first Southern flag to be flown over conquered territory. Not exactly "flown," perhaps, because the Storm Flag's pole had been taken down in order to lower it, so Private John S. Byrd, Jr., of the

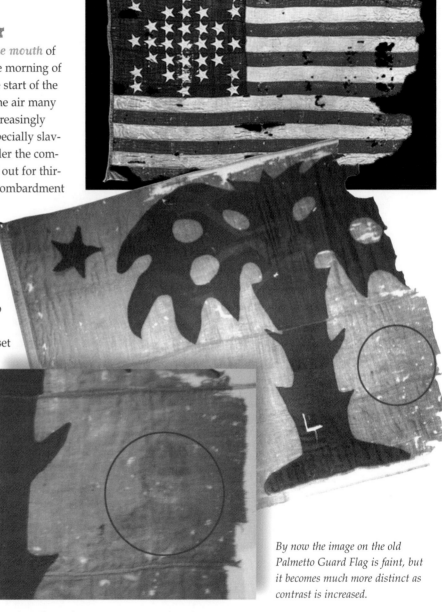

By now the image on the old Palmetto Guard Flag is faint, but it becomes much more distinct as contrast is increased.

Palmetto Guard draped the flag over the upper ramparts of the fort. This flag featured a green palmetto tree and a red star against a white background. The tree had been a symbol of South Carolinian resilience ever since the Revolutionary battle of Fort Moultrie, when British cannonballs had bounced off or sunk harmlessly into the tough, fibrous palmetto logs that formed Moultrie's walls. It is still featured on the state flag today.

The Storm Flag, also known as the Fort Sumter Flag, is now on display at Fort Sumter National Monument's museum, facing the old Palmetto Guard flag that replaced it. Both flags are ragged remnants of their former selves, torn to shreds by artillery, wind, and the passage of time. And each contains a mystery.

Two soldiers who played a historic role at Fort Sumter seem to have somehow transposed their images into the two old flags. If you look carefully just to the right of the centermost star on the Storm Flag, a small patch has somehow lost its original deep blue dye and now looks just like the silhouetted image of a Union soldier. Some say it's the image of Private Hough and it appeared there the day he died in the salute. And if you look just as carefully to the right of the trunk on the old Palmetto Guard flag, you can also make out another faint image, stained into the weave of what was once its snow-white field, now dingy with age. It is an almost photographic image of a face—could it be Private Byrd? If so, that would certainly make for a nice symmetry. Perhaps the voices sometimes heard at the fort are those of their spirits still trying to sort it all out, one asking the other why it took exactly four years for Hough, who witnessed the surrender and then died that day, to win in the end, while Byrd, who triumphed, to ultimately lose. When the war began, most folks guessed that at most it would only last four months. But wars often have a way of getting out of hand.

Lavinia Fisher

The old Charleston jail, sitting now incongruously in the midst of a housing project, seems like some grim remnant of the Middle Ages, a medieval-style aboveground dungeon for those nervously awaiting their trials and those dreading to hear their sentences. Among the earliest and most infamous residents of the Old Jail were a young couple named John and Lavinia Fisher, who operated a roadhouse and inn in Charleston's rowdier days. Six-Mile House sat on the part of the Charleston peninsula where the land thins down to a slender neck. Even now, it's a kind of no-man's-land of junkyards and cemeteries, but two hundred years ago it was the jumping-off place to the mostly undeveloped frontier of the fledgling state. Well outside the city walls, the Fishers' tavern was situated so that anyone proceeding overland from downtown Charleston would have to pass by. As it turned out, the couple had established a little routine to supplement their income. If they thought they could get away with it, Fisher and his attractive wife would occasionally murder and rob their overnight guests. Their preferred victims were ignorant people fresh off a ship from elsewhere, traveling alone, who hadn't made any local friends yet and so weren't expected anywhere else anytime soon.

For quite a long time, the Fishers had a good scheme going. Whenever someone fit their preferred-victim profile, Lavinia would signal her henchman husband and

People who had been standing close enough to look her directly in the eyes later said they'd never forget her wicked stare or the chilling sneer that froze on her face when she died.

put something in the visitor's food to knock him out or at least send him off to his room feeling dizzy. A short while later, husband John would quietly let himself in and smother or strangle the unlucky traveler. After rummaging through the lodger's belongings for valuables, the enterprising couple would then burn any identifiable clothing and bury the body in one of several lime-filled pits dug beneath the tavern. This scheme worked as long as their guests were new to the area and relatively innocent of its dangers. However, they eventually made the mistake of trying to kill a man who was heading in the other direction and had been in the Carolina backcountry long enough to learn a thing or two about tricks and traps.

On the evening of February 12, 1819, a storm was coming on when a lone deerskin trader named John Peeples stumbled into Six-Mile House and asked if he could stay the night. Peeples had just guided a string of pack mules, laden with dried animal skins, through the mountains of north Georgia and didn't want to risk having the valuable skins soaked in the storm. Lavinia Fisher gave her husband the signal and then invited Peeples to leave his mules under the cover of their shed. After the visitor had secured them, she told him that she'd make him a dinner. Peeples, who'd brought provisions with him,

declined, but Lavinia persisted. "It would be our pleasure," she said, smiling flirtatiously. "We won't even charge you for it. We're just delighted to be able to entertain a handsome-looking fellow as charming as you."

That kind of line might work on some greenhorn fresh off the boat, but if there was one thing Peeples had learned, it was that there was no such thing as a free lunch. He was immediately put on his guard, although he kept a smile on his face. But when dinner came (since there seemed to be no way to politely refuse it) he only pretended to eat.

Later, after Lavinia showed him to his room and left, Peeples piled extra blankets on the bed and pulled the coverlet over them to make it look as if he were sleeping in it. But then he lay down on the floor to sleep fully clothed. A few hours later, the trader heard a key turning slowly in the lock and felt the boards creak as big John Fisher crept into the room and stood over the bed in the pitch dark. Then he heard Lavinia whisper fiercely, "Do it!"

John pounced on the bed to smother another victim but let out an enraged grunt when he felt nothing but blankets. In the few seconds of confusion it took to realize the bed was empty, Peeples leapt up and managed to get away and clamber onto his horse. Pumped up with adrenaline, his weariness left him as he rode through the dawn as quickly as he could toward the walls of the city.

The following day, the sheriff's men were easily able to track the Fishers' own footprints in the rain-softened soil to a hiding place near the river, where they caught them and four other members of their band and took them into custody. Six-Mile House was burned to the ground.

At this point, only John Peeples' tale was counted against the Fishers. They quickly received a jail sentence and were in the midst of appealing the decision a few months later when some people poking around in the ruins of Six-Mile House found a trapdoor leading down to the old beer cellar. And in the floor of the cellar were a series of pits with the partly dissolved corpses of

between seventeen and twenty-six former guests (many of the skeletons were too far decomposed to reassemble with any certainty). The Charleston papers soon announced that the city jail held the worst criminals since the founding of the Carolina colonies.

The verdict of the new trial was then pretty much a foregone conclusion. The Fishers were sentenced to be hanged, the execution set for February 18, 1820.

Hangings were public events then, on the theory that seeing criminals punished was morally instructive for the rest of the population. February 18 would be a double feature, promising the unusual prospect of seeing a woman hanged as well as a man. The streets were

packed as a big crowd gathered for the show. They were not to be disappointed.

First to mount the scaffold was John. He turned to the crowd and begged for forgiveness. In jail he'd found religion, and he told the throng gathered around the gallows that God already knew that he was sorry for what he had done. He also said, jerking his head toward Lavinia, "I only done it for her. She made me! I was a good person till she come along!"

And then Lavinia jumped off the scaffold herself, almost but not quite reaching the ground as she dangled down in the crowd, just inches away from the closest horrified onlookers.

The crowd began to laugh and jeer, and someone yelled, "Act like a man!" Then they hauled him up by the neck to kick and squirm for several minutes before he finally ceased to move.

Next it was Lavinia's turn. And as it turned out, John was right. She really was the tougher of the two. After the executioners had dragged her husband's still-warm body off the platform, she proudly mounted it as if onto a stage, wearing her finest outfit, which happened to be her wedding dress. Before they could tighten the noose around her neck, she turned to the crowd and said, "If any of you's got a message for the devil, better give it to me quick 'cause I'm about to meet him!"

Realizing that this wasn't providing quite the kind of moral uplift a public hanging was supposed to encourage, the execution crew quickly finished their preparations before she could say anything else. And then Lavinia jumped off the scaffold herself, almost but not quite reaching the ground as she dangled down in the crowd, just inches away from the closest horrified onlookers. People who had been standing close enough to look her directly in the eyes later said they'd never forget her wicked stare or the chilling sneer that froze on her face when she died. Never, they said, had such an evil look appeared on the visage of such a once beautiful woman. Lavinia Fisher was only twenty-seven the day she was hanged.

Evidently she left her mark on Charleston, for even people who weren't there for the execution began to see her face floating behind the bars at the window of the cell where she'd been held awaiting her final day among the living. And after her cell's walls were cracked open in the Great Earthquake of 1886, people often said they could see her wandering around in other parts of the neighborhood, like the old Unitarian Church cemetery just a few blocks away. She was buried there in an unmarked grave because no other church would take her.

Tourists visit the area now, and uninformed guides sometimes tell them that she was the first woman hanged in America. That's not true. Lavinia Fisher's execution was roughly the fortieth recorded public hanging of a woman since the first English colonies were established. Long preceding her execution was that of Jane Champion, the first female hanged in the colonies (in Virginia in 1632). The oldest female ever hanged in America was seventy-one-year-old Rebecca Nurse, one of thirteen women hanged as witches in Salem, Massachusetts, in 1692. The youngest ever hanged was twelve-year-old Hannah Ocuish, hanged in New London, Connecticut, in 1786. Female executions in the U.S. didn't end with Lavinia Fisher, of course. Approximately 465 more women would be officially executed before 1900, the vast majority by hanging. More than fifty women remain on death rows around the country today.

Unitarian Graveyard

The Unitarian Church on Beaufain Street in Charleston is the oldest church of that denomination in the country. It also has one of the creepiest cemeteries in the country, overgrown with wandering rose brambles and muscular-looking crepe myrtles draped in Spanish moss. In addition to the evil phantom of Lavinia Fisher, the kinder, gentler spectre of Annabelle Lee, Edgar Allan Poe's true love, is often seen roaming wistfully among the stones. Stories say that the cemetery served as their secret meeting place early in their doomed relationship. If you find yourself encountering any ethereal females in this place, it would be prudent to ascertain first just whom you might be dealing with before approaching too closely. If she shivers as if chilled by the wind, then it's probably Annabelle, but if it looks more like she's quaking with malicious laughter, look out for Lavinia.

Atmore Oliver House Ghost

The Atmore Oliver House in New Bern, NC, is one of the most haunted buildings in the city. There are two explanations for the poltergeist-like noises and disturbances that are said to occur with some frequency in the upper floors and attic. One is that during a smallpox epidemic in the late 18th or early 19th centuries, a girl and her father were quarantined in the attic. They themselves did not have the full-blown disease, and would have lived except that the people who were to deliver their food and drink came down with smallpox and died before telling anyone about their duties. Locked in the attic, the man and his daughter died of thirst, after days of pounding on the walls. And that frantic pounding sound, intermingled with quieter moments of rattling—presumably the girl playing with her toys—continues to this day.

The other (admittedly weird) explanation we've heard is about Mary Oliver, the last resident of the house before it became a historic property. As she aged, she neglected more and more of the large house. At some point, a colony of cats got established in the shut-off parts of the house and Mrs. Oliver decided to hire a handyman to get rid of them. He came to the house and quickly eliminated the feral critters down to the last one. But when he went to Mrs. Oliver for his check, she refused to pay him the agreed amount since the job had taken less time than either of them had thought it would. In revenge, the man buried the cats in her yard, each in a shallow hole. The holes were so shallow that the animals' heads poked out of the ground, facing the house. When Mrs. Oliver looked out her window and saw the choir of dead cats facing her, she began stomping around the house in fury. They say she's still upset about it, and begins stomping around the place whenever she remembers the handyman's payback.

Claw Marks on the Wall

Premature burials probably never occur these days, but in the days before modern embalming techniques, they did happen from time to time. It's likely that the vast majority of cases went undiscovered, because most bodies are buried the traditional six feet under. Once in a while, however, there is evidence of a horrific tragedy that might otherwise have gone undetected.

The old Legare family mausoleum at the back of the graveyard behind Edisto Presbyterian Church on Edisto Island, SC, is said to have been one of those sites. According to the oral history of the place, back in the 1850s a girl was visiting relatives on the island when she fell ill. Some say it was diphtheria, others say yellow fever, or others cholera. In any case, the disease progressed rapidly, and within days she slipped into a coma and then died. Or so they thought. The fear of contagion from the corpse was so great that her body was given a hurried funeral and then placed in a makeshift coffin on one of the shelves of the mausoleum as quickly as possible. The door to the multiparty tomb was sealed to prevent any contagion leaking out, and then everyone began the long, slow process of healing after the loss.

Many years passed before another family member died and it became time to reopen the mausoleum for a new occupant. Everyone gathered around the door of the tomb as the oldest son, now the keeper of the key to the mausoleum, produced a penknife to scrape out the wax that decades earlier had sealed the keyhole. He inserted the key and shouldered the creaking, humidity-swollen door. His eyes were closed against the swirl of dust that billowed out of the chamber, so he wasn't the first to see what happened next. That honor fell to those at the front of the throng, who let out a collective gasp of horror at what they saw.

A small skeleton had tumbled out of the tomb onto the ground in front of them, still draped in a ragged shroud. After the shock of the finding, there was ample evidence to cobble together the bones of the story. At some point after the girl's funeral, she had awakened. She had managed to force the lid of the hastily constructed coffin in which she lay, and then clambered out. But that was as far as she had gotten. Weakened by hunger and disease, she'd been unable to force the door of the mausoleum and escape. No one had heard her screams, since the mausoleum sits at the edge of a swampy woods. No one knows how long she lingered there, but there's permanent proof of her utter panic. Her fingernails, which had continued to grow in her comatose sleep, had left long, frantic scratches in the hard, cold stone of the tomb walls.

Now some people believe the place is haunted. Something, since that day, has kept the tomb from ever being sealed again. Every attempt to mount a door, brick

it up, place a slab, chain it, lock it, or otherwise close it off hasn't lasted through the night. The ghost of the girl, they say, is determined never to be trapped again.

Even Saran Wrap Doesn't Work

A friend of mine worked on Edisto, and he and a friend attempted repeatedly to wrap Saran Wrap around the mausoleum in order to cover the door. The wrap ripped down the center of the entryway every time. Hearing this, I assembled another group of friends to take the 45-mile pilgrimage to visit the restless soul. We came bearing flowers and nail files. When we arrived, we got out of the car and felt so spooked that we dropped our offerings and got right back in said vehicle and sped home as fast as we could.
—Molly Matlock

Screams in the Graveyard

Many times through many different means they have tried to permanently mount the door to the mausoleum, but it always reopens. I have seen this too, and the door is now cemented in the ground in front of the mausoleum because they never could get it to stay shut. The story also goes that at times screams can be heard coming from the graveyard and it is the screams of the little girl. And it is because she doesn't ever want anyone buried in the mausoleum again that the door keeps reopening every time it is mounted. —Stephen Aaron

Residential Properties Now Available

In 1899, W. B. Smith Whaley & Co. built Olympia Mills in Columbia, SC, to be the largest and most up-to-date textile mill under one roof. Trainloads of raw cotton were brought to the mill in huge bales, and within hours finished cloth emerged from its more than 1,200 power looms in the most efficient manner available. One of the finest textile mills of its day, everything about it was the most modern technology and design for the times. Except, that is, for its labor practices.

A number of residents who have moved into these "luxury loft spaces" have reported some disturbing phenomena, including hearing the sounds of crying children.

Children as young as seven or eight years old labored in the vast spinning room of the Olympia Mills. Many met the (extremely) minimum weight requirements only by showing up to work with stones in their pockets, and then stood on crates to reach machines that had dangerously high-speed moving parts. Hours were long and breaks were short in the sweltering and noisy mill. In this tough environment, overseers threatened children who dawdled that if they failed to meet their quotas, they would be fed into the furnaces.

While most workers considered these threats as merely motivational incentives, not everyone is so sure they were purely figures of speech. Now that the old mill is being turned into an upscale apartment complex, a number of residents who have moved into these "luxury loft spaces" have reported some disturbing phenomena, including hearing the sounds of crying children or of running feet in empty hallways, mysterious disappearances or rearrangements of toys and tools in locked spaces, and images of small hands or faces appearing in the moisture of fogged-up windows. One explanatory story making the rounds has it that while it's probably unlikely that an overseer actually put any living children into a furnace (despite the threats), he could have burned the bodies of children who had died of exhaustion in order to destroy any evidence that might trigger an investigation of the harsh conditions at the mill. Child labor continued at Olympia Mills for nearly forty years.

S 156

Underwood & Underwood
New York & London

(20)-5670—In a great spinning room (104,000 spindles), Olympian Mills, Columbia, S. C.   Copyright Underwood & Underwood.

Lady of Lockhart

The water tower of Lockhart, SC, stands high atop a steep hill overlooking the town, which until the late 1990s was one of the last company-owned mill villages in the Carolinas. According to a local legend, about a century ago a woman who was jilted in love hoped to end her troubles by climbing the old water tower and leaping off it to her death. But now she seems to be stuck in something like limbo, for even though the current tower replaced an earlier one that dated back to the late 19th century, she's still hanging around in the vicinity. Sometimes around midnight she'll be found at the base of the tower, holding a rose in her mouth, but if she thinks she's not sufficiently appreciated, she'll climb to the top, brandish the rose one last time in defiance, and then leap—but she never quite touches the ground before she vanishes.

—*Thanks to Tally Johnson*

Lydia

One of the most popular ghost stories of all time is the tale of the phantom hitchhiker. There are versions of it from all over the world, with all kinds of variations. We should keep in mind, though, that the fact that something may be a well-told story doesn't mean it couldn't have happened again for real. After all, Sleeping Beauty wasn't the last person to wind up in a coma.

The version we know best dates from the early 1920s and involves Lydia, the vanishing hitchhiker of Jamestown, NC. The site where it took place is certainly believable. It's an old barrel-vaulted, single-lane tunnel, its entrances now all but hidden under a blanket of rampant kudzu beneath the railroad tracks near Jamestown. It was here, according to the story, that late one foggy night in 1924, a young driver was making his way along the old highway that used to go through this tunnel when he spotted a bedraggled-looking girl in a party dress standing by the roadside. He pulled over to give her a ride, and she hopped in. She explained that she had been at a party in Raleigh, had had an argument with her boyfriend, and was now just trying to get back home to High Point.

As they rode along, the girl relaxed a bit and told the guy that her name was Lydia. When they approached her neighborhood, she gave him instructions on how to get to her parents' house. After he stopped the car and cut the engine, he got out and walked around to open the passenger-side door like a gentleman. But the seat was empty.

Thinking she'd somehow slipped out at the same time he did, the man went to the front door to make sure she had made it into the house safely. But when he rang the bell, a sad-eyed older woman answered it. "Good evening, ma'am," he said. "I just wanted to make sure Lydia got in okay. I just gave her a ride."

The older lady looked at him and shook her head and sighed. "When will it ever end? You're not the first, son, and I'm so afraid you won't be the last. You must have come by way of

the old tunnel bridge, like all the others."

"I certainly did," said the young man. "She was hitching and told me she needed to get home."

"Lydia never comes home," said the lady. "She was killed on that road about a year ago, and almost every night someone like you tries to bring her back here. As soon as they pull into the drive, she's gone again, gone to spend another cold night out by the road."

Lydia has been hitchhiking along High Point Road heading from Greensboro into Jamestown ever since. The underpass where she is now seen most frequently is a new undercutting under a railroad bridge and is easy to spot because of all the graffiti. To see the old original tunnel, park here and make your way through the kudzu and underbrush about forty or fifty feet from the road. Some people say the old tunnel is the more likely place to see the hitchhiking apparition, but we sort of doubt it. If she's really still looking for a ride—and we assume that she is—then like any other sensible hitchhiker, she'd put her thumb out where more traffic is likely to pass.

Spirits at Cap'n Charlie's Station

On the point of land that forms North Carolina's Cape Fear there was once a light tower, of which now only the foundations remain. Three small cottages at the site are collectively called Cap'n Charlie's Station after lighthouse keeper Charles Swan, who lived there with his family between 1903 and 1933. One of the three houses is haunted by the island's most famous nonliving resident, a red-haired beauty that residents call Mrs. Cloden.

According to Larry Pace, some time in the 1930s a newlywed couple from New York City had the romantic idea of sailing down the East Coast on their honeymoon. Offshore from Bald Head (then called Smith Island), they struck Frying Pan Shoals, a famously treacherous hazard that extends nearly twenty miles out to sea and has been the undoing of many a ship over the centuries. Unable to free themselves from the shoals and with a hurricane fast approaching, they abandoned their boat and rowed its dinghy to the nearest visible shore, making landfall near Cap'n Charlie's just as the storm struck.

No one was around, since the station had been decommissioned a few years before, but they managed to break into the middle of the three sturdy buildings and weather the storm in it. Or at least they thought they had. Although the husband had been a reasonably skillful sail boater in northeastern waters, he wasn't familiar with the structure of hurricanes and didn't understand that the calm and often bright and sunny weather in the middle of the storm wasn't the end of the tempest. It was only the eye, the highly misleading intermission between two violent and opposing acts. In the illusory calm, he set off in the dinghy once more to get help, leaving his wife in

the cottage. When the eye finally passed and the other side of the storm struck, the wife barricaded herself in the house, knowing that her poor husband was almost certainly lost in the worst of the gale.

He was, in fact, and his body and the battered pieces of the dinghy were found washed up on Caswell Beach eight days later. When the corpse was discovered, local rescuers guessed that there might have been others with him and began scouring the shore for any potential survivors. Within a day or two, they made their way to Cap'n Charlie's Station, where they discovered that the center cottage had been entered. They forced the door to try to rescue the dead man's young widow.

Unfortunately, it was too late. And even more unfortunate was the fact that the poor woman had apparently died of dehydration. The inexperienced couple had not known about the cistern system that lighthouse stations used to catch rainwater and store it, and she had died without realizing that just a short distance away were hundreds of gallons of drinkable rainwater.

Ever since then, people who have stayed in the middle cottage at Cap'n Charlie's Station have occasionally reported seeing a tall, red-haired, and apparently friendly young woman who seems to be waiting nervously for someone to appear. Sometimes she's seen in an upstairs window, sometimes in a faint reflection in the mirror, or out of the corner of the eye on the stairs. She seems especially kind to children, probably because she had been looking forward to raising a family of her own with her lost husband. Occasionally she speaks, they say, and has even mentioned a name, though it's not certain if it's her first name, last name, or that of her husband. People also disagree as to whether it's spelled Cloden, Clodin, or Culloden, since the voice is so soft and faint and often muffled by the sound of the wind or waves.

—*Thanks to Ann Mills and Gayle Tustin*

That Awful Night at Bostian Bridge

Every August 26, a small gathering of people with interests in the supernatural heads out Buffalo Shoals Road on the southwestern edge of Statesville, NC, to gather at Bostian Bridge and wait to see if the terrible events that took place on August 27, 1891, repeat themselves. On that night, North Carolina's worst railroad disaster left two unsolved mysteries.

The first mystery has to do with how it could have happened. Bostian Bridge was built in 1857 and in its day was considered an engineering marvel. Sixty feet high and 260 feet long, it spans Third Creek far below it in a series of gracefully graduated arches. For its first thirty-three years, thousands of trains chugged across it without any trouble whatsoever.

On that fateful night, however, a train was running thirty-four minutes behind schedule when it pulled out of Statesville. Perhaps because he was running late, engineer William West opened the throttle a bit more than usual. We'll never know if some action on the part of West or his fireman, Warren Fry, had anything to do with the disaster, since both were killed that night. What we do know is that only five minutes after the train left Statesville Station, the entire train—locomotive, tender, baggage car, passenger cars, and the private car of the

Richmond & Danville Railroad superintendent—left the track just as it headed over Bostian Bridge. Investigators later determined that it flew 154 feet through the air before landing sixty feet below the bridge, injuring or killing everyone aboard.

Once the train had fallen, the nightmare was only beginning, for the wreckage had dammed the creek, and its currents were beginning to fill up the compartments. In all, twenty-two people died that night. A subsequent investigation offered a variety of conflicting possibilities for how the wreck could have happened. Engineer's errors, rotten timbers, loose rails, vandalism, and intentional sabotage were all blamed. Six years later, two inmates at Central Prison in Raleigh were tried and given additional sentences for the disaster after they'd bragged to fellow prisoners about committing it. However, there is some suspicion that investigators only made scapegoats of them in order to close the case. The mystery of why Engine No. 9 left the tracks with the entire train behind it will probably never be solved.

But perhaps it might. Apparently it's sometimes possible to watch the event happen all over again, as if in some kind of cosmic replay. How and why this takes place is the second mystery.

Columbia, SC, residents Larry and Pat Hayes were on their way through Statesville in the wee hours of August 27, 1941, when they noticed that their car had a flat tire. They pulled off on the side of Buffalo Shoals Road at the point just before it crosses Third Creek, and Mr. Hayes jacked up the car and took off the flat. He began walking back to town with it to get it fixed, while Pat stayed in the car with the kids.

As she sat on the passenger side with the windows rolled down, she heard a train heading down the tracks that parallel the road about two hundred yards to the north. She saw the light of the train come into view and

illuminate the top of Bostian Bridge. Then, to her horrified shock, she saw the train leap from the bridge and fall with an incredibly loud crash into the creek. Within seconds, she heard the screams and cries of the injured. She had already jumped out of the car and run partway to the bridge when one of the conductors came limping up to her and begged her for help. She then saw a car coming from the direction of town. As it slowed down, she realized it was her husband, getting a lift back with the patched tire. She ran to tell him about the train wreck and turned to point toward the railroad man. He was gone. Suddenly the night was completely quiet except for the sounds of katydids and the gurgling creek.

By then it was nearly dawn, and the Hayeses decided they would rest in Statesville after what had been a more than ordinarily stressful night. They mentioned Pat Hayes's puzzling experience to someone they met at breakfast, and that's when they first learned about the tragedy that had happened exactly fifty years earlier.

Now early in the morning on every August 27, in the hours just after midnight, people gather near the bridge. Call them ghouls, but what they really are, is seekers after the unknown. *—Thanks to Phyllis K. Moss, Joel Reese*

Cemetery Safari

There's something inherently fascinating about almost any cemetery, whether it's a Victorian masterpiece that looks ready for the next remake of *Frankenstein Meets Dracula* or one of those E-Z-care modern spreads with the plaques set at ground-level to facilitate mowing. And yet, almost anything we do in a cemetery—exploring old graves, appreciating the art, hunting ghosts—is, by any way you measure it, akin to tightrope walking over the Grand Canyon, all the time knowing that someday you're going to fall into it. Thrilling, but a little nuts when you get right down to it. Or maybe it's more like a carnival ride or a horror movie: In a perverse way, we enjoy the close encounter with danger.

In any case, the Carolinas have thousands upon thousands of graveyards, each fascinating for all the tales they tell. Each one speaks of some kind of membership, from big urban spreads of the dead to relatively smaller graveyards next to old churches. Only a neglected few speak sadly of a past forgotten or ignored. Here's just a sampling of the tales a good Carolina cemetery can tell.

Tale of Two Cities . . . of the Dead

The places where we choose to spend eternity say a lot about us. Take two cemeteries as examples of what we mean. At one end of the spectrum is God's Acre, the traditional term for Moravian burying grounds, like the one located just north of the old Moravian stronghold of Salem, NC. First laid out in 1766, it reflects the values of the community and its members. The sect originally organized its communal living and church attendance in groups defined by age, sex, and marital status. Believers largely identified their roles in life by the groups they belonged to, ahead of their identity as individuals or as members of families. Even after death, the group was the main thing that identified you. Different sections of God's Acre were designated for married men and widowers, married women and widows, single men and boys, single women and girls, and infants. Within each section, the dead are set out in long, straight rows according to the order in which they died.

For Moravians, death is the great equalizer. Tombstones in their cemeteries therefore lie flat and in uniform rows, with those of adults being only slightly larger than the children's (in order to include the names of spouses and offspring). At first this kind of regimentation may seem almost military, but a truer comparison would be to farming. As you enter the cemetery, you step out of the shaded walkway into a light space open to the sun and sky, where the dead lie planted like seeds in a garden. The term God's Acre comes in fact from an old Moravian saying that at the Second Coming, Jesus will "harvest" the souls of the righteous. Meanwhile, the place is easy to weed and maintain.

At Charleston, SC's, Magnolia Cemetery, and the cluster of other eerie necropolises surrounding it, death is anything *but* uniform. Here each grave expresses the individual's personal history, as well as his wealth, family connections, and any other odd thing he or his relatives wanted to include. The sheer variety of tombs is staggering, ranging from simple rows of white stones (for the nuns buried here) to only slightly scaled-down replicas of Egyptian temples, Roman pyramids, Greek ruins, medieval towers, and Norman chapels. Farthest out, a section called Buzzard Island outclasses any Hollywood horror movie set in terms of sheer Gothic spine-chilling creepiness. Here are giant rattlesnakes

wrapped around columns, Druidic dolmens, cannons, stone baby carriages with mourning wreaths for wheels, and even glassed-in crypts where you can look down into shelved recesses and see corpses turning back into their original elements.

Through all this intricate variety, Magnolia reflects the history of Charleston, which, of course, is quite different from Salem's. While Salem was founded as a religious colony, by one group for one united and predetermined purpose, Charleston was a seaport and a mercantile free-for-all, overflowing with all kinds of people from all over the globe. Nearly surrounded by water on its narrow, marshy peninsula, by the mid-19th century it was overflowing with its own dead as well.

Property for a new cemetery outside the city was acquired in 1849 and plots went on sale immediately. Magnolia became one of the first purpose-built cemeteries in the nation, a city for the dead, a showplace for the living. Nothing, it seems, was more delightful to the morbid Victorian mentality than a carriage ride out to the tombs for a Sunday picnic among the ancestors. And as a true Land of the Dead, it's still a fun place to explore.

To visit Magnolia head north on Meeting Street from downtown Charleston and turn right on Cunnington Avenue. It is free and open daily 8–5. Listen for the bell, which indicates the gates are about to close—you won't want to be locked in.

A replica of the Pyramid of Cestius in Rome was created for the William B. Smith family. Mausoleums based on Egyptian and classical themes were popular in the 19th century and were considered the ultimate in status housing for the departed. Since this photo was taken, the figure atop the entry was stolen.

Hunley Crews

Among the some 2,300 Confederate soldiers buried at Magnolia Cemetery are all three crews of the *H. L. Hunley*, considered the world's first "successful" submarine (though the men who drowned while hand cranking her propeller during her various voyages may have thought otherwise). The *Hunley* itself disappeared after its last run, during which it sank the Union warship *Housatonic*, and was rediscovered in 1995. The remains of the crew from that voyage were buried in Magnolia in 2004. The submarine is now undergoing a multimillion-dollar restoration.

Friends Forever

On June 26, 1875, best friends Dora Staton and Hester Pippen accidentally drowned together. Both girls were fifteen years old, born in Tarboro, NC, just two months apart, and grew up as inseparable as sisters. Because of this, they were buried side by side in identical tombs, each marked with a cross sinking beneath the waves. Epitaphs on the back of the markers read, "It is well," and "Thy will be done."

Old Ford's Glowing Cross

Several times a year, a cast-iron cross in the graveyard of the Old Ford Baptist Church near Cross Hill, SC, glows brightly and changes colors for several minutes before fading back to its normal dark shade of rusted metal. Theories abound as to why this happens, including various weather conditions, calendar dates, and historic events, but so far none have proved conclusive. Could it be some kind of signal?

The individual whose grave it marks died at the age of 70, in 1913. The epitaph, "Precious in the sight of the Lord is the death of His saints," provides no clues. It is also not known whether the cross ever glows when no one's there to see it. Short of setting up a camera to constantly monitor the site, we may never find out.

Mourning Their Mother

A tombstone in St. Michael's churchyard, in Charleston, SC, bears the epitaph

HERE LIES THE MOTHER
OF 23 CHILDREN.
SHE HATH DONE WHAT SHE COULD.

Headboard Headstone

When Mary Ann Luyten died in 1770, her grave in St. Michael's churchyard was marked with the head of her bed, extending lengthwise down the stretch of the gravesite. Why, we have no clue. It stood more than two centuries in the open, humid air of Charleston before finally requiring replacement. The new marker is a replica of the original and should be good for another century or two. The words engraved on it read the same as the original:

IN MEMORY
OF
MARY ANN LUYTEN WIFE OF WILLM LUYTEN
DIED SEP 9TH 1770 IN THE 27TH YEAR OF HER AGE.

Curse of the Witch's Wall

At the Old Stone Church on Highway 76, halfway between Clemson and Pendleton, SC, is a singular grave, isolated and walled off from all the others. It's the burial place of Eliza Huger, but none would call it her "resting place," for no one believes she's ever really been at rest, hence the wall. It's this grave, though, that invariably draws visitors and about which so many legends have been told.

Eliza Huger and her husband belonged to the Old Stone Church. At some point she was accused of being a witch, and though she vehemently denied the charges, her persecution continued for weeks. Eventually she left the church, cursing it as she did so. Her husband, though, continued to go from time to time, and when Eliza died, he expected his wife to be buried in the church graveyard, since they were still technically members.

The other good people objected, not wanting a witch buried in their churchyard. After some discussion, it was settled that Eliza could be buried on the far side of the graveyard, away from all the others, and that a wall would be built up around the grave to keep her spirit in. The husband unhappily agreed, but at the same time he made an offhand comment about how impossible it would be to trap her spirit.

Today, the grave is still set off by itself, though its stone wall is crumbling. Rebar keeps it from falling down entirely. The huge stone tablet across the grave is badly cracked, and it is impossible to make out the words. And as it turns out, it *was* impossible to trap Eliza's spirit. Her curse on the church was that the wall around her grave would never stand. From all appearances, the curse was effective and the church has to rebuild the wall every few years.
—*Thanks to Stephen Aaron and Paul Matheny*

Eliza and the Judas Tree

Eliza left the Carolina upcountry for New Orleans, where she became a "lady of the evening." When her brothers went to find her, she was found with a "client" and both were killed in a resulting skirmish. Her body was brought home to be buried at Old Stone Church. Because of her scandalous reputation, the church elders required that a stone wall with no entrance surround her grave, to keep her spirit from mingling with the righteous spirits in the churchyard.

A Judas tree sprang up and continues to grow inside one corner of the wall, and no amount of herbicide will kill the weeds and briars that grow around the grave. The gravestone has been frequently struck by lightning, breaking the marble where her name is inscribed. *—Betsy Dunkle*

Before it was cracked by lightning and eroded by weather, Eliza Huger's slab read:

A BROTHER'S SORROW
DEDICATED
THIS MARBLE TO THE MEMORY
OF HIS SISTER.
BENEATH IT ARE THE REMAINS
OF
ELIZA HUGER
WHOSE SPIRIT RETURNED TO
HEAVEN
OCTOBER 19,
1819.

Visitors sometimes toss a few coins onto the slab if they need any kind of special favors done for them in the underworld, but these are invariably quickly swept off the stone by an unseen hand. And despite the slab's claim that her spirit went to heaven, the money is soon blackened, as if by hellish heat or brimstone. But leave the change you see scattered around the grave alone — if you try to take back Eliza's "pay" you'll be cursed yourself. Don't stand or sit on the wall, either. She's had it with entertaining any more company.

Love Finally Blossoms in the Afterlife

In an old graveyard atop a little rise along old Tommy's Road north of Goldsboro, NC, there is a strangely haunting image that seems to have been

formed from the raw material of desire itself. Its story starts back in 1856, when seventeen-year-old Rachael Vinson fell achingly in love with the man of her dreams, a local fellow in his mid-twenties named George Deans.

Unfortunately, George seemed oblivious to the hints Rachael dropped, indicating her affection for him. In time, she felt there was no other recourse than to ignore the social customs of those days and make the first move. She confessed her love. George, taken by surprise or else just plain insensitive, bluntly turned her down. He claimed he was already in love with someone else, even though no other girl had ever been seen with him. His thoughtless refusal broke Rachael's heart.

In those less jaded days, hearts did actually seem to break. After Deans's rejection, young Rachael Vinson went into an immediate and rapid decline. Within months, it was clear she was approaching the end of her life. In her final days, she sent for her hoped-for lover. And when he came into the room where she lay, she sat up and said what were very nearly her last words, "I may not have won your heart in this world, George

Deans, but you will be forever mine in the next." A day or so later she passed away and was buried in the little graveyard above Tommy's Road.

Deans tried to put her out of his thoughts and go on about his life, but he'd underestimated the power of Rachael's love. About a year after her death, he was returning home after a night out carousing with friends. The young men were stumbling along the road that passed below the graveyard where Rachael lay. Suddenly a glowing column of something like fog rose up from the graves and began drifting toward them. Everyone scattered except for George. He was so frightened he was unable to speak or run as the apparition moved closer and closer. Finally it came so near he put out a hand to stop it. When he touched the fog, he felt only the painful coldness of empty space. He screamed in pain and then collapsed in shock. The glowing form retreated and vanished.

His companions heard his screams and came back, only to find him lying in the road, unconscious. As they lifted him up, they discovered that his right hand had frozen solid, though the other had kept its normal warmth.

George Deans lived another thirty-two years, but as a damaged man. The frozen hand withered and dangled uselessly for the rest of his life, reminding him of his failure to return Rachael Vinson's love. Any woman who might have entertained notions of sharing a future with Deans soon dropped any such ideas. Not only would he be a poor breadwinner with only one good hand, but he was a man cursed by someone who considered him spoken for. He never married, dying a single man in 1889. He was

Each flower had a distinct meaning, in the symbolic language of 19th-century tombstones.

buried in the same cemetery as Rachael Vinson, just a few paces from her mortal remains.

Whoever carved both their tombstones—and they are undoubtedly from the same workshop, perhaps even by the same master carver—must have known their tragic story, for the symbolism hewn in bas-relief tells exactly its main points. On Rachael's grave is an upright hand clutching a bouquet of three flowers: a lily, a lily of the valley, and a rose. Each flower had a distinct meaning, in the symbolic language of 19th-century tombstones. The lily stood for purity of heart, chastity, and virginity, as Rachael had undoubtedly saved herself for George, her first and only love. The lily of the valley stood for hope and eternal promise—not only the promise of rebirth in heaven, but for Rachael the hope she must have had that Deans would someday promise to be hers. The rose, still in the bud, speaks of a love never allowed to blossom. The whole bouquet is a bit wilted, too, which tells of her grief and disappointment.

And yet, the hand is upright. Anyone in Rachael Vinson's day would have understood immediately what this was meant to say: "The reward is yet to come."

George Deans's stone also includes a symbolic statement. It seems almost certain that over the years he must have regretted his actions and searched for some way to respond to the meanings carved into her marker. It appears that he ordered one remarkably similar to hers for himself before he died.

Above his name, a man's hand gently and lovingly holds the delicate hand of a woman. In old tombstone symbolism, clasped hands meant both "farewell" and "we shall meet again, in eternity." Furthermore, the male right hand is shown whole and functional again, which seems to speak of George's hopes for healing in the hereafter. Most importantly, the joined hands also offer a kind of proposal. There's little doubt for whom it was intended.

Apparently his offer was accepted, since there's even more to George Deans's tombstone than he could have planned. As the stone aged, a mysterious image began to appear on its dark and weathered reverse side. It's especially easy to see on rainy days, when the stone is wet. Among the lichens and darkened minerals, the unmistakable form of a 19th-century woman has gradually appeared. She seems to be waiting calmly, swirling in some kind of shroud or fog. People who have seen the old daguerreotypes of Rachael Vinson say that the face of the woman looks exactly like her. So, it would seem, Rachael has finally accomplished her goal: She has managed at long last to make George Deans hers. *—Thanks to Daniel Barefoot*

Weeping Arch of New Bern

Cedar Grove Cemetery is easily the most haunted place in the smallish coastal city of New Bern, NC. Graves dating back to the early 1800s fill the huge, undulating space, in the center of which is an unusual mass grave containing the remains of at least three hundred Confederate soldiers who died during the battle to save the city. What makes it unusual, at least for the South, is that it's an ossuary—the soldiers were originally buried directly in the battlefield, wherever they'd fallen, but years later their bones were retrieved and transferred to Cedar Grove.

Citizens of New Bern know better than to linger for long under the peculiar triple arch leading into their cemetery. The Weeping Arch, as they call it, is made of marl, a porous conglomerate of compacted fossil seashells, which absorbs moisture from rain and everyday humidity and drips almost constantly. If one of the drops ever falls on you, they believe, you'll be returning to visit Cedar Grove again quite soon, and . . . dead!

Elephant Man

One of the more curious tombstones in Charlotte's old Elmwood Cemetery is that of John King, a performer and elephant trainer in the great Robinson Circus. On September 22, 1880, King's elephant, named Chief, suddenly attacked him. King's colleagues in the circus raised the funds to have a marker erected over his grave featuring his beloved assassin, then the show went on.

Log Cabin Likeness

Elmwood includes a number of other peculiar monuments, among them a granite log cabin dedicated to Henry Severs. The cabin is extremely detailed, down to the growth rings in the logs and the proper orientation of flat nails in the faux board sign (across the grain). It seems quibbling to point out that the roof should have been made of split shakes or shingles, and that the chimney should have stood outside the "logs" at the end, but it suggests that whoever designed it had only dreamed of the simple cabin life without having actually lived it. Better late than never, though.

Little Mary

Four-year-old Mary DeGraffenreid was outside her Chester, SC, home dancing around a trash fire in April 1857 when her dress caught fire. She died from the burns. Her devastated parents decided to erect a monument in the town's Evergreen Cemetery to perpetuate her memory. They commissioned an Italian sculptor to render the likeness as if the girl were napping in a four-poster bed holding a bouquet of flowers, under a marble sheet. For nearly sixty years a glass enclosure kept the carving a snowy white, but after the glass shattered, some time in the 1920s, the stone began to weather to the color of living skin. *—Thanks to Jean Muldrow*

OUR FIRST BORN.

Billy and Benny McCrary, with a combined weight of 1,300 pounds, stop to air their spare tires after an afternoon of uneasy riding.

World's Largest Twins

On December 7, 1946, trucker Frank "Throttle Boy" McCrary became a proud dad when his wife, Virginia, gave birth to two boys. Billy Leon and Benny Loyd McCrary soon grew into normal rambunctious kids, just like all the kids in their hometown of Hendersonville, NC. Except for being identical twins, there was nothing particularly unusual about them. Until they were nine, that is.

At that age, they both contracted the measles. The disease, though extremely rare today, was so common in the mid-1950s that most people regarded it then as little more than a kind of childhood rite of passage. But it hit the McCrary boys severely, and later it was discovered

that the disease had somehow damaged their pituitary glands. One of the myriad things this tiny gland does is regulate growth, and with their regulators damaged, the boys began growing at full throttle.

Less than a year later, they each weighed more than two hundred pounds. By the time they entered high school, they had doubled that to four hundred pounds apiece, and soon they had passed the five-hundred-pound mark. Walking became so difficult that they got around town on minibikes. A photograph taken of the two of them on their bikes wound up in *Life* magazine, and their careers as showmen were launched.

With their massive size to provide an ongoing spectacle, everything they did—dancing, telling jokes, playing music, wrestling, or just getting up out of a chair and moving around—seemed awesome and spectacular. Audiences would gather, whether in Las Vegas or their own hometown, to watch the eight-hundred-pound twins do nearly anything. Life on such a scale was often difficult, however. According to Jerry Bledsoe (in *North Carolina Curiosities*), they had to drive individually in "separate, reinforced, and specially equipped cars. . . . Their own furniture had to be reinforced and they carried small jacks to put under motel beds to keep them from collapsing."

The twins refused medical attention that might have cured their problem because their livelihood depended on staying very big. Billy died when he was only thirty-two. He fell from his minibike and suffered injuries that led to a serious infection and then death. His brother Benny died of "natural causes" in 2001, at age fifty-four. They are buried side by side in a grave of epic proportions at Crab Creek Cemetery at the foot of Jeter Mountain Road, about eight miles west of Hendersonville. The *Guinness Book of Records* has proclaimed them the World's Largest Twins.

A KIND HEARTED MAN
SPREADING GOD'S WORD
IN A BIG WAY!
AN INSPIRATION AND A
SOURCE OF ENCOURAGE-
MENT FOR US ALL.
PHIL. 4:13

A BIG MAN
WITH A BIG HEART.
LOVED AROUND THE
WORLD. WITH A
LEGEND AS BIG AS
THE MOUNTAINS
AROUND HIM.

WORLD
RECORD
HOLDERS

BENNY
727

BILLY
747

McCRARY

THE WORLD'S LARGEST TWINS

Burns's Cannon

Otway Burns was, in essence, a U.S. government-licensed pirate. During the War of 1812, he was one of the most successful of such "privateers," raking in millions of dollars in seized ships and booty. The armaments on Otway Burns's privateering schooner, *Snapdragon*, included six heavy cannons, one of which lies embedded in marble atop his grave in the Old Burying Ground in Beaufort, NC.

Oldest Monument to Confederate Dead?

As far as we know, the old St. David's Episcopal Church in Cheraw, SC, is *not* haunted, which is actually even more peculiar than if it were. Certainly it has seen enough suffering, serving as a hospital during both the American Revolution and the Civil War. Its huge churchyard includes dead soldiers from all four sides of those conflicts.

On one edge of the cemetery is what Cherawians claim is the oldest monument to the Confederate dead, erected in July 1867. We note that this same claim is also made by the city of Fayetteville, NC, for a memorial they erected the following year. The determination of which is truly the oldest monument hinges on a small legalistic detail: Because the Cheraw monument was set up while the city was still under military occupation by Union soldiers, the fallen heroes of the South weren't exactly specified in so many words. Only a few poetic symbols—a partially uprooted oak with the words FALLEN BUT NOT DEAD arcing over it, an anchor surrounded by the words LOVED AND HONORED THOUGH UNKNOWN—were there to suggest that it was some kind of memorial, but without quite saying to whom.

Buried on the British Banks

There is a tiny piece of British soil on the island of Ocracoke on North Carolina's Outer Banks. It is the final resting place of four sailors whose bodies washed up on the island after the British navy corvette HMS *Bedfordshire* was sunk by a U-boat in May 1942. The land was deeded to England after the war so that the men might be buried in their native soil, and the Union Jack flies above it. During World War II, more than sixty ships were sunk by German submarines off the Carolina coast.

Roof over His Head (stone)

Near the intersection of Miami Church Road and Barrier–Georgeville Road in eastern Cabarrus County, NC, is a roadside family graveyard that includes a grave with a little shingled roof over it. The grave belongs to Dr. Solomon Furr, a first lieutenant in the North Carolina State Troops during the Civil War. Furr died in 1895 at the age of 73. Local lore has it that he and a comrade in the Confederate Army spent many a night together shivering in the trenches or trying to sleep in the rain. According to the story, they made a pact that the first to die would never have to sleep in the rain again, since the other would be responsible for building a roof over his grave. Solomon was the first to die—and has since stayed high and dry.

Girl in the Rum Keg

Near the back of the Old Burying Ground on Ann Street in Beaufort, NC, is a curious little grave with a crude marker made of wood. These days the date is difficult to read, but no matter, for there's no name, either. The epitaph says only: LITTLE GIRL BURIED IN RUM KEG.

According to the story, the girl's family moved to Beaufort from England when she was just an infant. As a child, she often heard stories of the old country and comparing its imagined magnificence with the small fishing town she found herself in, she began longing to see the place of her birth. She begged to be allowed to return for a visit, and finally her father, a sea merchant, relented. He promised his wife that their daughter would not be allowed to stay in England, but would only visit, and that he would bring her home to Beaufort again under any circumstances.

The visit, by all reports, went well. Unfortunately, the girl caught some illness along the way, and during the sea voyage back she died. The father remembered his promise to his wife to bring their daughter home no matter what, so he did the only thing he could do under the circumstances. To preserve her body for a proper funeral, he bought a keg of rum from the ship's master and sealed her little corpse inside it. When they landed in Beaufort, he told his wife the heartbreaking news, and together they buried their child. Today the grave is usually found sprinkled with trinkets, shells, coins, toys, or little souvenirs left by other children moved by the story of the little girl who had died to visit the place where she was born.

Death in the Fast Lane

We don't know if it was due to highway department oversight or bullheadedness on the part of the original landowners, but one of the least-restful places to wait out eternity must be the little graveyard just northeast of exit 95 on Interstate 85, a short distance from Gaffney, SC. It's also one of the least accessible burial sites in the Carolinas: right in the middle of the median strip between four lanes of traffic. If you're on the interstate you get a second's glimpse at seventy mph, but forget slowing down or stopping for a good look. *Weird Carolinas* took the exit and made the way along the frontage road, then waited nearly an hour to see if we could dart across the pavement between oncoming cars on foot. But the traffic was relentless and we finally gave up. We probably will never know who's buried there, for it seems like a place where even angels might fear to tread.

Buried Extremities

Captain Lemuel Cratie Arnold is buried in two places. Born in 1883 in Smithville (later renamed Southport), NC, he was diagnosed with something like spinal meningitis as a boy, and at age fifteen had both his lower legs removed. These were buried in the Old Smithville Burying Ground. By the time he died at a fine old age, in 1967, the plot where his legs had been buried was full, so the rest of his body was buried in nearby Northwood Cemetery. Captain Arnold was never handicapped by the loss of his legs; he was a commercial fish-

erman and well-known boat builder who made all his own crutches and prosthetics.

A belief in bodily resurrection at the Second Coming may have to do with other, similar burials of lower extremities in sanctified ground. Against the back wall of the Old Lutheran Cemetery in Salisbury, NC, is the grave of a foot. Late one night in the winter of 1893, eighty-eight-year-old James A. Reid was partially run over by a freight train. Although the accident severed his foot, Reid survived and decided to give his foot a proper burial rather than just throwing it away. A miniature tombstone marks the spot, which still vibrates frequently with the rumbling of passing trains. The rest of Mr. Reid was buried seven years later at Trading Ford Baptist Church, on Long Ferry Road.

Grave of the Unknown Graniteville Boy

There is a grave back in the southwest corner of Cemetery Hill above Graniteville, SC, that, though smaller than nearly all the others, stands out from the more prominent monuments surrounding it. It's covered with brightly colored toys, trinkets, and flowers that local people have been leaving there ever since a hasty funeral took place back in 1855. In October of that year, a train pulled into town and a little boy was carried off it, feverish with an unknown disease. He had been traveling alone, and by the time the conductor had found him slumped in his seat, he'd slipped into a coma. No one aboard knew who he was, where he'd boarded the train, or where he was headed. There were no papers or clues in his pockets to indicate who his relatives might be.

The proprietors of the Graniteville hotel took him in and attempted to care for him. The boy lingered for several days, tossing and sweating with fever as the local churches organized prayers for his recovery. But all to no avail. When he died, the mill workers built a tiny coffin and lined it with donated cloth, then took up a collection for a proper burial with a real stone. The words engraved on it are brief and direct: THE LITTLE BOY, OCTOBER 1855. For more than 150 years, anyone in the area who has lost a child or misses one, and even children themselves, have visited the forlorn spot at the back of the old cemetery and left a little something there for the boy who died far from home.
—Thanks to Mary Jane Lock

Little Boy Plays with His Toys

I attend college at the University of South Carolina–Aiken. One town over from me is a town called Graniteville, which has a cemetery called . . . the Graniteville Cemetery. This cemetery is bigger than most I've seen, and there are no lights in it whatsoever, so a walk through it at night sends chills down your spine. It is a normal cemetery until you walk all the way to the back, to the section marked "Unmarked Graves." Most cemeteries have them, but there is one particular grave that stands out above all the rest.

All the marker says is "The Little Boy," and it's dated October in the 1800s. The boy buried there was found dead, but no one knew who he was or where he came from. Today, the grave has a border around it that is lined with toys and many other things people have left.

It is said that at night the little boy comes out to play with his toys. One night, I was walking around with some friends, and my friend Josh went off by himself. He said he saw this little ball of light swoop up, zoom back down and then bam! It disappeared! At first he thought it was possibly a glare, and he tried to come up with every possible explanation. He stepped back and forth to see if he could catch the glare again, but he couldn't, so he got freaked out and kept walking. Then he heard a sound like someone sweeping a foot quickly back and forth through gravel. He thought it was our other friends, but at that time they were standing on grass and nowhere near a gravel grave. Another night when I was there I was taking photos and saw a light right next to me in the flash. It freaked the HELL out of me. *—Danette Oberg*

Cemetery Hill, Graniteville

The Little Boy may not be the only resident not quite resting in peace up on Cemetery Hill. In fact, the vast cemetery has been the locale for numerous sightings of wavering lights, fireballs, and blinding flashes. Some people attribute these to meteorological causes like lightning, pointing out that the graveyard occupies one of the highest promontories in the area and that the old Spanish moss–draped cedars and pines standing among the graves are natural generators for static electricity. Others aren't so sure the problem is purely physical. They feel restless or dissatisfied spirits could linger about the place and point to a couple of possible sources.

Like nearly all southern textile mill towns, Graniteville was purpose-built to answer all its inhabitants' needs—as well as the mill owners' needs for a nearly captive workforce. In a complete cradle-to-the-grave scheme set up for its employees, the owners included a town cemetery in their plans. The earliest graves, however, were marked with only simple wooden slabs, which over the years rotted away. Thus, the locations of most of the early graves are long forgotten, since the records also disappeared in floods that periodically ravaged the region. It's these forgotten dead, say some, who must be unhappy with their lot and return from time to time to vent their upset at descendants who no longer remember them.

Others point to more recent troubles and say that perhaps the dead are merely trying to offer the living some kind of solace. A train loaded with chemicals wrecked in the middle of town not long ago, releasing a cloud of poisonous gas that killed a number of people and sickened hundreds of others. Meanwhile, the great mill, famous for making the gray uniform cloth for the Confederate Army, and built of white granite with fountains and towers so grand and striking that visitors often compared it to a palace, had fallen on hard times long before it finally closed in 2006. The train accident, the bad luck, and the economic worries that have plagued the town have not only led to a rash of mysterious health problems but may have upset the cosmic balance of the place, so long regulated by the pounding rhythms of the looms and the signals for the changing of work shifts. Whatever the cause, the old graveyard up on Cemetery Hill is now one of the more paranormally active necropolises in the state.

When in Doubt—Overpack

Eccentric South Carolina planter Francis Cordes left his rice plantation Cachan—on the west bank of the Cooper River—to his young nephew, on the condition that he never attend college. In 1803, as Cordes lay dying, he left more strange instructions with his body servant, Jack: "I am going on a long journey. When they coffin me, I want you to load and place in my hands my double-barreled pistols. Put my hunting knife in my pocket and my hickory stick by my side. I don't know what sort of people I may fall in with."

Holy Cross's Traveling Ghost

The Episcopal Church of the Holy Cross near Statesburg, SC, is one of the tallest *pisé de terre* (rammed-earth) buildings in the country. It was erected on the site of the old Claremont Church in 1850, but the graveyard surrounding it was already well established long before it was built. In 1851 Joel Poinsett, a botanist who had discovered a plant later to be known as the poinsettia, was buried here. The old graveyard is said to be haunted by a lone male figure who is often observed at a distance strolling among the tombs even in daylight and vanishes as soon as anyone attempts to approach him. Some believe he is one of the Confederates whose remains lie in the graveyard. Others say he is one of the Friersons whose coffins were exhumed and moved here from their old Wiboo Plantation in Clarendon County in 1941 when the Santee Reservoir permanently flooded their land. But it may be Poinsett himself. After all, as a trained naturalist and professional diplomat he was an inveterate world traveler who had roamed throughout Asia, Europe, and the Americas. Maybe too much dust had begun gathering on his traveling shoes—even if the dust was his own.

Abandoned
in the Carolinas

Who hasn't stared at the hollow-eyed shell of some abandoned house or hospital and thought about the people who once lived or worked there, and who are no more? Maybe it's the mysteries that hide behind the darkened windows that light our imaginations. Or maybe it's the kick we get out of pondering the futility, bad timing, or bad luck involved in their creation and demise.

Whatever the reason, there are plenty of places in the Carolinas to tease us with their stories. But here, explorers may find that they are not the only life poking about the ruins. The invasive vine kudzu is also there, covering everything that doesn't move. It's a pest to many, but to some it introduces elements of magic as it drapes and shadows large swaths of landscape, turning old tobacco barns and millhouses into enchanted castles or Mayan ruins. An empty building may just be temporarily vacated. But a building covered with vines is *abandoned*—and beckoning. Follow the kudzu, if you dare.

Seven Springs

The little town of Seven Springs, NC, takes its name from an old spa where people once came to enjoy the health benefits of an extremely unusual natural phenomenon. Seven water sources—each with remarkably different tastes, mineral compositions, and healthful properties—burbled out of the ground within a few feet of each other. *Weird Carolinas* can vouch that this is true. Water from one of the springs tastes strongly of iron, another of sulfur, another salty, one almost sweet, one with no taste at all, and so on. Some of the springs emerged with more force than others, as well, possibly coming from different strata of the groundwater aquifer.

In the late 19th century, Seven Springs was run as a spa, with the waters said to cure a host of illnesses and generally add vim and vigor to Victorian life. Visitors traveled by steamboat up the Neuse River, docking just a few miles downstream from the Cliffs of the Neuse, the highest river bluffs in the eastern part of the state. They'd stay in a hotel that still stands (though it's in bad condition) on private land a few hundred yards from the springs, and in between jaunts down to drink "recipe" mixtures of the waters they'd play games, sing songs, listen to lectures, and have a good time in the outdoors.

As water cures fell into disregard in the years following World War II, people stopped coming to the Seven Springs hotel. The building where the springs sprang, the old picnic grounds, and a bottling facility gradually fell into disrepair and disappeared behind a veil of rampant vegetation. In 1999, Hurricane Floyd caused the Neuse to flood, inundating the spa site, along with much of the rest of the town. The system of floor channels that drained the springs was clogged and has not been cleared since. The springs are flooded, with their waters mixing of their own accord.

With recent discoveries that some of the old health cures actually worked better than modern people thought, it may be time to revisit the springs. *Weird Carolinas* hopes someone with vision will help the property spring to life once again.

Vesuvius Furnace

Looking a bit like wizards' tombs, a few massive remnants of the early days of the Industrial Revolution lie scattered across the Carolinas.

Vesuvius Furnace is one of the easiest to get to and one of the most impressive. It's on Lick Creek, north of Iron Station in Lincoln County, NC. The name gives its purpose away; it's an iron-smelting furnace.

To make iron back in the 1790s, when Vesuvius was built, this huge structure was filled with alternating layers of charcoal and iron ore dumped into the top via a wooden ramp across a trestle. Once the charcoal was burning hot enough to stay alight, giant bellows squeezed by a waterwheel blasted air into the whole thing, bringing it up to white heat and sending smoke and cinders out the top like a volcano (hence the name, after the famous volcano Mt. Vesuvius near Pompeii in Italy). When the hot charcoal had melted the iron, a clay plug that sealed a hole in the bottom of the furnace was broken open, and molten iron would pour out into a ditch that channeled it off into small pits. The usual form of the molds was a branched structure with many individual ingots at angles to a central channel or runner. The whole thing bore some resemblance to a litter of piglets suckling on a sow. When the metal had cooled and hardened, the smaller ingots (the *pigs*) were broken from the runner (the *sow*), hence the name *pig iron*. Voila!

All of the old iron furnaces were similar in size and design, and they all demanded access to the same basic elements: not only iron ore, but stone for constructing the furnace, water to power the bellows, and vast forests to supply enough wood to be converted to charcoal. When all the trees had been cut and the forests gave out, most of the inland ironworks closed, but some of the old structures still stand, reminding us of sooty days gone by.

nearly all heavy machinery. And wherever the water-powered mills were, towns grew up around them. Until the hydroelectric dam came along.

Hydroelectric dams require a great deal more water to turn their turbines than the old mill wheels. The lakes

Submerged Towns of the Carolinas

Thanks to Hollywood, everyone knows what a ghost town is supposed to look like: a row of false-fronted buildings with a wooden sidewalk, rails to tie up the horses, and a tumbleweed or two blowing in the wind. But in the Carolinas, the much more likely scene is this. Everything is a shade of green; a dappled light plays over the remains of former homes and work places; a wrecked car sits without tires, its hood rusted permanently in the raised position; an old wringer-washer lies tipped on its side with a bass lazily swimming out of it . . . That's right, a bass. For most of our old Carolina ghost towns are underwater.

Early settlers founded their towns along waterways for transportation, drinking water, and power. Until steam power, gasoline, and electricity made it possible to site industries away from water, waterwheels powered

they needed were much larger and deeper than any old-time millponds, and to create them, valleys, river basins, and entire regions were flooded, including the old towns. Other than the Carolina Bays and a few other natural lakes like Pungo and Mattamuskeet, almost all of the lakes in the Carolinas are artificial, and nearly all of them have a town or an important historic site at the bottom.

Lake Norman covers towns like Long Island and East Monbo, along with the battlefield where General William Davidson fought the British at Cowan's Ford. Under Lake Logan is the town of Sunburst. Under Lake Tillery is Allenton. The old Cherokee village of Keowee is under Lake Keowee, along with pre-Revolutionary Fort Prince George. Fort Charlotte is hidden under Lake Strom Thurmond. Lake Marion drowned Pond Bluff,

Francis "Swamp Fox" Marion's old home place, along with the town of Ferguson's Landing and Benjamin Schenkingh's Fort. The site where botanist André Michaux discovered the rare Oconee bell flower is now under Lake Jocassee.

The government promised the people who lived in the communities now at the bottom of Lake Fontana access to their old cemeteries via a road that was to go around the lake's north side from Bryson City. But after only a few miles were completed, the road was abandoned and construction came to an abrupt halt. The famous Road to Nowhere or Road of Broken Promises still generates angry resentment among old long-term inhabitants.

The Lake Murray Bomber

On April 4, 1943, when America was deep into World War II, Second Lieutenant William Fallon took off from Columbia Army Air Base in his Mitchell B-25C twin-engine bomber. He was headed toward Lake Murray, twelve miles away, on what was supposed to be a routine bombing practice run. Fallon and his crew were practicing a technique called skip bombing, which involves flying at very low altitudes to drop bombs that skip across the water like stones on a pond. Keeping low meant the planes could sneak up on the enemy. It was a dangerous but highly effective technique if done well.

Practice was going along routinely until the left engine suddenly began failing. Despite Fallon's giving full throttle to the right engine, the plane began to lose the little altitude it had. It was going to crash, and Fallon yelled at the crew to prepare for a water landing. He pointed the plane into the wind and let it down onto the surface of the lake as smoothly as he could.

Perfectly preserved inside it were radios, machine guns, and navigation charts, along with that day's Columbia newspaper (still readable).

The landing was anything but smooth, and the crew barely managed to scramble free and launch a life raft before the damaged plane sank out of sight. They were about two miles west of Dreher Shoals Dam, giddy to be alive, but anxious to get out of the water before anything else went wrong.

Luckily, they were rescued almost immediately, by businessman Sewall K. Oliver, who happened to be home from work since it was a Sunday. Oliver got into his motorboat and pulled the crew to safety. The plane, however, had settled in water too deep to make recovery feasible, and was given up by the Army Air Corps as a total loss.

But it wasn't lost to history. At 150 feet, the fresh water of the lake remained cold enough and deoxygenated enough to suspend the plane in a remarkable state of preservation for decades. It would remain in silent darkness on the bottom of Lake Murray, partially buried in silt, for the next sixty-two years.

Pediatrician Dr. Robert Seigler first heard about the bomber on the bottom of the lake when he was in high school and spent summers boating and water-skiing there. His interest in the story eventually grew into an obsession as he tracked down old documents, military reports, and even eyewitnesses to help him relocate it. In 1992, a Naval Reserve sonar team finally found the wreck. Seigler raised the funds to hire an experienced salvage crew, and just before midnight on September 19, 2005, the wings of the twin-engine bomber felt the rush of air for the first time in over sixty years.

Several days later, the plane was sent to the Southern Museum of Flight in Birmingham, Alabama, for cleaning and stabilizing, in preparation for being mounted on permanent display. The bomber is not only a good example of a very rare plane (only four like it are known) but it also turns out to be an unintended time capsule of a very specific moment in history. Perfectly preserved inside it were radios, machine guns, and navigation charts, along with that day's Columbia newspaper (still readable), some of the crew's leather flight jackets, a portable toilet, and copilot Robert Davison's watch, with an inscription his wife had engraved on it when she'd given it to him. He'd owned it for only a month before it went to the bottom of the lake. *—Thanks to Ron Donald*

The Charlotte Observer

Foremost Newspaper Of The Carolinas

WEDNESDAY, MARCH 12, 1958

Cloudy

E CAROLINAS—Partly cloudy
ol tonight and Thursday.

CHARLOTTE AREA — Partly
; expected high today 62, low
st 35.

High 64; Low 28
High 73; Low 35

—Ago

Vol. 89, No. 335

30 Pages

5 Cents

The Observer is served by the ...
ciated Press, United Press, Chicago
News World Service, Washington,
Raleigh, Columbia and Gaston County
bureaus.

Unarmed A-Bomb Hits S. C.;
6 Hurt As Trigger Explodes

Bldg "a" Rear View

Oops! Bombs Away!

After dropping the first atomic bomb on Hiroshima, Japan, on August 6, 1945, the U.S. waited just three days before dropping a second bomb, on Nagasaki. Then the U.S. waited eleven and a half years before dropping the third atomic bomb—on an inhabited area that, luckily for international relations, was on U.S. soil. And luckily for a sizable chunk of South Carolina, this bomb didn't explode with a full-scale thermonuclear reaction. It exploded, but in a relatively underpopulated area: the rural community of Mars Bluff, SC, a few miles east of Florence.

The story starts at 3:53 p.m. on Tuesday, March 11, 1958. Four B-47s took off from Hunter Air Force Base near Savannah, Georgia, en route to a practice bombing exercise over England. Though it was just an exercise, the planes were fully loaded with 30-kiloton MK6 atomic bombs, each nearly eleven feet long and five feet in diameter.

A design flaw in B-47s meant that after the planes took off, they would be unable to land until they had used up nearly all their fuel. Once in flight, they'd have to stay in the air long enough to burn off the fuel, or else crash. Because crashing with atomic bombs aboard is always a bad idea, the planes were designed to be able to dump their weapons in an emergency.

No one is sure exactly how it happened, but somehow a 7,600-pound bomb was released, bashed open the bomb bay doors, and headed down toward the earth below. Oops. The cockpit crew knew immediately that something terrible had happened. Out the window, they could see a circular shock wave radiating from a black cloud far below them. The plane's commander issued a coded message to his mission controllers at Hunter AFB, but they didn't understand it (as it had never been sent before). He had to contact the Florence municipal airport tower in order to get the message to Hunter that the plane had "lost a device" seven miles east of town. He also told the Florence tower to send police, fire, and ambulance services and "all other constituted authorities" to the site immediately.

For the next several hours, the crew was forced to fly in circles burning off fuel before they could safely land, not knowing what was going on below or if they had vaporized an entire community. They assumed the worst when, as they landed, military police surrounded the plane, demanded their sidearms, escorted them to a windowless room, and told them they wouldn't be going anywhere or talking to anyone until everything was sorted out. The people on the receiving end of the accidental drop had a rather different experience. It had been a pleasant afternoon, and Bill Gregg was out in his workshop while his three young children played in the garden with their cousin. Bill's wife, Ethelmae "Effie"Gregg, was at her sewing machine in the house they had built together just five years before, the family cat playing beside her. Catherine Coker, their part-time maid, was in a corner of the yard burning household trash in a barrel.

pass high overhead, followed by a strangely familiar whistling noise, and then suddenly felt the most massive explosion of his life. He barely had time to grab his screaming boy and huddle over him when part of the workshop roof collapsed around them, accompanied by a rain of mud.

Gregg was injured by one of the rafters but stumbled out of the ruins of his workshop, half carrying his son. All he saw before him was a dust storm of "green, foggy haze, followed by a cloud of black smoke." When the house emerged from the dust and smoke, it looked as if it had been hit with a giant sledgehammer. But Effie Gregg was still alive, and clambered out of the ruins covered with plaster and embedded with asbestos insulation. The Gregg kids and their cousin were frightened and wheezing from having inhaled a lot of dust, but at least they were all present and accounted for. Knocked down by the blast, Catherine Coker had sprained her back, but she survived as well.

Around four o'clock, the kids left the garden playhouse and continued their play in the side yard, closer to the main house. Gregg's son came into the workshop to see what his dad was up to. At 4:19 p.m., Gregg, who had served as a paratrooper in World War II, heard a plane

CHILDREN PLAYING

GREGG HOUSE

CAR

WORKSHOP AND GARAGE

PRIMARY BLAST ZONE

CRATER

BLASTED TREES

'Daddy,' He Cried As A-Bomb Struck

After establishing that everyone was alive, Bill Gregg saw that 250 feet away, where his garden had been—and where his children had been playing just twenty minutes before—was a smoking crater almost seventy feet in diameter and thirty feet deep. Both the playhouse and a chicken house were gone. All the pine trees within two hundred feet of the crater were flattened or stripped of bark and needles. Closer by, his car and pickup truck were totaled. The house itself was beyond repair.

Emergency workers and government radiation-contamination experts appeared shortly after the dust settled. The family was treated for injuries and examined for signs of radiation, while men with Geiger counters cordoned off two square miles of land around them. The only joy the family experienced that day was when the family cat came out of hiding from the wreckage of the house.

The Greggs weren't the only people in the area to suffer from the bomb. Reports of broken windows, smashed mirrors and pictures, and cars being spun completely around in the shock wave were reported from as far as two miles away. The cloud of smoke and dust was large enough to be seen eight miles away. For months afterward, local people were tested for radioactive contamination. Fortunately, the chances of the bomb going off with a nuclear fission explosion were remote. Creating that kind of bang requires a complex series of procedures, which were not executed here.

Still, it all could have been much worse. One of the things that saved them was rain.

It had rained a lot in the previous weeks, and the ground was soft enough that the bomb burrowed into it before exploding. This funneled most of the force of the explosion straight up, instead of sideways. If not for the rain and soft ground, there would have been little left of the entire neighborhood. And if the worst had occurred—nuclear fission—fallout from scattered radioactive materials could have caused a health risk disaster for centuries.

The air force was quick to point out that this didn't happen—too quick, according to some, who say the air force made this assessment before the reports of the con-tamination-assessment teams had been submitted. Others point out that radioactive fragments of the bomb scattered and have even appeared for sale on eBay.

For three days, the event made worldwide head-lines. And then it all just went away. The journalistic silence and lack of follow-up after the incident seems almost eerie these days. The news was so muffled, in fact, that the family stumped the contestants on the *I've Got a Secret* TV show less than a month later. Their secret was, of course, "Our house was hit by an atomic bomb." They won eighty dollars for appearing.

The U.S. government seems to have taken advantage of the lack of journalistic interest to deny decent com-pensation for destroying the Greggs' property, interrupt-ing their lives, and leaving lasting physical and emotion-al scars. After three and a half years of legal battles, the government begrudgingly paid the family $56,000. It didn't cover the family's $29,000 attorney's fees.

The plane crew was left with lasting scars as well. Though eventually exonerated, the stigma of having been the only crew to drop an atomic bomb on the U.S.

followed them for the rest of their military careers.

The crater is still there, and if you look closely at the ground, you can see where the house once stood. Oblivious to the radiation contamination potential, apartment blocks and housing developments have sprung up in the plots surrounding the crater. To find it,

'RELAX FOLKS—IT'S ONE OF OURS'

take Highway 301 to Francis Marion College, seven miles east of Florence. Across the highway, north of the campus, enter Lucius Circle. Envisioning Lucius Circle as a clock face, go to one o'clock and then head off in that direction on foot about a hundred feet. It's not much to see—just a big, mucky, sixty-year-old pit in the ground—but what a weird moment in history. If you own a Geiger counter, bring it. Maybe you'll find an interesting souvenir from the Cold War.

—*Thanks to Effie Gregg, Louise Davies, Alice Beaty*

Goldsboro Bomb

On the west side of Big Daddy's Road, halfway between Faro and Musgrave Crossroads in Wayne County, NC, is a soybean field that looks like any other in the surrounding countryside. Except *this* field has concealed the abandoned remains of a four-megaton hydrogen bomb beneath its sandy soil ever since the early 1960s.

The years leading up to the Cuban Missile Crisis were a peak of Cold War activity, and one of the busiest

projects was something called Operation Chrome Dome. In this mission, the U.S. Air Force countered the threat of Soviet sneak attacks by keeping a fleet of B-52 bombers in the air as long as possible, fully loaded with atomic weapons. The name of the mission jokingly referred both to Soviet premier Nikita Khrushchev's bald head and to the route taken by the planes, which flew over the North Pole toward Russia, and then turned back at the last possible moment. Refueling in the air, the planes would stay aloft and complete the circuit as long as their crews could avoid exhaustion.

The near-constant flying took a toll on machinery as well as men. As one B-52 was on its way back to Seymour Johnson AFB near Goldsboro, NC, metal fatigue caused a leak in the right-wing fuel tank. Fire erupted in the plane just after midnight on January 24, 1961, when 37,000 pounds of jet fuel poured from the tank. The eight-man crew bailed out just before an explosion broke up the plane, but three members died in the incident. As the huge bomber was blown to pieces at an altitude of about 8,000 feet, two MK39 thermonuclear bombs separated from the wreckage and landed some distance from where the rest of the fragmented aircraft hit the ground.

Both bombs were equipped with parachutes, theoretically allowing time for a bomber to escape the scene before the atomic blast would go off. The parachute of one of the bombs deployed, and it was quickly found and recovered.

The other parachute did not open. Its bomb slammed into the rain-softened ground of a soggy field at an estimated eight hundred miles an hour, leaving an impact crater about five feet deep and ten feet wide. But there was no weapon in sight. By 1:30 p.m. that day, full-scale recovery efforts began as munitions specialists began frantically—and secretly—digging for the bomb. To avoid panicking the local population or creating a sightseeing nightmare, press and politicians were told that the excavators were only looking for a missing seat from the airplane crash. Terrible conditions—freezing rain, loose high explosives, potential radioactive contamination—combined to slow the salvage operation.

Eight feet below the surface, the first pieces of the bomb were discovered. The next day, more fragments were found at depths of twelve and fifteen feet. Four days after the crash, at nearly twenty feet deep, pieces of detonators and arming devices were discovered. The excavation pit continued to grow, and two weeks later, it was two hundred feet in diameter and nearly fifty feet deep. The massive pumps and heavy equipment brought in to assist the excavation were no match for groundwater rushing in from nearby Nahunta Swamp, or the quicksand.

At the end of May, the government gave up. The hole had already cost at least half a million dollars to dig and showed no sign of ever yielding the rest of the weapon, which was probably almost two hundred feet underground. The government refilled the hole and bought an easement on the land. The farmer who owned it could continue planting crops but he was banned from ever digging near the site. It'll be too bad if property values go up and development encroaches on the area, since the weapon's missing pieces—some of them plutonium—will need to remain untouched for the next 24,000 years.

A (Mostly) Abandoned Land of Oz

Almost seventy years have passed since Judy Garland trooped down the Yellow Brick Road with the rest of the crew on their way to the Emerald City, in what now seems like the quintessential American film. It's hard to believe that *The Wizard of Oz* wasn't always the family cult classic that it is now, but in the years after its 1939 release it was just another film, and not all that commercially successful at that. It was the introduction of color TV that resuscitated its reputation and turned its annual rebroadcasts into great excuses for parties and get-togethers.

Meanwhile, the Carolina mountains in the early 1960s were finally losing their reputation as a scary land of feuding and inbred moonshiners and were becoming a wholesome holiday destination. Improved roads brought hordes of people to see the Great Smokies and surrounding countryside. But while looking at leaves and shopping for churns and quilts was fun for Mom and Dad, the kids were a bit bored. It wasn't long before entrepreneurs decided to address (and profit from) this problem, and mountain theme parks were born.

The Land of Oz, atop Beech Mountain near Banner Elk, NC, was one such theme park where you got to walk on the "actual" Yellow Brick Road and encounter the movie's characters along the way, just as Dorothy did.

The heyday of these places lasted less than twenty years. By the late 1970s, most had closed, done in by higher gasoline prices, cheap airfares, and even video games. The Land of Oz, like several others, shut its gates and went out of business.

But as it turned out, not quite. For ten years, the attraction sat abandoned and was frequently looted and vandalized. Then new owners acquired the property in the early 1990s and die-hard Oz fans wheedled them into a deal. One weekend a year (the first weekend in October) the aging theme park would stage a festival during which the gates would be briefly reopened. Proceeds from the festival go to restoring and maintaining the old, abandoned site the rest of the year.
—Thanks to Karen Ciccone

Powell Theater: Abandoned and Haunted!

When one of our tipsters sent us off to downtown Chester, SC, to check out the old Powell Theater, he warned us ahead of time that the site was "active." Although no longer in use as a theater, it's got just about everything a truly creepy place should have. Its creepy location, to start with. It is said the public gallows once stood here, and its neighbor is an abandoned funeral home. In fact, you can open a door off the costume-changing room on the second floor of the theater and step directly into the old embalming room, still complete with sinks, tools, worktables, and a drain in the middle of the floor.

There are creepy sensations at the Powell too. It has about as many "cold spots" as a walk-in freezer. People have spoken of being shoved from behind, touched atop their heads, feeling like air has been sucked out of their lungs, and tripping for no apparent reason, often in the very same place as others just did.

Strange sounds abound. When the theater was in regular use, actors and stagehands heard noises of all kinds that weren't connected to ongoing activities. Thumps, crashes, banging noises, the sound of babies crying, the whir of projectors running years after the old carbon-arc units were removed. It's amazing that the Chester Little Theater group, which once performed here, managed to stage any productions in the midst of it all.

One event the theater group still talks about with noticeable unease happened during a rehearsal of *Man of La Mancha*. Actor Dick Blair told *Weird Carolinas* that in order to learn the songs, they had already played a tape of the musical a number of times when all of a sudden one of the songs *in the middle of the tape*—a Psalm, as it turns out—played backward, so that the words sounded demonic. As everyone listened in troubled concern, the next song played in the normal forward manner. When they tested the tape again, it was okay. No one had any idea why that happened—or how.

The ghosts of various dead people are said to haunt the place now. Some people report observing the translucent figure of an elderly lady wandering around the back of the ground floor. A black woman who came to a violent end on one of its dark stairways is said to still lurk. And then there's that funeral parlor.

It doesn't take much imagina-tion to see how easy it would be for any roaming spirits to enter the premises. Adjacent to the back of the stage is a loading dock for hearses and ambulances. It leads directly to a "corpse elevator" or "dumbwaiter for the dead" once used to hoist bodies up to the funeral parlor's second-floor prep rooms (which are next to the actors' rest area). Just beyond that are the extra-deep shelves that line the coffin stockroom. The corpse-viewing platform and a spare coffin are still sitting right where they were left when the mortuary was abandoned. If they left all that, there's no telling what else may have been left behind. —*Thanks to Tally Johnson and Dick Blair*

most difficult of which were to go through the solid granite of Stumphouse Mountain. Work began on three tunnels in 1852, and by 1859 they were about eighty percent complete. Unfortunately, pre–Civil War unrest caused the withdrawal of funding for the project. Work never resumed. Today the Stumphouse Mountain Tunnel deadends 4,260 feet from where it was intended to emerge on the other side of the mountain.

For eighty years, the tunnel served only as a residence for bats drawn to the pitch darkness at the back of the unfinished tunnel. Then in 1940 a professor at Clemson University came up with the idea of using the deep cave for making bleu cheese. Its dark, damp, cool conditions were perfect for growing the blue mold that gives this cheese its peculiar, intense flavor. The cheese was formed on campus from milk from the university's dairy herd, then trucked thirty miles to be cured in the tunnel. In 1956, facilities for artificially duplicating the conditions in the Stumphouse Mountain Tunnel were built on campus, at which time the genuine "cave aging" ceased.

Nowadays, the town of Walhalla runs the tunnel as a park. If you visit, be sure to bring a flashlight, since it's been returned to much the way it was in 1859 when work stopped—a long passage into the dark, ending only in frustration.

Cheese Tunnel

An abandoned railroad tunnel partway through Stumphouse Mountain near Walhalla, SC, is all that remains of the dashed hopes of a consortium of entrepreneurs in Charleston and Cincinnati, Ohio. In the middle of the 19th century, these visionaries had a plan to link Cincinnati's access to the harvests of the Midwest with Charleston's access to the sea. And so the Cincinnati and Charleston Railroad Company was founded in 1837.

Surveyors had plotted a route through the mountains to Cincinnati that required digging thirteen tunnels, the

Transit of Venus

In Aiken, SC, stands a strange-looking cage on stilts that not many people could identify. Mounted on the plaque below it is the following, baffling inscription:

> VENUS—DURCHGANG, 1882
> DEUTSCHE STATION 11
> 5H, 26M., 6W. 33° 33' 51" N.

So what is it?

In the late 1870s, German astronomers had calculated that something extremely unusual was going to happen in the skies on December 6, 1882, and they wanted to be sure they observed it clearly, unhampered by bad weather. The only way they could be reasonably certain of that was to send various teams to a variety of places in the world, all equipped to take the measurements they wanted to record. What they were so anxious to see was not a comet or a supernova. It was only the planet Venus coming between the earth and the sun.

It may not sound like much, but by measuring exactly how long it took for Venus to cross in front of the sun, it would be possible to calculate how far the earth was from the sun, how far away Venus was, and a host of other bits of information that would help us figure out where our planet was located in the solar system. If they missed this opportunity, it wouldn't happen again for a long time (in fact, the next Transit of Venus will occur about a century from now). Teams were sent to the sunniest places that meteorology could recommend in those days: Tahiti, Africa, and Aiken, South Carolina.

The Aiken-bound team created quite a lot of local interest as they began erecting their portable observatory. With German thoroughness, they commandeered a city block bounded by Laurens and Newberry streets and Barnwell and Edgefield avenues and turned it into a remote scientific research station. They set up three prefabricated towers and their equipment, and then they settled in behind a wall they'd built to keep out annoyingly inquisitive kids.

When the day of the interplanetary event finally arrived, armed guards were hired to hold everyone away from the camp until Venus had made her celestial crossing. Horses and wagons were routed blocks away to avoid jiggling the delicate instruments of measurement. Even the mayor of Charleston was denied access, after he

had come all the way to Aiken to witness the achievement of a scientific landmark.

When it was over, the Germans put away their notes, packed up their instruments and departed. The only thing left as a souvenir of their peculiar visit was the tower of their largest observatory. In following years, the tower served many purposes as it wandered around to several locations in Aiken: a trellis, a gazebo, and a pseudo–jungle gym. In 1995, its value as a historical artifact was finally recognized, and it was moved to stand next to the Aiken County Museum. It's been there ever since, awaiting the next time the goddess of Love decides to come between us and the light of day.

INDEX Page numbers in **bold** refer to photos and illustrations.

ACKNOWLEDGMENTS

For their hospitality as well as help, I thank Woody Connette & Jane Harper, Tom & Jane Hatley, Tom Patterson, Molly Renda, Mark Sloan & Michelle Van Parys, Liza Plaster, Tom & Kathe Stanley, Gayle Tustin, Tom Meyer & Jonathan Williams, Tom Whiteside, and especially Cici Stevens, who met me at the airport after many a flight. Leads came from all over, but Julie Adair, Grace Morris Cordial, Charles Di Perna, Jason Hart, Sam Hodges, Victor Jones, Jr., Pelham Lyles, Paul Matheny III, Tom Maxwell, John Schelp, and Maury York were unusually thoughtful. Kathie Whitley and Dan Partridge made working from overseas possible. I'm especially indebted to my parents, Richard and Zora Manley, who spent time on their own exploring old cemeteries, researching court records, and sending me weird clippings. It's no exaggeration to say they raised me to write this book.

Other leads and assistance came from Everett Adelman, Claire Ashby, Kathy Bahnsen, Ruth Bardon, Jan Blodgett, Tim & Linda Bost, Grace Britt, Susan Broili, Betty Broughton, Faye Bumgarner, Leslie Burns, Fay Byrd, Gloria Caldwell, Roy Campbell, Lucille Carabo, Lindsey Carlson, Linda Carnes-McNaughton, Karen & Chris Ciccone, Susan Cloer, Allen Coleman, John Coles and Mark Tiedje, Martha Creighton, Patricia Curl, Sudy Dressler, James Dulin, Cori Dulmage, Kathy Dunlap, Susan Edwards, Tom Elmore, Karen Flowers, Michael Frank, Jim Gabel, Gary Garvin, Ruth Ann Grissom, Michael Hardy, John Hawkins, Laurie Hayes, Lowell Hayes, Alison Hinman, Yvette Howard, Laura Ingram, Dot Jackson, Lauren Jackson, Lisa Kobrin, Mary Jane Lock, Nancy Luquire, Janet Meleney, Angela Michol, Ann Mills, Vickie Millsaps, John & Nancy Moorer, Jean Muldrow, Tim Nance, Joyce Joines Newman, Mary Noel, Larry Pace, James Peeler, Hilary Perez, Patricia Poland, Gary Presley, Karen Proctor, Ann Pursley, Jane Pyle, Sue Rainey, Brenda Reed, Joel Reese, Zoe Rhine, Naomi Rhodes, James Rion, Michelle Robinson, Donna Roper, Buff Ross, Jennie Schindler, Neal Seegars, Sandy Semans, Ran Shaffner, Debrah Shaw, Betty Sherrill, Philip Shore, Terry & Jan Smith, Debbie Spears, Sarah Spruill, Helen Stahl, Wanda Stalcup, Linda Blue Stanfield, Stephanie Stewart, Lisa Stillwell, Julie Stovall, Susan Swiggum, Anne Taylor, Bill Taylor, Troy Taylor, Donna Thompson, Connie Troutt, Ann Vaughn, Jennifer Vaughn, Louise Watkins, Louise Watson, Sally Watts, Dianne Welch, Robert Welch, Jerry West, David Wheeler, Marlene White, Johnathan Wiener, James Williams, Ann Wills, and Mary Lou Worley. Many, many others too numerous to list offered clues, ideas, and information, and I thank them sincerely.

The author's dad, Richard Manley, with his own contribution to Carolina weirdness.

PICTURE CREDITS

SHOW US YOUR WEIRD!

Do you know of a weird site found somewhere in the United States, or can you tell us about a strange experience you had? If so, we'd like to hear about it! We believe that every town has at least one great tale to tell, and we're listening. It could be a cursed road, haunted abandoned site, odd local character, or bizarre historic event. In most cases these tales are told only in the towns in which in they originated. But why keep them to yourself when you could share them with all of America? So come on and fill us in on all the weirdness that's lurking in your backyard!

You can email us at: Editor@WeirdUS.com,
or write us at:
Weird U.S., P.O. Box 1346, Bloomfield, NJ 07003.

www.weirdus.com